THE COMPLETE BOOK OF
HOLD 'EM POKER

THE COMPLETE BOOK OF
HOLD 'EM POKER

A COMPREHENSIVE GUIDE TO
PLAYING AND WINNING

———◆———

Gary Carson

LYLE STUART
Kensington Publishing Corp.

LYLE STUART books are published by

Kensington Publishing Corp.
850 Third Avenue
New York, NY 10022

Printed in the United States of America

ISBN 0-7394-4830-7

CONTENTS

PART THREE: SPECIAL SITUATIONS

PART FOUR: PLAYING SOME HANDS

PART FIVE: CONTINUING EDUCATION

THE COMPLETE BOOK OF
HOLD 'EM POKER

1

Introduction

Given the number of poker books on the market, this is probably not your first poker book. Why another book on Hold 'Em? After all, you can win at poker without much of an understanding of the game. All you really have to do is learn some basic guidelines for playing tight, then find some weak opponents. You can win that way, but weak opponents are getting hard to find.

If you want to maximize your wins and be able to win against almost any nonexpert opponents (and some experts), you'll need to do more. Hopefully this book will help start you down that road.

WHY PLAY POKER?

It's likely that anyone reading this book has already played some poker. After all, most people have their first poker experience long before they've read a book on the subject. You're reading this book because you want to learn more about the game. Ask yourself why.

Before we start learning the nuts and bolts of the game of Hold 'Em, it helps to understand why we care, why we even want to play the game. The standard answer is that we play poker to win money, but that's not really an answer. There are many ways to earn money that are easier than playing poker. For many players winning money is necessary for enjoyment of the game, but it's not sufficient and for some players it's not even necessary. If you're enjoying the game, then you're getting something out of it besides the money. You're getting a psychic reward, but what is that psychic reward? I don't know. You do, though. Self-awareness is an important element of poker, and an awareness of the motivations of others is an even more important element.

There are different reasons why people play poker. Think of a hunting analogy for a minute. Some people enjoy the hunt itself more than the kill, and some people don't see much reason to hunt if you don't kill something. Some just like having the neatest gun; others get their thrill from being able to make a clean kill with a single shot.

Poker is the same principle. Some people play because they want to win money. Money won really is much sweeter than money earned. Others play because they enjoy the thrill of the gamble. They want to win also, but they simply want to gamble even more. A third group plays because it gives them an opportunity to demonstrate a knowledge of the game. This group thinks they want to win also, but it's really more important to them to be correct, to show off. To some, poker just provides an escape from everyday concerns.

We'll try to get to know all these players. While we're doing that, you should be thinking about the question: Why do you play poker? Once you can answer that question, honestly and completely, you'll be a big step ahead in removing the major emotional roadblocks to maximizing your win. No matter what your reason for playing is, winning is important. Some of us just couldn't play if we didn't win.

UNIQUE FEATURES OF POKER

Poker is a game of *skill*; luck and psychology also play a part, but unlike other casino games that rely entirely on luck, winning poker requires skill. A skillful poker player can change the odds in the game to his favor by using position, psychology, bluffing, and other methods to increase his chances to win the pot and increase the size of the pots he wins. No other casino game allows the player to manipulate the odds—only poker. *Poker is a game of money management*. It more closely resembles the board game of Monopoly than any other casino game. It is also a game of *patience* that most closely resembles hunting and has no analogy in any other casino game. A knowledge of the critical features of poker is necessary to form an understanding of the game.

Like other games in a casino, *poker is a gambling game*. Unlike most other games, bets are made among the players, not between the players and the house. The casino is essentially renting the space to players. Casinos collect rent by either taking a small amount from each pot, by charging each player a small hourly rate, or by variations of the two collection methods.

Table games, games where you bet against the house, are designed so that the house always has an edge. You can get lucky and win at table games, but over the long haul you will be a loser.

The result from an individual poker session has a lot to do with luck. The structure of the game, however, is such that a player with an understanding of the game can be a long-term winner, whereas those who don't really understand the game will be losers. That makes poker an ideal gambling game for those willing to work to improve their understanding of the game. Note that I didn't say you will be a winner. Many players understand the game very well, but engage in enough self-destructive behavior at the table that they almost never win. We talk about how to avoid some of those self-destructive tendencies later in the book.

Those without an interest in learning about the game should probably just buy lottery tickets if they want to gamble. The fact that you're reading this book suggests that you're interested in understanding the game, which is the first step toward becoming a winning player.

POKER VERSUS OTHER CASINO GAMES

Of course, it's possible to win at other casino games. Blackjack can be a winning game if you count cards. Progressive jackpot slot machines are profitable when the jackpots get large enough.

Poker is a preferable gambling game for a few reasons. First, a winning poker player has a large statistical edge. A counting blackjack player can also achieve an edge over the casino, but poker typically gives a larger edge than blackjack. It can be as much as 5 percent (or larger) for poker players, while blackjack players typically play with an edge of about 1 percent (or less). Winning poker players profit from huge mistakes which are often made by opponents. The only mistake the casino makes is allowing the winning blackjack player to play, and they can correct that error by simply ejecting the player from the casino.

Because of their larger edge, winning poker players also experience smaller fluctuations in their results than do blackjack players or players of progressive slots. We discuss risk in more detail later in the book. There are two characteristics of a game that create risk. One is even-money bets. Statistical variance reaches its maximum on even-money propositions. The other is when the range of possible outcomes is very large. Blackjack is very close to an even-money game, hence it has large risk. Progressive jackpot slots have low probability but very high dollar payoffs, hence a large risk. Poker is based on neither even-money bets nor low probabilities.

KEEPING SCORE WITH MONEY

There are other games where bets are made directly among players—golf, pool, tennis, backgammon, and gin come to mind—but these games exist without bets, they aren't really about money. Poker is about money; without money it just wouldn't exist. It's sometimes said that poker is not a game of cards played with money—*it's a game of money played with cards.*

Just because poker is a game of money doesn't mean money is always the point. When you get your competitive juices flowing, winning is the point. Winning means money, but at some point the money often becomes a secondary aspect of your motivation. A similar process occurs when you lose. The late Jack Strauss, a well-known poker player from San Antonio, said it best, "The bad thing about losing isn't the money, it's the embarrassment."

The idea that poker is a game of money but isn't always about money is another topic we come back to later in the book. As I pointed out earlier, the game attracts many players, not because of the opportunity to win money itself, but because *they enjoy the risk* associated with an opportunity to win money. This is a very important concept.

For these players it's the game itself that is important, not the winning. You'll see many losing players who seem to behave irrationally. If you keep in mind that, for some, the hunt is more thrilling than the kill, you'll see that their behavior is often quite rational, and you'll do a better job of reading these players. Again, we'll come back to this subject.

THE BASICS OF POKER

Poker is a card game involving both cards and money as basic elements of the game. It is not a game of making big hands; it's a game of winning large pots. It's not a game of winning a lot of pots; it's a game of winning the big ones. This is an important distinction between poker and other card games. In poker, money is not just the objective—it's an integral part of the game. Often new players, and even some not-so-new players, look for a magic formula or system based on the cards that will make them a winning poker player. There isn't one. When Kenny Rogers sang, "Know when to hold 'em, know when to fold 'em" in the song "The Gambler," he only got it half right. You also need to know when to bet or raise. Money does matter.

War

As children, most of us played a card game called war. I recall the game as a two-player game where each player got half the deck, face down. The top card in each player's stack was turned face up, the player with the highest ranking card won the cards, placing them on the bottom of his stack. Ties were broken by comparing a second card. The winner was the player who ended up with all the cards.

War is not poker, but a slight modification of the game transforms it into a primative form of poker. It simply requires adding money bets and peeking at your next card to transform it into a form of poker.

War as Poker

For example, each player could put up one cent (the ante) then receive a card. The first player looks at his card and decides whether to bet or check. The second player looks at his card and decides whether to call or fold (or bet if the first player checked).

Even without allowing a raise, we now have a simple form of poker. Note that just adding money to the game in the form of an ante was not sufficient to create a poker game—the option to bet is a key element of the game that makes poker what it is. Once we've added the concept of a bet to the children's game of war, the entire nature of the game has changed. In the game of war, the winner is the one who ends up with all the cards. When we are allowed the option to bet or fold, it should be easy to see that the player who gets all the cards may not end up as the player who wins the most money. This is also true in poker. The player who wins most of the pots is seldom the one who wins the money. The reason is that to win most of the pots you have to play most of them. Playing too many hands is one of the quickest routes to losing at poker that you can choose. *Remember this*. It's probably the most important fundamental truth about poker that a new player can learn.

MATHEMATICS OF POKER

If it's a game, mathematicians have tried to analyze it. Poker is no exception. Although it's probably impossible to completely analyze poker as a mathematical problem, most individual decisions that arise in poker can be profitably analyzed from a mathematical (or probabilistic or statistical) point of view. At various points in the book I do that. At least a basic concept of some of the mathematical principles of poker is needed to excel at the game; however, I do keep the math simple. Even the math-phobic reader should be able to follow the mathematical concepts used in most of the book.

Later in the book, I do provide an introduction to probability, statistics, and other mathematical concepts and their application to poker. For those who want to do their own probability or statistical analysis of the game, this material at least provides a beginning. You should do this if you want to extend your understanding of the game.

GROWTH AND CHANGE IN POKER

Until recently most poker was played on kitchen tables among friends and relatives. Often the stakes were low enough to be trivial, and the major activity of the game was social. Those games are still being played, but casino and cardroom poker has been popping up all over the country and has essentially replaced home poker in most areas. When you have a casino cardroom just down the street, you don't need to go to the effort of gathering seven to ten people to play for a few hours. The cardroom gathers them for you.

It wasn't that long ago that the only time most of us would have an opportunity to play poker in a legal cardroom was on a trip to Las Vegas or a handful of other locations that had legal poker. Even Atlantic City waited years before adding poker rooms to their casinos. Now most Americans are within a short drive of a legal cardroom.

You aren't playing for quarters anymore. Even the lowest limit casino game involves more money than the typical kitchen table game. Although you might very well find your friends and neighbors at the table with you in a public cardroom, it's not something you can depend on. Public cardrooms are public. Games are usually not by invitation. Some of your opponents, and in many places most of them, you'll probably never see again, so the social interaction is often superficial. Even if you're used to playing for the same stakes in a friendly home game, you will find yourself winning less or losing more in a casino game. This is not just because the games are tougher, although they are, it's because the house dealer is raking from $3 to $5 from each pot. In a fast-paced game, as much as $200 per hour (it's usually closer to $90) is leaving the table rather than being circulated among the players. Somebody's going to be losing that money. Make sure that it's not you. This is a different kind of poker.

HOLD 'EM

Although many of the concepts in this book apply to any form of poker, this book isn't a general poker book; it's about Hold 'Em, a particular form of poker that has gained tremendous popularity in North America and Europe. This popularity probably originated in the no-limit Hold 'Em championship event held at Binion's Horseshoe in Las Vegas every May.

It was originally called Texas Hold 'Em. The origins are obscure, but the game probably began in the old private cardrooms of South Texas. One of the features of the game is that it's typically played with ten players. Because each player only gets two unique cards, the other cards are community cards placed faceup on the table. You could play as many as twenty-two players if you could get that many around a table. You seldom see more than ten at a table in a casino game. I've played with as many as fourteen in private games.

Why Hold 'Em?

Why should you choose Hold 'Em as your game and not Seven Stud, Five Card Draw, Omaha, or some other poker game?

First, Hold 'Em is a much simpler game than any of the aforementioned poker variations. In Seven Stud you have to pay close attention to the cards that have been played and what was folded. It requires a great deal of memorizing, something that is not easy to do given the pace of the game in a cardroom, especially for a beginner. Five Card Draw also requires that you remember which player took how many cards. Omaha requires that you keep in mind that two of the four cards in your hand *must* be used with three community cards to make your hand. This is something that can easily be confused in the fast-paced atmosphere of the cardroom, where players think they have a hand only to find out at the showdown that a card on the board or in their hand is not valid in making their hand. Hold 'Em only requires that you know what you have in your two-card hand and how it meshes with what is on board. There are no discards, folded cards, or anything else to memorize, nor are there extraneous cards that can cause confusion.

Second, during any given hand in Stud the position of the bettor varies with the high hand, but in Hold 'Em, the position of the bettor doesn't vary during a hand. If you know that your position will not change, it allows you to play your position to its maximum effectiveness.

Third, in a Hold 'Em game, more players will stay in the game as opposed to Stud or Draw. This is chiefly because there are usually ten or eleven players as opposed to seven or eight in Stud or Draw; additionally, because of the five community cards, the hands are more promising to more players. Because more people tend to stay in the game, it yields bigger pots. Of course, with bigger pots you have a better chance to make more money. One winning hand in Hold 'Em can make up for hours of lost blinds and folded hands.

Fourth, it is a much quicker game than most other poker variations. For instance, you can play nearly twenty hands of Hold 'Em in the same amount of time it would take to play ten hands of Seven Card Stud. With the faster turnover of the cards, it gives you more opportunities to win.

Fifth, it's just more fun.

SOURCES FOR THIS BOOK

The first book devoted solely to Hold 'Em poker was a pamphlet written by David Sklansky about twenty-five years ago. Since then dozens of books on Hold 'Em have appeared. Many of the ideas expressed in this book have at least been inspired by these previous books.

A later chapter of the book discusses a number of other Hold 'Em and poker books. For now I recommend four that I think every serious Hold 'Em player should read (besides this book): *Winning Low-Limit Hold 'Em* by Lee Jones, *Hold 'Em Poker for Advanced Players* by David Sklansky and Mason Malmuth, *The Theory of Poker* by David Sklansky, and *The Book of Tells* by Mike Caro. Read them if you get the chance, but go ahead and read this book first.

Most of the original ideas expressed in this book were formed while I played in the cardrooms of Northern California, Northern Nevada, Southwest Louisiana, and private games in South Texas. Most of what I know about poker I learned the hard way, with my money.

The Internet has been a rich source of ideas and a place to refine ideas. There is an active Internet newsgroup, rec.gambling.poker. Although they usually stick to poker, recent posts have ranged in topic from values of vintage cars, to bankruptcy law, to the geography of Europe. Mostly it's about poker, though. Also, TwoPlusTwo Publishing maintains an on-line forum (www. twoplustwo.com) for the discussion of poker theory and strategy. PokerPages.com (www.pokerpages.com) also offers on-line discus-

sion forums, in addition to news on poker events and
wide range of poker writers.

While writing this book I used an Internet E-mail discussion
group to provide me with a forum to discuss the ideas and Hold
'Em strategies in the book. A number of poker-playing acquain-
tances from the Internet participated and helped immensely in my
ability to make some of my thoughts coherent. In parts of the
book, I also relied heavily on simulations using the computer software, specifically Turbo-Texas Hold 'Em for Windows, available
from Wilson Software (www.wilsonsoftware.com).

Good luck.

PART ONE

Hold 'Em for Beginners

The first part of the book is aimed at the beginning Hold 'Em player. The first two chapters provide an introduction to the mechanics and procedures of a typical cardroom Hold 'Em game. Whether addressing topics of interest to readers who are new to Hold 'Em, to cardroom games, or to both, the focus is on procedural aspects of the game, not strategic or tactical issues. More experienced players may benefit from parts of these chapters, but most will probably want to just skim them.

Beginners should strive to play a tight, simple game. That's also usually the best initial stratagy for an experienced player sitting in a new game for the first time. Four chapters of Part One present the playing requirements for such a tight, straightforward, aggressive playing style.

Part One is aimed at the beginner. More experienced players might want to just skim Part One, although parts of it may be interesting even to many experienced players.

2

Entering a Public Cardroom

PICKING A ROOM

Once you've decided you want to play poker in a casino cardroom, the next step is to decide which cardroom. Not all cardrooms are the same, and the choice of a cardroom can be critical to your success, especially if you're a novice player.

The most important decision you make in poker is your choice of table. Your profits depend on mistakes made by the other players at the table. Because your profits depend on your opponents, it's important to pick them carefully. Your choice of a room can determine the range of tables you have to choose from. Some cardrooms offer better choices of games than others. In particular, the more players in the cardroom, the more chances you have of finding opponents who are making a lot of mistakes. That's one of the reasons that larger cardrooms are often preferable to smaller ones.

Most cardrooms are well managed. They're clean and pleasant and provide an enjoyable environment. Unfortunately, some are really dingy, unpleasant, gloomy rooms. You'll need to check out the cardrooms near you and make a choice. Not all cardrooms are alike. If you have a bad experience at one, don't give up. Try another room. The best way to choose, of course, is to get a recommendation from a friend.

If you're computer literate, an alternative is to check the Internet newsgroup rec.gambling.poker. Its archives contain a number of player reviews of cardrooms; www.pokerpages.com is also a good source for cardroom reviews. If you can't find any recent reviews of cardrooms in your area, post a request for a recommendation on the newsgroup.

A third way to find a good cardroom is to just pick the largest in your area. In most cases you're more likely to have a good experience at a large cardroom. They will tend to have a wider selection of games, and game selection is the most critical decision you'll make when playing poker. Larger cardrooms also tend to put more effort into customer relations. They have a lot of tables to fill and need happy customers to maintain repeat business.

This isn't a slam against small cardrooms. Many of them are very good rooms, with very good games. Once you've gained some experience, you should at least check out the smaller cardrooms in your area. In fact, in some locations, the smaller rooms often have the better games. That's particularly the case in Las Vegas.

In Las Vegas the larger cardrooms tend to offer a wider range of limits. The local pros and semipros tend to be attracted to the rooms with the higher limit games. The smaller rooms in Las Vegas, which tend to offer exclusively low-limit games, often don't attract the local pros or regulars, relying almost entirely on tourist players.

This is often not the case in locations without the extensive tourist trade found in Las Vegas. If you're new to cardroom play, you should usually start with the larger ones unless you have a specific recommendation from a trusted friend.

INITIAL VIEW OF THE ROOM

When you walk into a large cardroom for the first time, it can appear chaotic. The noise and the people can be disorienting. Relax; it'll soon just be part of the scenery for you.

Most rooms have a railing that separates the playing area from the waiting area of the cardroom. It's often a good idea to spend a few minutes standing at the rail, just getting an overview of the room. Don't stand right next to a table unless the rail separates you from it, and don't stand directly behind a player. It bothers some players.

The particular procedures involved in getting into a game are not standardized—they vary from room to room. In this chapter I give you an idea of what to expect, but the specifics depend on the room. Don't hesitate to ask a cardroom employee if you are unsure of a procedure.

SIGN-UP PROCEDURES

Somewhere in the room will be a floor manager or host, usually called the "brush" in a poker room. Before you can take a seat at a table, you'll have to find him. He maintains a sign-up sheet for the waiting list in each game.

You'll need to be prepared to tell the floorman or brush what game (Hold 'Em) and what limit you want to play. Ask him what limits are available. Put yourself on the list for any limits you will be comfortable playing. A beginner should probably start in a 2/4, 3/6, or 1-4-8-8 game. (In the next chapter I explain what these numbers mean.)

I sometimes put myself on the waiting list for every game and limit that the room has available. If I decide I don't want to play a certain game, I can always turn the seat down when my name comes up, but getting on all the lists leaves my options open.

You can't just sit at an empty seat; just because a seat is empty doesn't mean it's available. It may be that a new player is on his way to take the seat, or there may be some other reason the brush will want you to take a seat at a different table. Generally you will not be allowed to take a seat without referral by the brush, so don't try.

The form of the sign-up sheet varies from cardroom to cardroom. Some use a large blackboard or acrylic writing surface, and players can add themselves to the list. More commonly someone is standing near the board, and they will add your initials or name. Sometimes the floor manager keeps a clipboard that contains the waiting lists.

If you see a large board that looks as if it might be a sign-up board, go to it. You should find a floor manager nearby. If you don't see such a board, look for a podium either near the front or middle of the room. If all else fails, just ask someone where to sign up for a game.

Whenever you're in doubt about something, don't be hesitant to just ask whoever is available. Because every cardroom has a slightly different sign-up procedure, you won't be identifying yourself as a novice by asking. Even the most experienced player may have to ask if it's his first visit to that particular cardroom. You'll usually get a receptive reaction to questions from players and employees alike.

Once you've signed up for a game, don't leave the cardroom area without first telling the brush. Some cardrooms will give you a beeper to carry if you intend to wander to other areas of the casino. Sometimes they'll page you over the casino loudspeaker. Some of them are even starting to keep computerized lists shown on monitors scattered around the room. If you don't tell them you will be out of the area, many cardrooms will simply cross your name off the list if you don't quickly respond when your name is called. It all depends on the procedures in use at the particular cardroom. *Ask*.

TAKING YOUR SEAT

Once a seat is available, your name will be called out or you'll be paged. When you respond, you'll be told at which table to take a seat. Usually the tables are numbered on signs hanging over the table which also gives the game and limits and the buy-in. Sometimes they are numbered on a small plaque, face-up on the table next to the dealer.

Buying Chips

In some cardrooms players buy chips from the dealer, and in some the brush will take your money and get chips for you from the cage. Some rooms have chip-runners who carry chips around in a pouch to sell to players. If you're not sure of the procedure in your cardroom, just get out your money, and someone will get you some chips. Again, you just might need to ask.

The minimum buy-in in the smallest games in most cardrooms is $40. Typically a minimum buy is either $40 or ten times the smallest bet allowed. I recommend you buy either $100 or about twice the amount of the minimum buy-in, whichever is larger.

Rebuys

You won't be able to go into your pocket to buy more chips during the play of the hand. So, you always want to make sure you have enough chips before a hand is dealt, and it's always a good idea to have a few more chips than you'll probably need. You can buy chips between hands. If you haven't run out of chips, there is usually no minimum amount to buy for an add-on.

How Much Money to Bring?

One of the worst things that can happen to a poker player is to be in a good game, have a short run of bad luck, and run out of money. It's a good idea to make certain that you have enough cash to cover any normal runs of bad luck. Generally I like to have between three to five buy-ins in my pocket for a poker session. For a game where the normal buy-in is $100, I won't play if I don't have $300 in my pocket, and I like to have $500.

That might seem like more money than a winning player would need, and it usually is, but the nature of poker is such that you will lose more pots than you will win. The amount of money in the pot when you do win will more than make up for the amount of money that you might lose in three or four losing pots. The fact remains that it's not unexpected to lose quite a few pots in a row. Often, in the better games where the players are a little loose and wild, you might lose a lot of pots in a row. Sometimes the pots get big enough in these games that you can break even by just winning one out of ten pots that you contest, but if you don't have enough money in your pocket to keep playing, you won't have that opportunity. *Bring enough money.*

Posting the Blind

When you first sit down, you won't get a hand right away. Because the two blinds take the place of an ante, you won't be eligible to be dealt a hand until you have posted a blind. Blinds are put up in turn, so you'll have to wait until the blind position moves around to your seat. Because Hold 'Em is typically played without an ante, in most games you won't be dealt a hand until you've posted a blind. You will have the option of posting an amount equal to the big blind (as an extra blind for that hand) or simply waiting until it's your turn in the normal rotation of the button to post the big blind. Most players just wait. At some cardrooms this rule is not enforced at the lower-limit tables. The reason for the rule is to prevent players from taking shots by sitting in at a table, getting free cards until it's their blind, then getting up and cashing out.

KNOW THE RULES

"A wildcat is only good once a night." That's the punch line from an old poker joke. A player goes to a draw poker card club for the first time. After a couple of hours, he gets four Aces and bets heavily. He gets called by a player who shows a hand of Q9732, four different suits. The dealer starts to push the pot to the player with the Q high hand. Our hero says, "Hey, I've got four aces." The dealer says, "Yes, but he's got a wildcat," pointing to a sign on the wall that says, "A wildcat consists of Q9732 and is the best hand."

Well, as you might have guessed, later our hero gets a Q9732 himself and, after much betting, gets shown the sign that says "A wildcat is only good once a night."

Although few clubs have a wildcat rule these days (although some California clubs do have some weird house rules), a novice casino player does need to realize that the house rules aren't going to be the same as the rules at home games. String betting is an example. Showing all your cards at the showdown, even when you aren't using them all to make your hand, is another. Sometimes a violation of these rules will cost the novice a bet. Sometimes the pot.

Knowing the house rules is important. Watch, listen, ask questions. Some rules are relatively standard and I discuss a few of them here, but there is always the possibility of a weird house rule. It pays to ask.

Protect Your Hand

Sometimes, particularly if you're in a seat adjacent to the dealer, the dealer will accidentally grab your cards and put them into the muck. If that happens, then your hand is dead. It's as if you have folded. It's your responsibility to keep control of your cards. You can't move your cards over the edge of the table, so the best thing to do is to place a chip on top of your cards whenever you leave them lying on the table. That will prevent the dealer from accidentally scooping them up.

Keep Your Cards on the Table

Don't pick your cards up and hold them close to your chest to look at them. Leave your cards on the table, cup your hands over them, and bend up the edges of the cards to look at them. Watch the other players to see how it's done.

The reason for this is a rule that says that no card can cross an imaginary barrier at the edge of the table. If you do move your cards behind the edge of the table, your hand can be ruled dead. Most cardrooms do not strictly enforce this rule at the low-limit tables. But you will be corrected if you do it, and if you persist in doing it, you will eventually have your hand declared dead. Just don't do it.

On a related note, should the dealer accidentally deal your card to you in such a way that it flips off the table onto the floor, do not reach down and pick it up. You are not supposed to touch any card that's off the table. The floorman will come over and pick up the card. The reason for these rules is to protect the integrity of the deck.

Show Both Cards

Your hand consists of the two cards you're initially dealt. You don't have to use both those cards to make up your poker hand, but you must have both of them to win. Show both your cards at the showdown by simply turning them face up. Do this even if only one of them is being used to form your poker hand.

One Player to a Hand

Don't ask a friend for advice at the table and don't give advice to a friend, even if one of you is not involved with the pot, or even if your friend isn't playing at the table. Consulting with another person about how to play a hand isn't allowed. Also don't show your hand to another player, even if he is not involved in the pot and even if you are folding.

String Bets

A string bet is a bet that's made in two motions. It's common in home games to see a player say, "I call your dollar," put a dollar in the pot, then say, "And raise you a dollar," as he reaches into his stack of chips for a second chip. That's a string bet. In a casino, if you're going to raise simply state "raise." Don't say something like "I'll call your bet and raise you." Just say the one word, "Raise," and put all your chips into the pot at one time, not in two motions of your hand.

The reason for this rule is to reduce the chances for players to engage in what's called angle shooting. Without this rule players can call a bet, wait to see your reaction to the call, and if you react in a way that suggests you didn't want to be called, they will raise. Not allowing string bets reduces the opportunity for this kind of unethical move.

Raising

A raise must be at least the size of the bet. For example, if I bet $4 in a 1-4 game, then you must raise by $4 if you want to raise. If I had bet $2 then you could raise $2, $3, or $4. You cannot make a $2 raise if the original bet was $4.

Be Careful What You Say

Verbal declarations usually count. "Call and raise" is the verbal equivalent of a string bet, and, in some cardrooms, if you say that before you put your chips in the pot, you will be limited to a call.

Splashing the Pot

When you make a call or bet, just place your chips in front of you. Don't toss your chips into the pot. The dealer will count your chips before putting them into the pot to ensure your bet is the correct amount. Just throwing your chips directly into the pot is called splashing the pot because of the bouncing of the chips that usually results. Don't do it. Again, the purpose of the rule is to protect you.

Act in Turn

In Hold 'Em, the action at each betting round begins with the first player to the left of a designated dealer. Each player then acts in turn. Don't act until it's your turn—don't fold or bet early.

Table Stakes

All cardroom games are played at table stakes. That means you can't reach into your pocket for more money during the play of the hand. You can't be bet out of the hand either; you remain in competition for whatever the pot is up to the point where you've run out of chips. This is called creating a side-pot. You can buy chips to add to your stack at any time between hands. You cannot add to your stack during the play of a hand.

Ratholing

"Ratholing" is the poker term for taking money off the table and slipping it into your pocket. It's not allowed. Except for incidental uses, such as tipping the cocktail waitress, taking money off the table is not allowed.

Short Buys

Every table has an established minimum buy-in. Your first purchase of chips must be at least that amount. At some cardrooms, after the initial purchase, it is permissible to buy less than the minimum buy. This is called a short buy. Almost all cardrooms will allow a short buy if you are not out of chips. Some will allow a short buy when you run out of chips but only once.

Dealers

The dealer is an employee of the cardroom and is at work. If you have a question about the game, ask the dealer. If you want to talk about last night's football game, talk to one of the other players. The dealer's job is to keep the game running smoothly, not to provide you with conversation.

Making Friends, Avoiding Deadbeats

Most cardroom players eventually make some friends of people they meet in the cardroom. My advice is don't be too quick to do this. Poker attracts a complete cross section of society. You'll meet all kinds of people from all walks of life. Although most of them are great people, some really are thieves and deadbeats. Be careful about extending your friendship, and *don't loan money*.

3

The Play of the Game

In most areas of the country, the most popular form of casino or cardroom poker is Hold 'Em. Hold 'Em is being played in cardrooms more and more. Because of this the procedural details are becoming more and more standardized. This chapter gives an introduction to the mechanics and procedures of Hold 'Em as typically played in a cardroom.

In a cardroom players are generally expected to follow fixed playing procedures which are designed to keep the game moving at a regular pace. Most players act in turn and act quickly. If you aren't used to playing in a cardroom, the play may seem to be moving very fast to you, but you'll quickly become acclimated to the routine. Because cardrooms typically charge their fee by raking a small amount from each pot (there are some exceptions to this), the more pots, the larger the total rake. So they have a financial incentive to keep the games fast paced.

THE DEALER BUTTON

Both to keep the game moving smoothly and to guard against card manipulation by the players, the casino provides a nonplaying dealer. In Hold 'Em the action at each betting round begins with the first active player to the left of the dealer. There is a large disadvantage to having to go first and a large advantage in going last. So a player-dealer is designated for each hand, and the designation is passed around the table with each hand. This player-dealer doesn't actually deal the cards, but the deal and the play proceeds as if that player were the dealer.

This player-dealer is designated by having a large, round "button" placed in front of him. The button is passed to the left after each hand. The player who has the button in front of him is said to be "on the button." He is last to act for each betting round except the first round.

BETTING LIMITS

There are two kinds of betting limits in Hold 'Em: structured and spread limit. The most common at the low limits is "spread limit," for example 1-4, which means, at each betting round, you can bet anywhere from $1 to $4. Typically in spread-limit games, the bets on the first round will be at the minimum, and players will bet the maximum on later rounds.

Typical spread limits you might see are 1-4, 1-5, 2-5, 2-10, 1-4-8, 1-4-4-8, or 1-4-8-8.

Games designated by two numbers, such as 1-4, allow bets in the range of $1 to $4, at any betting round. A designation such as 1-4-8 means that bets up to $4 are allowed at any round until the last round, when the allowable range is $1 to $8. Most cardrooms would designate that game as 1-4-4-8. When describing the limits of a spread-limit game, a 1 is the first number in the description. There are a few exceptions, such as 2-10 and 2-4-8-8, but many clubs will designate games as 1-4-8-8 even if the actual minimum bet is $2.

"Structured limits" are where the bet at every round is fixed, 10/20 is an example. Here the bet on the first two betting rounds is $10, on the second two, $20.

A "variation" is structured betting with an option on the last bet, for example, 3/6/12 or 10/20/40. In 3/6/12, the bet on the first round is $3, the bet on the flop is $3, on the turn $6, and the river bet is either $6 or $12 at the option of the bettor. Spread-limit games also sometimes have the limit double on the last betting round.

Hold 'Em is sometimes played as a pot-limit or no-limit game, or sometimes as a variation such as pot-limit with a cap on the maximum allowable bet. Most casino games, however, are played as either spread- or structured-limit games.

The strategic advice in this book is mostly geared toward the typical structured game with two betting levels. However, spread- and structured-limit games with three betting levels each have some important strategic considerations that are unique to the betting structure. These issues are addressed separately in Chapters 20 and 21.

THE BLINDS

Typically cardroom games are played without an ante. The reason for this should be obvious to those of you who are familiar with the common mantra of home games, "Who didn't put their ante up?"

Because poker is basically a struggle among the players for the right to the money in the pot, without some seed money for the pot there's nothing to struggle over and no game. We need some procedure to get the pot started. In Hold 'Em, blind bets are what's used to get some initial money in the pot.

The action in Hold 'Em at each betting round begins with the first active player to the left of the dealer button. Blinds are forced bets put out by either the first or the first two players. Usually it's the first two players. The blinds replace the function of an ante in getting some initial money into the pot. Some games only use a single blind, most use two blinds, the second one larger than the first. In a structured game, the second blind (called the big blind) is the size of the pre-flop bet. In a 10/20 game, the big blind is $10, and in a 3/6/12 game, the big blind is $3.

The small blind is put out by the first player to the left of the button and is half the big blind. In a game such as 3/6, where the big blind is an odd number, the small blind is sometimes rounded up, sometimes down, $1 or $2. It's usually rounded down. Spread-limit games usually have smaller blinds than a corresponding structured-limit game does.

Blinds are "live," which means that the player posting the blind will be last to act during the first betting round. Even if no player raises—that is, they all only call the large blind bet—the player who posted the large blind has an option to raise.

Straddles

A "straddle" is a third blind, voluntarily put out by a third player. It's sometimes referred to as a "kill." Cardrooms do not have standard procedures about straddles. Some don't allow them at all. Some allow them, but only by the player to the immediate left of the big blind, the under-the-gun (UTG) position. Some require them under certain conditions. Although the term kill is sometimes used for any straddle, it is usually reserved to refer to a required straddle.

Sometimes straddles are live, sometimes not. When they are live, you are essentially buying last position in the betting; you have the option to raise after everyone else has acted. Some cardrooms consider a straddle put out by the UTG player as live, but other straddles must act in turn, without the option of acting after everyone else.

Some rooms have games with a required kill if certain conditions are met, such as winning the last pot. These are called kill games, or winner blind games. Depending on the cardroom, if a pot reaches a certain threshold size or if the same player wins two pots in a row, the winner is required to straddle an amount twice the size of the big blind, and the betting limits for that hand are doubled. This can sometimes change the ratio of bet size to initial blinds enough so that significant changes in playing strategy are called for.

Sometimes a straddle is the size of the big blind, sometimes twice the big blind. Sometimes it doubles the limits of the game, sometimes it doubles the bet size before the flop only. Sometimes it has no effect on the bet size.

Are you confused? You should be. The range of straddle rules is confusing. If you are a beginner, my only advice is to avoid straddles or kill games until you gain some experience. If you find yourself in such a game, just ask lots of questions.

BETTING ROUNDS

Hold 'Em has four betting rounds, each corresponding to a different stage of the deal. You start with two cards dealt facedown. These are the only two cards that will be uniquely yours, hidden from other players. All other cards are community cards, dealt faceup in the middle of the table. There will be five community cards faceup at the showdown. These are cards placed in the middle of the table and shared by all players. The community cards are called the board and are dealt faceup in three stages:

1. Three cards are dealt at once, called the flop.
2. Then the fourth card is dealt, called the turn.
3. Then the fifth card is dealt, called the "river" (or end).

Before each of the three stages, the dealer will burn a card, that is, he discards a card facedown. After each stage of dealing, there is a betting round.

Your poker hand is formed from the best five cards chosen from any combination of your two-card hand and the five-card board. You can use zero, one, or both of your cards in your final poker hand.

Your Hand and the First Betting Round

Each player is dealt his two-card hand. The first round of betting begins with posting of the blinds. These blind bets are required; they are automatic and must be posted by the first two players to the left of the button. The first player to the left of the big blind is the first player with discretionary action. Each player, in turn, can either fold, call the big blind bet, or raise. The play proceeds around the table to the blinds. The small blind can fold, call for the difference between the current bet and his small blind amount, or raise. When it reaches the big blind, if there has been a raise he can either fold, or call the raise, or reraise. If there has not been a raise, he can either check or raise—his blind is already the amount of the first bet.

If no one calls the big blind, then the big blind wins the pot, consisting of the two blinds.

The Flop and the Second Betting Round

After the first round of betting, three community cards are dealt faceup. These three cards are called the "flop." Once they are spread faceup in the middle of the table, the second round of betting begins with the first active player to the left of the button. The bet size is usually the same size as it had been on the flop betting round. In Hold 'Em, the flop defines your hand. During the first round of betting you have only two cards, and different two-card combinations have different potentials. The combinations (A♥A♠), (A♥K♥), and (T♠6♥) all have some potential to develop into different poker hands (the potential of T♠6♥ is very weak). Once you've seen the flop, you know something about whether any of the potential is likely to be realized.

The Turn and the Third Betting Round

The fourth card (or turn) is put faceup on the board after the flop betting round is completed. Then a new round of betting begins. In structured betting games, the bet size doubles on the turn betting round.

The River and the Last Betting Round

The river card is the last community card. After the card is dealt, there is a round of betting and a showdown.

THE POT

The pot goes to the highest hand at the showdown.

Split Pots

Because of the community cards, Hold 'Em has more ties than most other forms of poker. An example would be if the board contains four Aces and a King. It's not possible for anyone to hold a card in their hand that is better than that hand. Even if a player has a King in his hand, every player can play the King on the board and tie. In some home games, it's common to break ties by giving the pot to the player with the high card for the sixth card, using the Bridge rank of suits (Spades, Hearts, Diamonds, Clubs) to break ties in ranks. That's not the generally accepted way to do it in poker. In a cardroom ties aren't broken—the pot is just divided among the active hands.

There are other ways for a tie to result in Hold 'Em other than all players simply playing the five cards on the board as their best hand. Players frequently have the same two pair, or the same straight, or similar ties. And example of this would be if the board contained an Ace, King, Queen, Jack, and Deuce. Here any player who has a 10 in their hand has an Ace-high straight, and if more than one player holds a 10, then the pot is split among them.

Poker hands are five-card combinations. No tie-breakers are used. The pots are just split when players tie.

Side Pots

Casino poker is played with the table-stakes rule. This means that you cannot be required to call a bet for more money than you had on the table before the hand began. Similarly you aren't allowed to bet more than you had on the table before the hand began. If a player runs out of money during a hand, and more than one other player remains, then a side pot is created. A player who runs out of money is said to be "all-in."

If a player is all-in and only one other player remains active, then the cards are simply dealt out, you have a showdown, and the best hand takes the pot. If two or more other players are still active, then action between those players can continue.

When a player runs out of chips, then the pot at that point is pushed aside by the dealer. This pot contains all the chips for calls and bets up to the amount corresponding to the all-in player's calls. All bets and calls after that point are kept in a separate pile until the showdown. This is the "side pot." The original pot is called the "main pot."

The side pot is awarded to the best hand among the players who put money into that pot. The all-in player cannot win any of that money. Once the side pot is distributed, the winner of that pot shows down with the all-in player. The best hand of those two takes the main pot. If more than one player goes all-in during a hand, multiple side pots are created. The showdown starts with the players active in the last side pot created.

The Rake

In a casino, the casino will collect a fee for playing poker. This fee is generally called a "rake" because most cardrooms collect the fee by raking a certain amount from each pot. Whenever this is the procedure, the amount is typically either 5 or 10 percent, up to a maximum of $3 to $5. In most games you can count on almost every pot getting large enough so that the maximum rake will be taken.

Two other collection methods are in common usage: a time charge and a button charge. "Time charges" are a fixed amount, collected from each player every half hour. They typically range from $3 to $7 per half hour, depending on the limits of the game. Button charges are collected each hand from the player on the button; $3 is a typical charge. Sometimes the button charge is a live bet; it counts as a call of the initial blind bet.

TIES AND SPLIT POTS

Since Hold 'Em uses five community cards, shared by all players, it's not unusual to have two or more hands of the same rank competing at the showdown: two full houses, two flushes, sometimes even two straight flushes. It's only a tie if all five cards are identical. Suits don't count in the rankings. One suit does not outrank another.

For example, say the board is 4♠4♥4♦4♣7♦. Every player still active in the pot (anyone who hasn't folded yet) has four 4s. The tie is broken by the fifth card. Anyone holding an Ace in their private hand has an unbeatable hand. If two players hold an Ace, they split the pot. If no one holds a card higher than a 7, then all active players split the pot.

Full houses are ordered by the rank of the triplet. That means 3, 3, 3, 4, 4 will beat 2, 2, 2, A, A. In poker variations that don't use community cards, the rank of the pair never enters into a comparison of two full houses. Not so in Hold 'Em. Let's say we have a flop of 2♠2♣7♥Q♥K♠. One player has a K♥2♥, another has Q♦2♦, and a third player has 7♠7♣. The player with the 7, 7 has the best hand, 7s full of deuces (7♥7♠7♣2♠2♣). The second best hand is deuces full of Kings (2♠2♣2♥K♠K♣), and the worst hand of the three is deuces full of Queens 2♠2♣2♦Q♥Q♦.

Another frequent occurrence is two players having the same two pair. For example, say you have A♦J♦. I hold A♥T♥ and the board is A♠5♦4♥4♣9♣. We both have two pair, Aces over

RANK OF POKER HANDS

Straight flush	Five cards of the same suit, in sequence	An example is 10♣9♣8♣7♣6♣	Rank is determined by the highest card. A royal flush, such as A♦K♦Q♦J♦T♦, is the highest straight flush.
Four of a Kind	Four cards of the same rank, with the fifth card any rank	An example is 3♠3♥3♦3♣7♠	Rank is determined first by the highest quads then, if if the quads are on board, by the rank of the fifth card.
Full House	Three cards of one rank and two of another	An example is 3♠3♥3♦7♠7♣	Rank is determined by the highest triplet, then, if two players have the same triplet, by the rank of the pair.
Flush	Five cards of the same suit, not in sequence	A♣J♣9♣4♣2♣ is an example	Rank is determined by the highest card, then, if the highest card is on the board, by the second highest card, then the third highest, or fourth highest, or fifth card.
Straight	Five cards in sequence, not all of the same suit	An example is J♣T♥9♦8♣7♦	Rank is determined by the highest card.
Three of a Kind	Three cards of the same rank, the other two are any other cards that don't form a pair	K♥K♦K♣Q♥8♥ is an example	Rank is determined by the triplet. If two players have the same triplet, then by the rank of the highest odd card, then the rank of the other odd card.
Two pair	Two cards of one rank, two cards of another rank, and an unmatched card	K♥K 9♠9♥A♣ is an example	Rank is determined by the largest pair. If two players have the same largest pair, then by the rank of the other pair. If both pair are the same, then by the rank of the odd card.
One pair	Two cards of the same rank and three unmatched cards	A♥A♣K♥Q♠4♦ is an example	Rank is determined by the pair, if two players have the same pair, then by the rank of the highest odd card, then the second highest odd card, then the third.
No pair	Five cards without any pair, not all of the same suit, not in sequence	A♣T♣9♥4♥2♥ is an example	Rank is determined by the rank of the highest card, then the second highest, then third highest, etc.

fours. But your five-card hand gives you A♠A♦4♥4♣J♦, beating my A♠A♥4♥4♣T♥. The fifth card, called a "kicker," breaks the tie. Hold 'Em is often referred to as a game of kickers. It's that tie-breaking role of the kicker that's being referred to. It happens more often than you might think.

Note that in the above example, if the last card on the board had been a King rather than a 9, we'd both have a King kicker and would split the pot. You don't go beyond the five-card hand to break ties.

Sometimes, no one can beat the poker hand consisting of the five cards on the board. An example would be a board of K♠K♥ K♦K♣A♠. Another example is a board of A♥K♥7♥4♥2♥, and no one holds a Heart in their hands. Whenever this happens, it's a tie and all active hands split the pot. Note that if anyone had a Heart they would have a higher flush than the board.

4

The First Betting Round

My definition of a good poker player is one who can recognize and exploit advantageous situations and recognize and avoid situations that are not advantageous. You can get some help toward developing the skill of a good poker player from books, but books will not be enough. You need experience. You're going to have to get in there and mix it up.

Beginning Hold 'Em players should follow a basic plan of playing tight. Your bottom line is affected just as much by avoiding a loss as it is by winning a pot. Playing very tight is one way to avoid losses. By playing only very strong hands, you'll avoid many of those decision points that require the judgment of an experienced player. Because many of those tough decisions require knowledge of the playing habits of your opponents, playing very tight is also the preferred style for even an experienced player if you're not familiar with the playing habits of your opponents.

Just playing tight is not an approach that will maximize your win in most games, but it is an optimal learning strategy for players who are new to Hold 'Em. You should not, however, play too tight. Part of learning the game is getting involved in some hands and making a few mistakes. Don't plan on making mistakes, do what you can to avoid them, but realize that they will happen and try to learn from them.

Tight play starts with the first two cards. It's a strategy based primarily on the idea that poker is a struggle among the players for a claim on the initial money in the pot (the blinds). The focus is on the random distribution of the first two cards on the deal. It's a risk-averse approach that does not explicitly exploit any probable or observed errors that your opponents might be making.

POSITION

At a ten-handed table, I usually think of the seats as divided into five pairs.

PLAYING POSITIONS

Number of chairs to the left of the dealer button	Playing position
1 & 2	The blinds
3 & 4	The under-the-gun positions (first two players to act after the blinds)
5 & 6	Early position
7 & 8	Middle position
9 & 10	Late position and the button

DECIDING TO PLAY

If you're a new Hold 'Em player, or just new to the table and haven't yet been able to identify the game conditions, the best approach is to just play tight.

There are three things you should take into consideration when deciding whether to play a hand.

1. Your position
2. How many players have already called
3. Whether the pot has been raised

Depending on these three things, tight play means different things. It doesn't mean wait until you get pocket Aces. Tight play means that you should only get involved when the situation suggests that the hand you've been dealt has an edge over the hands the other players have been dealt.

When you're in early position, you should generally play fewer hands because of the lack of information you have about others' hands and the risk of a weak hand being raised by a better one. In late position, you have more information about others' hands and can often play weaker hands if no one has raised. Actually, in late position you can usually play weaker hands even if someone has raised.

How the number of players affects your hands depends both on how many of them have called and the position they've called from. If others have called from an early position, you generally need a stronger hand. That's because most players who open from an early position will have a strong hand themselves. However, if many players (generally five or more) have called, then you can play many weaker hands because you're getting fairly good odds on your money.

If the pot has been raised, you should generally play few hands. This is especially true if the raiser came in from an early position.

In the tables, I list some minimum hand requirements to open the pot or to call an opener under various situations. Don't memorize these tables. The cut-off hands I suggest are just that— suggestions. In most cases you should be playing either tighter or looser than the tables suggest—depending on how well the others at the table play. The better your opposition plays, the fewer hands you should play. The worse your opposition plays, the more hands you should play. Use these tables as guidelines, not as a set of rules about playable hands.

In cases where your opponents all play badly after the flop, then you can usually loosen up even on these minimum requirements, but in many games the minimums given in these tables are probably too loose. You should play tighter than the tables suggest. In Chapter 12, where I talk about a theory of starting hand values, I give some other hand groupings based on game characteristics that give hands value. My best suggestion is to take the tables in this chapter and adjust them for play in the game in which you typically play based on the hand groups I give in Chapter 12. Do your own table of starting hands based on game characteristics and on how well you play relative to the other players. The simplest decisions are when no one else has called yet, meaning the only thing you need to take into consideration is your position.

When You're First to Call

The criteria to use when deciding to play when no one else has called yet are different from the criteria that are important when deciding to call when another player has already opened the betting. When no one else has opened yet, there will be some players who have folded, leaving you with a smaller field to worry about beating, and the only money that's in the pot is the money from the blinds.

Under the Gun

When you're under the gun, the very first player to act, there are nine other players who have not yet acted. You're in a vulnerable position, and you'll be in a vulnerable position at every betting round. Only your best hands should be played—those that figure to be good enough to beat eight or nine random hands. In first or second position, you just shouldn't be playing many hands, the risk of getting raised by a better hand is just too great.

Early Position

In the next two positions, when one or two players have folded and seven or eight players are yet to act, you're still in a pretty

MINIMUM OPENING HANDS WHEN YOU'RE FIRST IN

Suited Cards

	Pairs	Ax s.	Kx s.	Qx s.	Jx s.	10x s.	9x s.	8x s.	7x s.	6x s.	5x s.
Under the gun	7,7	A♠9♠	K♠10♠	Q♦10♦	J♦T♦	—	—	—	—	—	—
Early position	6,6	A♠8♠	K♦9♦	Q♦9♦	J♦10♦	10♦9♦	—	—	—	—	—
Middle position	5,5	A♦2♦	K♦7♦	Q♦9♦	J♦9♦	10♦9♦	9♦8♦	—	—	—	—
Button	4,4	A♦2♦	K♦6♦	Q♦8♦	J♦8♦	10♦8♦	9♦8♦	8♦6♦	7♦6♦	6♦5♦	—
Small blind	2,2	A♦2♦	K♦2♦	Q♦7♦	J♦7♦	10♦7♦	9♦7♦	8♦6♦	7♦4♦	6♦3♦	5♦4♦

Unsuited Cards

	Ax	Kx	Qx	Jx	10x	9x	8x	7x
Under the gun	A♠Q♦	—	—	—	—	—	—	7x
Early position	A♠J♦	K♠J♦	Q♠J♦	—	—	—	—	—
Middle position	A♠10♦	K♠10♦	Q♠J♦	—	—	—	—	—
Button	A♠4♦	K♠7♦	Q♠7♦	J♠9♦	T♠9♦	—	—	—
Small blind	A♠2♦	K♠2♦	Q♠2♦	J♠6♦	T♠7♦	9♠6♦	8♠6♦	7♠5♦

Legend: Ax s. means an Ace and another lower card of the same suit.
Kx s. means a King and another lower card of the same suit
Ax means an Ace and another card of a different suit from the Ace.
Kx means a King and another lower card of a different suit from the King.

NOTE: An entry like A♠9♠ means that hand and any better hands. A♠9♠ represents A♠K♠, A♠Q♠, A♠J♠, A♠10♠, A♠9♠, of course, of any suit. The next four tables are to be read in the same way. The entry 6♦3♦ means 6♦5♦, 6♦4♦, or 6♦3♦, again of any suit.

vulnerable position. You can open with a couple of additional hands that are slightly more risky than the hands you can open with under the gun. At a tough table, all these added hands have a potential to make an expensive second-best hand. Waiting until a couple of early players have folded reduces those chances enough to make them profitable hands, even at a somewhat tough table.

Middle Position

Once two or three players have folded, you're in a little better position. You've only got five or six players yet to act and two of them are in the blinds, who will be in a weak position relative to you after the flop. You can add a lot of hands to your list of hands to open with.

Late Position

Infrequently, you'll be in late position, and everyone who has acted ahead of you has folded. If this happens frequently, you're in too tight a game and should move to another table. Or go home and watch reruns of *Gilligan's Island*. When it does happen, you can safely open with a lot more hands than you can in early position.

The Small Blind

If everyone has folded except the blinds, and you're in the small blind, you should aggressively go after the blinds at least half the time. The tighter and the more passive the player on the big blind tends to be, the more often you should attack the blinds when the situation arises.

Opening Hands When You're First In

In the last table, I suggest K♦6♦ as a minimum-suited King to open with from late position, when you're either last or next to last before the blinds. To many people K♦6♦ doesn't seem to be all that much different a hand than K♦2♦. This is because, if you flop a King, then in either case if someone else also has a King, your hand will likely be beaten by a better kicker. The flush draw potential of the two hands is the same, and the difference between a pair of Kings with a 6 kicker and a pair of Kings with a 2 kicker isn't much. Also, two pair with Kings and 6s aren't much different than two pair with Kings and 2s. All that's true, but the difference between a 2♦ and a 6♦ is still fairly large, particularly when you're opening from late position.

I suggest the K♦6♦ as a minimum if you're one of the last two players (the button and one to the right of the button). In this case you've got two or three possible callers. You're not really looking to flop a flush draw—your odds are pretty weak for that with at most two or three callers. The flush possibility only adds a very little when you're first in from late position. In the same position I suggest K,7 unsuited as a minimum opening unsuited King.

Against such few opponents, the King can sometimes even win just with its high-card value. Flopping "second pair" (pairing the second highest card on the flop) is a good hand in a short-handed game, and if only three or four of you haven't folded, that's the situation you're in. So, pairing the King is probably enough, and you won't need a kicker.

The King is actually the kicker here. The 6 can flop second pair, and second pair with a good kicker is a strong hand in a short-handed confrontation. A deuce or trey isn't going to be flopping second pair much. That's the difference between K♦6♦ and K♦2♦. Very small cards like 2 through 5 will flop "bottom pair" too often. Very small pairs will often be beaten by second pair, but a small card as large as 6 or 7 is often just large enough to make a difference.

Another major difference between the 6 and a 2 is overcards. If you pair a 2 on the flop, then every card that comes on the turn or river is an overcard to your pair, bringing a risk of beating you by pairing a card in the hand of an opponent. If you flop the bottom pair with a 6, then only six overcards might make someone a larger pair on the turn or river. This is a big difference.

When Others Have Called

The situation is a little different if players ahead of you have already voluntarily entered the pot. Now you're no longer against

Minimum Calling Hands With One or Two Early Position Limpers

Suited Cards

	Pairs	Ax s.	Kx s.	Qx s.	Jx s.	10x s.	9x s.	8x s.	7x s.	6x s.
Under the gun	n/a	n/a	n/a	n/a	n/a	n/a	n/a	n/a	n/a	n/a
Early position	9,9	A♠J♠	K♠Q♠	Q♦J♦	J♦10♦	—	—	—	—	—
Middle position	9,9	A♦J♦	K♦Q♦	Q♦J♦	J♦10♦	—	—	—	—	—
Button	8,8	A♦10♦	K♦J♦	Q♦10♦	J♦9♦	10♦8♦	9♦8♦	8♦7♦	—	—
Blinds	6,6	A♦6♦	K♦10♦	Q♦9♦	J♦8♦	10♦7♦	9♦7♦	8♦6♦	7♦6♦	6♦5♦

Unsuited Cards

	Ax	Kx	Qx	Jx	10x	9x	8x
Under the gun	n/a	n/a	n/a	n/a	n/a	n/a	8x
Early position	A♠K♦	—	—	—	—	—	
Middle position	A♠K♦	K♠Q♦	—	—	—	—	
Button	A♠Q♦	K♠J♦	Q♠J♦	J♠10♦	10♠9♦	9♠8♦	8♠7♦
Small blind	A♠J♦	K♦10♠	Q♠10♦	J♠9♦	10♠9♦	9♠8♦	8♠7♦

Legend: Ax s. means an Ace and another lower card of the same suit.
  Kx s. means a King and another lower card of the same suit.
  Ax means an Ace and another card of a different suit from the Ace.
  Kx means a King and another lower card of a different suit from the King.

random hands, you're against a few random hands and one or more hands that are probably fairly good hands. Because of this it usually takes a much better hand to call when another player has entered the pot than it does when you are first to enter. This is true even though the other player entering the pot has made the pot slightly larger.

If four or five players have come into the pot, the pot is often large enough to gamble a little, to play hands that would not be strong enough to open the pot with but have the potential to develop into a very strong hand. However, if only one or two players are in, you generally need a very strong hand to call.

Notice that it makes a large difference whether one or two players have entered the pot rather than four or five. With only a few players competing for a pot, Hold 'Em is very much a high card game and premium high cards are needed if you're against a couple of other players with probable high cards. When many players are competing for the pot, however, Hold 'Em becomes more a game of draws. It becomes more important for your cards to work together as suited cards than as premium high cards.

Again, don't memorize these tables, especially the last table. This table assumes that the opener is a typical to fairly tight player. The idea is that you shouldn't call except with hands that are at least one or two notches better than the worst hand that player would open with.

Against a very tight player, you should play tighter than the table suggests. Against a loose player, you should call with more hands than the table suggests. Pay more attention to learning the habits of your opponents than to memorizing the tables.

When Someone Has Raised

Usually you need a stronger hand to call a raise than you would need if you raised yourself. That's usually the case, but not always.

If you open with a raise, you're putting in two bets to win one and a half bets (the two blinds). That's 3-4 odds. If you call a raiser,

Minimum Calling Hands With Four or Five Limpers

Suited Cards

	Pairs	Ax s.	Kx s.	Qx s.	Jx s.	10x s.	9x s.	8x s.	7x s.	6x s.
Under the gun	n/a	n/a	n/a	n/a	n/a	n/a	n/a	n/a	n/a	n/a
Early position	n/a	n/a	n/a	n/a	n/a	n/a	n/a	n/a	n/a	n/a
Middle position	4,4	A♦2♦	K♦6♦	Q♦8♦	J♦8♦	10♦7♦	9♦8♦	8♦7♦	7♦6♦	—
Button	3,3	A♦2♦	K♦4♦	Q♦6♦	J♦7♦	10♦6♦	9♦7♦	8♦6♦	7♦4♦	6♦4♦
Blinds	2,2	A♦2♦	K♦2♦	Q♦5♦	J♦6♦	10♦6♦	9♦6♦	8♦5♦	7♦3♦	6♦3♦

Unsuited Cards

	Ax	Kx	Qx	Jx	10x	9x	8x	7x
Under the gun	n/a	n/a	n/a	n/a	n/a	n/a	n/a	n/a
Early position	n/a	n/a	n/a	n/a	n/a	n/a	n/a	n/a
Middle position	A♠J♦	K♠10♦	Q♠10♦	J♠10♦	10♠9♦	—	—	—
Button	A♦9♦	K♠9♦	Q♠J♦	J♠8♦	10♠8♦	9♠7♦	8♠6♦	7♠6♦
Blinds	A♠9♦	K♦9♠	Q♠10♦	J♠8♦	10♠7♦	9♠6♦	8♠6♦	7♠6♦

Legend: Ax s. means an Ace and another lower card of the same suit.
   Kx s. means a King and another lower card of the same suit.
   Ax means an Ace and another card of a different suit from the Ace.
   Kx means a King and another lower card of a different suit from the King.

Minimum Calling Hands With an Early Position Raiser

Suited Cards

	Pairs	Ax s.	Kx s.	Qx s.	Jx s.	10x s.	9x s.	8x s.	7x s.	6x s.
Under the gun	n/a	n/a	n/a	n/a	n/a	n/a	n/a	n/a	n/a	n/a
Early position	9,9	A♠Q♠	—	—	—	—	—	—	—	—
Middle position	9,9	A♦Q♦	K♦Q♦	Q♦J♦	J♦10♦	—	—	—	—	—
Button	8,8	A♦J♦	K♦J♦	Q♦10♦	J♦9♦	10♦9♦	9♦8♦	8♦7♦	—	—
Blinds	6,6	A♦8♦	K♦10♦	Q♦9♦	J♦9♦	10♦8♦	9♦7♦	8♦7♦	7♦6♦	6♦5♦

Unsuited Cards

	Pairs	Ax	Kx	Qx	Jx	10x	9x
Under the gun	n/a	n/a	n/a	n/a	n/a	n/a	n/a
Early position	—	—	—	—	—	—	—
Middle position	A♠K♦	—	—	—	—	—	
Button	A♠Q♦	K♠J♦	Q♠J♦	J♠10♦	10♠9♦	9♠8♦	—
Small blind	A♠J♦	K♦10♠	Q♠10♦	J♠9♦	10♠9♦	9♠8♦	8♠7♦

Legend: Ax s. means an Ace and another lower card of the same suit.
Kx s. means a King and another lower card of the same suit.
Ax means an Ace and another card of a different suit from the Ace.
Kx means a King and another lower card of a different suit from the King.

48

Minimum Calling Hands With a Late Position Raiser and Three or Four Limpers

Suited Cards

	Pairs	Ax s.	Kx s.	Qx s.	Jx s.	10x s.	9x s.	8x s.	7x s.	6x s.
Under the gun	n/a	n/a	n/a	n/a	n/a	n/a	n/a	n/a	n/a	n/a
Early position	n/a	n/a	n/a	n/a	n/a	n/a	n/a	n/a	n/a	n/a
Middle position	n/a	n/a	n/a	n/a	n/a	n/a	n/a	n/a	n/a	n/a
Button	6,6	A♦2♦	K♦4♦	Q♦6♦	J♦7♦	10♦6♦	9♦7♦	8♦6♦	7♦5♦	6♦5♦
Blinds	4,4	A♦2♦	K♦2♦	Q♦5♦	J♦6♦	10♦6♦	9♦6♦	8♦5♦	7♦4♦	6♦4♦

Unsuited Cards

	Ax	Kx	Qx	Jx	10x	9x	8x	7x
Under the gun	n/a	n/a	n/a	n/a	n/a	n/a	n/a	n/a
Early position	n/a	n/a	n/a	n/a	n/a	n/a	n/a	n/a
Middle position	n/a	n/a	n/a	n/a	n/a	n/a	n/a	n/a
Button	A♠9♦	K♠10♦	Q♠10♦	J♠9♦	10♠9♦	9♠8♦	8♠7♦	7♠6♦
Blinds	A♠9♦	K♠9♦	Q♠10♦	J♠9♦	10♠9♦	9♠8♦	8♠7♦	7♠6♦

Legend: Ax s. means an Ace and another lower card of the same suit.
Kx s. means a King and another lower card of the same suit.
Ax means an Ace and another card of a different suit from the Ace.
Kx means a King and another lower card of a different suit from the King.

you're putting in two bets to win three and a half bets. That's 7-4 odds to call a raise. Because you're getting better odds, you can sometimes call with weaker hands, but not always. It depends on who has done the raising. In fact, most of the time the slightly better odds you're getting just aren't worth going up against a hand that is probably very strong.

If someone has entered the pot from an early position you can usually be sure he has a stronger than average hand, especially if he entered the pot with a raise. Also, if someone else raises after a player has called from an early position, at least one of those two probably has a strong hand, often both of them. In that case, even though you might seem to be getting good odds, you've got a big hill to climb to beat the strong hand you're up against, and you should be selective with what kind of hand you're willing to call. You need a strong hand of your own.

If the original opener came in from the middle or late position, however, even with a raise, he often does not have a very strong hand. Also, if the raise came after three or four players have limped in, the raiser often does not have a very strong hand. Especially in the case where three or four players have limped in before the raise, where you're getting fairly good odds, it's often okay to call with a weaker hand than you would have raised with.

One of the risks of calling an early position opener from middle position is that there are still a few players after you who might reraise. You don't want to be caught in the middle of a raising war with a weak hand. The later your position, the less you need to worry about a raising war breaking out and the more hands you can play against an early position raiser.

TABLE OBSERVATIONS

You will often see pots being won with very weak starting hands, particularly in very loose games. Don't pay any attention to this, and don't draw any conclusions about it. It's true that any two cards can win, but some cards just won't win very often. Sometimes it seems that half the pots are being won by hands that all the books say are weak hands. Even if that's happening, that does not mean that weak hands have as good a chance to win as strong hands.

At a loose table, you might have six players seeing the flop. Two of the players might have fairly strong starting hands, hands such as 9♠9♦ or K♥J♦. The other four players are likely playing hands such 10♦4♦ or 6♠4♥. If half the pots are being won by the weaker hands, you might start thinking that they are just as likely to win as the stronger hands, but that wouldn't be the case at all. That's what you'd observe if the better hands each had a 25 percent chance of winning and the weaker hands each had a 12.5 percent chance of winning. In a loose game, you'll see many pots being won by weak hands because a lot of weak hands are being played. It's not because any two cards can win. Remember that.

HOW TO PLAY THE HANDS

If you're first in the pot, you should often open with a raise, but not always. It depends on the hand itself, on your position, and on the other players. Sometimes you should open by just calling the blinds, intending to reraise if someone raises. Sometimes you should open by just calling and just call if someone raises.

I can't give you any hard and fast rules for when to call, raise, or reraise. As a general rule, if you have any doubt, the best thing to do is probably raise. With your very best hands, such as a pair of Aces, if there is any chance at all that someone else will raise, then you should just call, intending to reraise. Such a "limp-reraise" often works well with other hands also, such as a pocket pair of Kings or Queens, but with less than a pair of Aces, you need to be more certain that another player will raise, giving you a chance to reraise.

With most strong hands, you actually make more money if you have more callers. Limping in helps drag in those extra callers, so it's often best to limp more from early position with strong hands and reraise. You actually want more callers when you open early—almost every hand makes more money with more callers (A,A makes the maximum profit with everyone calling). Your chances of winning that particular pot are greater with fewer callers, but average profit per hand goes up when you get more callers. The difference between getting four callers in for three bets versus two callers in for two bets is huge. Don't ever forget that poker isn't about winning the pot, it's about winning the money.

It's a different situation when you're opening from a later position, however. In a later position, it's usually best to just go after the blinds. Just raise and hope nobody calls. You're not likely to get many callers, they've already folded, and with most hands your edge is pretty small compared with the size of the blinds. Basically, whenever you probably have the best hand to start out, you should pick an action that is likely to get the most money in the pot from other players.

A SIMPLE APPROACH

For the first-time player, I recommend a much simpler approach to the play of the first two cards than I've outlined in this chapter. Basically it's to play only hands with two big cards, that add up to "21" if evaluated as blackjack hands. You can include large pairs in that. The basic hands would be an Ace with any face card or 10 and any pair of 10s or better.

Considering all the combinations of your cards, your position, and your opponents will eventually become second nature, but to the beginner it can be overwhelming. Limiting your play to just hands that contain an Ace and either a 10 or a face card greatly simplifies the things you have to remember.

There are some flaws in using blackjack hands as a hand selection rule, but the flaws aren't major. You won't be playing many hands using this rule, and that gives you plenty of opportunity to make observations about the game during your first hour or two of play. At that point you can use the information that you've gathered about the game and the suggestions in the tables to make modifications in your hand selection. Once you've gotten some experience, you can make some modifications to this simple approach.

From early position you should probably eliminate the weakest of the "21" hands, folding an Ace with a 10 or Jack. You can play those two hands from middle position if no one has called. From middle or late position, you should expand the hands to include those that give you a blackjack count of 20—any two 10-valued cards or an Ace and a nine.

Take it a step at a time. Don't try to do it all at once.

5

The Flop

PLAYING THE HAND

After you are dealt your two-card hand, and we have the first round of betting, a card is "burned" (discarded facedown), and the flop is dealt. The "flop" is three community cards dealt faceup in the middle of the table. Once it hits the board, your hand becomes pretty well defined. You should be able to formulate a good idea of your chances of winning the pot. The first step in playing the flop is reading it—determining what your hand is and what the likely hands of your opponents are.

When the flop hits the board, you finally have a poker hand—and so does everyone else. You need to be able to quickly determine your own hand and the possible hands of other players. Let's start out by looking at some flops and determine what hands are possible.

10♦9♦8♦

This is a scary looking flop—all of one suit and in sequence. A straight flush is possible with this hand—in fact more than one. Q♦J♦ makes a straight flush, as does 7♦6♦. The Queen-high

54

straight flush is the best possible hand, but so is a Jack-high straight flush with a J♦7♦. In that case having the Jack in your hand would block anyone from having a Queen-high straight flush. So there are three possibilities for a straight flush with this flop, and two of them could occur simultaneously.

The next highest hand would be an Ace-high flush. An A♦ with any other Diamond makes this hand. Any two Diamonds make a flush. The same card combinations that make a straight flush, without the Diamonds, would make a straight.

Of course, even if you don't have a made hand with this flop, if you hold a single A♦ you've got a good draw. Even a K♦ is often worth playing with a flop like this. A lot of hands are possible with this flop. If you don't have one of them, you're not going to like it much.

A♠K♠7♦

With this flop the best possible hand at this point is a set of Aces, three Aces for a player holding a pair of Aces in his hand. Any Ace, with a good kicker, however, is probably the best hand at this point.

With two Spades on the board, a flush draw is possible. However, with both the A♠ and the K♠ on the flop, a flush draw isn't likely unless your opponents tend to play fairly loose. Many players won't play just any two suited cards unless they are headed by an Ace or King.

What would be a good hand to hold with this flop? Well, other than the obvious pocket pairs that make a set or having two pair, an Ace with a good kicker is a good holding.

If your cards are of the right suit, that's even better. For example, A♦10♦ is a much better hand to have with this flop than A♣10♣. That's because the Diamonds give you a three-flush, a little extra way of winning by catching Diamonds on both the turn and river. Another hand that would give you a three-flush draw would be something like A♥Q♠. Also note that any of these hands give you three cards to a straight. These three-card straights or flushes on the flop don't have a lot of value on their own, but they add value to hands that are already fairly good. Small features like that can turn a good hand into a great hand.

On the flop, you still have two more cards to come. If your hand needs one card to make the probable best hand, then we'd say you have a draw. If you need both of the next two cards, then we'd say you have a backdoor draw, as with a A♦10♦ here. Backdoor draws by themselves are almost worthless, but, as I pointed out, they do add value at times, and players often overlook backdoor draws.

A♦10♦10♣

This flop has a lot of dangerous aspects to it. Of course there is a risk of someone having a 10. It's much more likely that someone has a 10 with a flop like this than it would be if someone had a 6 in a flop like A♦6♦6♣.

If you have a flush draw with this flop, then you have to worry about making your flush with a card that makes someone else a full house. With that in mind, a draw to a hand like J♦9♦ is probably a much safer draw then a draw to a hand like 7♦6♦. Although a Jack-high flush is better than a 7-high flush, that's not the reason it's a much better draw. It's because the J♦9♦ has two of the likely cards that might make a full house for someone with a 10, an important consideration.

There are similar risks to possible inside-straight draws with this flop. When a pair is on the board, the card that makes your straight not only might make someone a flush, but also might make someone a full house.

A♦9♥5♣

This flop isn't likely to give anyone any draws. If the pot was unraised before the flop, it's also unlikely anyone has an Ace in some games, depending on the particular players involved, of course. A hand like a 9♦7♦ is likely to be the best hand with a flop like this. Of course, if any of the other players are giving any significant action, you might have to revise that estimate.

Q♦J♥5♦

This flop is very likely a good one for someone. Anyone with two high cards has part of this flop, and it's got flush draw potential for someone with two Diamonds. This is a flop that you would want to play very aggressively if it fits your hand very well. Some hands that this flop would be excellent for would be A♦K♦, Q♣Q♠, K♦J♦, A♥K♥, A♦J♦, Q♥10♥. Some hands that might be in some danger with this flop would be A♣10♠, K♠J♠, Q♠10♠.

Note the distinction between Q♥10♥ and Q♠10♠. The three-flush with the hearts can make a difference with these hands.

That's not to say that you should automatically fold those hands that might be in some danger, but you should consider folding them if the action on the flop involves a lot of raising.

K♦10♣5♦

Again, this is a flop with a few possible draws. Possible flush draws and a possible straight draw are reflected in this flop.

J♦10♦7♣

This is another potentially scary flop. A lot of hands could have part of this flop. There is, of course, the flush draw possibility and straight draws. Someone may already have a straight. A hand like A♦K♦ is a great hand for this flop, and A♣K♣ is also a pretty good hand. The backdoor flush draw by itself isn't a good draw, but when it's added to the other possibilities of A♣K♣, it makes that hand all that much better. A hand such as 10♣ 9♣ is a good hand for this flop. A pair with a gutshot straight draw is usually a fairly good hand, and, again, the backdoor flush draw just makes it better. Whenever the flop has connected cards (the J♦10♦), you need to consider the possibility that someone has two-pair as those are the kind of cards most players tend to play. This is one of those flops that you shouldn't get involved with aggressively unless you have one of the better possible hands for it.

9♠5♥2♦

This is what's known as a garbage flop. It's very unlikely to have hit anyone. It has no big cards, no connected cards, and no suited cards. It's the kind of flop that many players like to bluff with.

BETTING OPTIONS

If you're first to act, or the round has been checked to you, then you have two options—you can check or bet. If someone has already bet, then you can call, raise, or fold.

Before you decide on which action to take, you need to think ahead. What's going to happen after you act? What are the other players going to do? Then what?

If you check, and another player then bets, will you fold? Call? Raise? Think ahead because your options are actually much broader than checking or betting.

Think about why you might want to take certain actions. The flop is the time to make an assessment of your hand. Do you have the best hand? If so, you probably want to take action that maximizes your chances of winning the pot right now.

STRAIGHTFORWARD PLAY

Especially when you're just beginning in the game, you will want to play your hand very straightforwardly. Bet or raise when you have the best hand, check when you don't have the best, and fold or call based on whether you are getting sufficient pot odds to draw. It's very easy for a beginner to develop what's called Fancy

BETTING OPTIONS TO CONSIDER

If no one has bet you can,

First Round	Second Round
check	fold to a bet
check	call a bet
check	raise a bet

First Round	Second Round
bet	fold to a raise
bet	call a raise
bet	reraise if raised

If someone has bet, you can,

First Round	Second Round
fold	
call	fold to a raise
call	call a raise
call	reraise if raised
raise	

Play Syndrome (FPS). That means you slow play too much, check-raise too much, semi-bluff too much, and generally spend too much time trying to be deceptive. It doesn't work.

Listed below are the symptoms of Fancy Play Syndrome

- *Slow play*
  Slow play means that you are playing a very strong hand weakly. You're checking and calling rather than betting and raising. There are times to slow play, but not many of them. You should consider slow play if you have an almost unbeatable hand like a straight flush, four of a kind, or the best possible full house. You should consider it, but not

always do it. With weaker hands you should seldom even consider it.

- *Check-raise*

   A check-raise is checking a hand with the intention of raising when someone else bets. For a check-raise to work you have to have a bet from another player. So if you aren't fairly sure that another player will bet, it's not usually a good idea to attempt a check-raise. Even when you're sure that another player will bet, you'll often do better by just betting yourself because they might then raise, giving you a chance to reraise.

- *Semi-bluff*

   A semi-bluff is a bet or raise where you probably don't have the best hand but do have some chance to make the best hand. It's a bet that has two ways to win. It can win as a bluff if the opponent folds, or, if the opponent calls, you can still win by improving on the next card. Raising with a flush draw when you think your opponent may be weak and might fold is an example of a semi-bluff.

- *Free-card play*

   A free-card play is similar to a semi-bluff. Like a semi-bluff, it's a bet or raise with a hand that is probably not the best hand but has some chance to make the best hand. The difference is that a semi-bluff depends on some chance that the other players will fold to your bet-raise. A free-card play depends on the others checking to you on the next betting round. A free-card play only makes sense if you are in late position, last to act. The idea is that the bet size on the flop is one half the bet size on the turn, so by making an extra bet on the flop, you save having to call a bet on the turn when the bet size is larger.

Excessive attempts at deceptive play actually make your hand easier for good players to read, and the bad players aren't paying any attention anyway. Play straightforwardly—they don't expect it.

It's also easy for a beginner who tries to play tight to become tight-weak. A tight-weak player is one who plays very tight, but when he does play a hand, he easily becomes convinced by aggressive opponents that he doesn't have the best hand. As I point out later in the book, there are many reasons other players may be betting or raising other than having the best hand.

You should play tight in your pre-flop hand selection. On the flop you should guard against two things: developing FPS and being pushed off a hand by a player with FPS. A major element of FPS is aggression when aggression isn't called for. Aggression just for the sake of aggression usually just isn't a good idea. Being deceptive just so that you can impress your friends or show the other players how tricky you are usually just isn't a good idea. Play aggressively, but don't develop FPS habits. At the same time, be aware that many players are infected with FPS, and there are some players who don't necessarily have much of a hand when they are betting or raising.

In most game conditions, your play on the flop is more of an important factor toward becoming a winning player than any other point in the game. It's the most important round to master.

Flopping a Pair

When one of the three cards on the flop matches one of the cards in your hand, you've flopped a pair. An example is if you hold A♦9♦ and the flop is K♠9♣4♥. You have a pair of 9s. We call that the second pair. Note that if the flop had been 4♥4♦3♥ you'd also have a pair, a pair of 4s, but every other active hand has at least a pair of 4s also. When we say you've flopped a pair, we're usually not referring to situations where the pair is on the board. Some pairs, however, are better than others.

Top Pair

"Top pair" is when one of your cards matches the highest card on the board. If the flop is Q♠9♥4♣, then any player who holds a Queen has the top pair. Your kicker (your unpaired card) matters in this situation. For example, if you hold Q♥2♥, then any other player with a Queen has a better hand than you.

When we're evaluating a hand, we generally think in terms of the top pair being the likely best hand on the flop. There are exceptions to this, but it's generally a good starting point. It's because of the increased likelihood of flopping the top pair that higher ranking cards are better to play than lower ranking hands. The next table illustrates this.

CHANCES OF FLOPPING THE TOP PAIR

If you hold an unpaired	Percent of the time it will be the highest card on the flop
Ace	16.6%
King	13.9%
Queen	11.3%
Jack	9.1%
T	7.1%
9	5.4%
8	3.9%
7	2.6%
6	1.6%
5	0.8%
4	0.3%
3	0.1%
2	0.0%

The smaller your cards are, not only are they less likely to flop the top pair, but when they do flop the top pair, they are more vulnerable. This is illustrated in the next table.

CHANCES OF AN OVERCARD HITTING THE TURN OR RIVER AFTER A FLOP OF THE TOP PAIR

Top pair holding a	Percent of time an overcard falls on the turn or river
Ace	00%
King	17%
Queen	32%
Jack	45%
T	57%
9	68%
8	77%
7	84%
6	90%
5	95%
4	98%
3	100%

If you are holding J♠T♣ and the flop is J♦7♥3♦, then you have the top pair. You've paired the highest card on the board, and the only way anyone could have a higher pair is if they hold pocket Aces, Kings, or Queens. Note, however, that 45 percent of the time at least one of the next two cards will be an Ace, King, or Queen, which will possibly give another player a higher pair. These midranked top pairs almost always need to be played very aggressively to force players with overcards to fold. Sometimes, however, too much aggression can backfire.

Generally the top pair is a good hand, but this hand isn't as good as it might look at first glance. If you're first to act and bet, then what hands that you can beat might call? Not many actually. If someone has Q♦J♥ or K♦J♥ or A♦J♥, then you're beat. They also have the top pair, but with a better kicker. You would have a

J♥9♦ beat, but hands with kickers smaller than the nine aren't likely to have been played by most players. *Kickers count, and in some cases they count for a lot.*

Of course, if you bet you might get calls from players with hands like 7♣8♣ or A♥3♥. You might even get calls from players with hands like K♥Q♥ or similar hands. Because you don't want to give players with hands like those a free chance to get a card on the turn that will beat you, you will want to bet this hand with this flop. If you get called, don't be too satisfied, and if you get raised, you might well be in big trouble. You'll be a lot more comfortable with that flop if you're in late position and everyone else has checked to you. You might still be check-raised, but generally you can be a little more certain that you have the best hand. This is an example of another reason that you will want to be more selective in the hands you play when you're in early position than when you're in late position.

Second Pair

You will encounter a lot of flops of second or third pair, for example, holding A♠T♠ with a flop of K♠T♦4♥ or holding T♣9♣ with a flop of J♠T♦5♥. In these examples, you should probably fold if someone bets unless the pot is fairly large. It's likely you don't have the best hand, and you're about a 9-1 underdog to improve. Even if you do improve, it may make someone else a better hand. For example, in the A♠T♠ example, an Ace on the turn could make someone a straight; in the T♣9♣ example, a 9 on the turn could make someone a straight.

It's important in Hold 'Em not just to have the best hand, but to be fairly confident that your hand is best. If you're not certain enough about your hand to bet or raise with it, then you aren't likely to be able to earn any extra bets those times you're best, but you'll be losing extra bets those times that you're not best. This idea of avoiding situations where you won't win much if you win but might lose a lot when you lose is a fairly common principle in Hold 'Em. Keep it in mind.

Missing the Flop with Pocket Pairs

When you play medium-sized or small-pocket pairs, you usually are looking to flop a set. Most of the time you won't do that. So, most of the time you'll be folding pocket pairs on the flop, but there are a few times that pocket pairs might be played past the flop. Of course, the most obvious time is when you have an over-pair to the flop, when your pocket pair is larger than any card on the flop. That sometimes happens even with fairly small pairs, like 7s, but the smaller the pocket pair, the more likely the flop contains straight danger if your pair is an overpair to the flop.

Another situation where you might call a bet on the flop with an underpair is if the pot is large. An example is a flop of 9♥8♥3♦ and you hold 4♥4♦.

If the turn card is a 4, you probably will have the best hand, but the odds of this happening are slightly over 22-1. If you do get lucky and spike a 4 on the turn, then you'll probably win a few extra bets. So, you need to be getting about 20-1 pot odds to make a call with this hand. If the pot is any smaller than that, and it usually is, then the call is just not worth it.

There are two other things you need to make sure of before you make this kind of call. It's important that one of your 4s be of the same suit as any flush draw on the board (in this case the 4♥). This is because you don't want to be in a position where the card that makes you three 4s also makes someone a flush.

It's also important that you are sure that no one is going to raise. A raise completely destroys the pot odds you're getting. If there are still players left to act behind you, then this call is usually not a good idea.

Another situation where you might want to play a small pocket pair past the flop is when the flop has a pair. For example, you might have 4♥4♦ with a flop of 8♠8♥3♦.

Only do this if the pair on the board is a middle-sized rank or smaller, decreasing the chances that another player has a card of that rank and if the odd card on the board is smaller than your pair. In the above example, your two-pair of 8s and 4s will beat the likely two pair of 8s and 3s of an opponent. You shouldn't always call in this situation, but you should often consider calling. Sometimes you should even consider raising.

FLOPPING DRAWS

Often the flop will fit your hand by giving you a draw rather than a made hand. By a draw, I mean a hand that probably isn't best right now but has the potential to develop into the best hand.

Do you have the best draw? If so, you probably need to get odds from the other players and you don't want to do anything that might cause some of them to fold, so that if you do complete your hand you'll win a large pot.

Flopping a Flush Draw

Suited cards are hands that very much depend on hitting a flop. They are drawing hands, and the best flop you can hit with them will usually be a draw.

If you flop a good draw, and a flush draw is almost always a good draw, then you often will want to play it aggressively. Once you've made your flush and three flush cards are on the board, the other players will tend to back off, and it's unlikely that you will get the betting to go over two bets. If the players are particularly passive, they'll often just check and call once the third flush card hits. The time to get the bets in is on the flop when you've flopped a draw.

One of the odds you need to know are the odds for a flush draw (see Chapter 11 for more odds information). At the flop, you're a 2-1 dog to make the hand. At the turn, you're a 4-1 dog to make the hand. So, if you're getting three or more callers on the flop, you should usually bet or raise with a flush draw. With only two callers a bet or raise is probably okay; with only one caller, betting a flush draw is not a bet for value, it's a bluff.

To call for a draw, you need to take pot odds into consideration. When you're considering pot odds, you also need to consider how many bets you're going to call. With a flush draw on the flop, in a loose game you don't need pot odds to draw. You are getting good enough odds just on the current betting round as long as you've got three callers. That's 3-1 odds on a 2-1 proposition.

That's 3-1 on the bet—not pot odds. That's 3-1 ignoring what's in the pot. You don't have to worry about counting the cost of the call on the turn, because that call will be getting good enough pot odds on its own.

With the better draws, such as flush draws, you almost always are getting the right odds to call on the flop. You'll be getting the right odds both on the flop and turn, but you need to make the pot-odds determinations one call at a time.

To take off a single card you need about 4-1. The only time you won't be getting that for calling one bet on the flop is when the two blinds are heads-up. So, calling on the flop with one of the strong draws is pretty much automatic. You'll be getting the right odds. Once there has been a bet and call on the flop, you'll also be getting the right odds to call on the turn.

If you know you're going to call, you should often think about raising. A flush draw (when the flop is unpaired) is a situation where you should almost always consider raising. The 2-1 odds with two more cards to come that I mentioned earlier comes into play when you're thinking about raising. If you do raise and get called by two or more players, then the pot size on the turn will almost always be big enough to give you 4-1 on the turn. If you raise, you know you'll be calling (and getting the right price to do so) on the turn.

In that case you raise if you are getting 2-1 or better on the flop from callers of your raise—not the pot odds.

You should think about pot odds when you think about a call. For a call you compare the pot odds to the odds of making the hand in one card.

You should think about odds on the bet itself (not pot odds) when you think about a raise. For a raise you compare the number of callers you expect (the odds you are getting) with the chances of making the hand in the next two cards. You can do that because you know the raise will make the pot big enough so that you'll be getting pot odds to call on the turn.

One consideration to making your flush is when someone else makes a bigger flush. It's a consideration—but it's not as an important one as many think. The major reason it's not as important is that it's not likely anyone is drawing to the same flush you are. Of the thirteen Hearts, you have two of them, and two are on the board. That only leaves nine unaccounted for. Contrast this to the situation where there are two Hearts on the board, and you don't have a Heart. Then eleven Hearts are unaccounted for, a substantial difference. Because of the combinatorial features of the mathematics involved, this difference is much larger than the 20 percent it might seem.

The other reason it's not as important as it might seem is that if two of you do actually have the same draw, it's now much less likely that you'll make the draw. Among you, the board, and the other players, you've accounted for six of the flush cards.

Flopping Straight Draws

Let's say you have 8♥7♥. Look at some of the flops you might get: K♣10♣9♠.

You've flopped a straight draw. Any Jack or any 6 will make a straight. You shouldn't like this flop and should probably fold if anyone bets. Not all straight draws are alike. They range from very strong hands to very weak hands.

What's wrong with the straight draw illustrated? Over half the cards that can make a straight for you might also make a better hand for someone else. Although any Jack or 6 will make your straight, that means eight cards, and two of those cards are Clubs, so one-fourth of the time that you make a straight, you might be beaten by a flush. Also a Jack would make anyone holding a single Queen a higher straight than yours. Add to it that someone may already have a higher straight than the one you're drawing to, and your prospects start looking bleak. The potential for a second-best hand is huge, and *second-best hands can get very expensive.*

With the 8♥7♥ in your hand, compare that flop with 7♣6♥4♦. Like the flop discussed, it's possible that someone flopped a straight, but if they did, you don't care because the straight you're drawing to is not a worse straight. Not only that, your top pair is probably the best hand right now.

Often you hear that you should not draw to inside straights, but that straights open on both ends are good to draw to. I've just shown you two examples of where that advice is reversed (the better of the two straight draws is the one that can only make a straight one way) with the inside draw for a 5.

In Hold 'Em, the key to drawing to straights is the consideration of how the cards that will make your hand will affect the hands of other players and whether you have the possibility of making the best possible straight.

Another example is, still with a 8♥7♥, a flop of 5♥4♣2♦. With this flop you have an inside straight draw, but also have two cards higher than any card on the flop, called "overcards." So, you have four cards that will make a straight for you, and six other cards that will make top pair for you. Top pair with an 8 or 7 is a little iffy because of the possibility that it will make a straight for someone else. This kind of draw (gutshot with overcards) can be a strong draw if you're not against more than two or three opponents.

For another example, compare 7♣6♦4♦ with the flop above when you're holding 8♥7♥. The two flops look much the same, but they can be vastly different, particularly in a loose game. Not only do you no longer have that three-card flush, but it's possible that someone has a draw to a diamond flush. A 7♦ makes three 7s for you, but may make a flush for someone else. A 5♦ makes a straight for you, but also has the flush risk.

In a typical game, where you have four or five active opponents on the flop, you probably still have the best hand, but it's vulnerable, and if it's not the best hand, you may not have many ways to win.

There is no one right answer as to how to play this flop—*but there is a wrong answer*. You should either play this very aggressively or not play at all. Calling a bet to see what develops would almost always be wrong in a typical game.

Overcard Draws

Overcards are the weakest draw of all. Overcards are when you have a hand like K♦Q♥ and the flop is J♦7♥3♠. Of course, if a King or Queen falls, then you have the top pair, but the risk is that the card that makes you the top pair will make someone else two pair. In loose or aggressive games, you should usually avoid playing overcards past the flop—not always, but usually.

An exception would be in a tight aggressive game where your premium overcards might well be the best hand. Premium overcards are hands like A♠K♠ or A♠Q♠ when the flop contains a spade.

You should be more likely to call with overcards if:

1. Your cards are suited and the flop has one of your suit.
2. The pot is large.
3. The flop is the kind of garbage flop when many players like to bluff.
4. You are last and won't get raised.
5. No one else has called.

Semi-bluffing Draws

Do you have a mediocre hand that might be the best hand but probably isn't? If so, now might be the time to think about a semi-bluff.

A "semi-bluff" isn't a bluff but it's close. A bluff is a bet that can't win if you're called. A semi-bluff is a bet that probably isn't the best hand if you get called, but your hand has some possibility of improving to the best hand. Bluffs are typically made when there are no more cards to come. Semi-bluffs are made on intermediate betting rounds; they depend on the possibility that future cards will improve the hand if the semi-bluff gets called.

CONSIDERATIONS FOR FLOP PLAY

Making the Pot Big

One advantage of playing strong hands aggressively and straight-forwardly is that it tends to make the pot large. A large pot is an incentive to other players to keep calling your bets with weak hands, which is always a plus for you.

Drawing Odds

In many situations where you're probably beat and should usually fold, the size of the pot often dictates otherwise. When the pot gets large, a lot of folding situations become calling situations. For example, when you've got the second pair, someone else bets, and you're fairly sure that the bettor has the top pair. We gave some examples of that earlier: One was when you are holding A♠T♠ and the flop of K♠T♦4♥.

It's likely you don't have the best hand and you're about a 9-1 underdog to improve.

How did I compute that? There are forty-seven cards you haven't seen (fifty-two minus the two in your hand and the three on the flop). Of those forty-seven cards, there are three Aces and two 10s that will improve your hand. That's five cards or five outs. So the next card can be one of five cards that help you or one of forty-two cards that don't help you; 42-5 is the same as 8.4-1. I round up to 9-1 to take into account those times when an Ace on the turn makes someone else a straight. In this case, if the pot has nine or more bets already in it, and you know that no one will raise after you call, then you should call a bet on the flop. You're getting the right pot odds for a call. This is also called getting the right price.

DANGER FLOPS

Some flops are very dangerous flops unless they hit your hand hard. That's because if they didn't hit your hand, then it's very likely they fit someone else's hand very well.

Flush on the Flop

When the flop has three cards all of one suit, then there is some chance that someone has a flush and very good chance that someone at least has a flush draw. So, if the flop is something like 9♥8♥4♥, then if you don't have A♥ or K♥ or a 9 in your hand, your hand probably isn't worth playing. You probably do not want to draw to a straight with this flop, because the chances of making your straight and having it beaten by a flush are just too great. With the A♥ you will want to draw to the flush, but you might not even want to draw to the flush if all you have is the K♥. With a hand like K♥9♦, you probably will want to play. Top pair and the King-high flush draw is a pretty good hand with a flop like this.

Not always, but generally, if the flop has three of one suit, you should not play further unless you have the top pair or a draw to at least one of the top two possible flushes. There are exceptions, but not very many.

When the Flop Has a Straight

A flop with three cards to a straight will often generate a lot of action. With a flop like 10♠9♦8♥, a lot of hands will play. Even if someone doesn't have a straight, it's very likely that players will have flopped combination draws like a pair, a gutshot straight draw, and a three-flush. If you've got a hand like A♣A♠, you might very well have the best hand even though two or three other players are raising. The problem with this kind of flop is that you can never be sure. I can't really give you a rule for how to play this flop.

If you've got a good overpair, you should probably be calling to the river unless some real scary cards hit and you're sure that you're beat. If you've got a hand like Q♥10♥ then you've probably got a pretty good hand, it might even be best, and even if it's not best, you have draws. Be careful with this kind of flop with hands like 7♣6♣ or 8♣7♣. Making the bottom end of that straight can often cost you a lot of chips with the second-best hand.

A Pair on the Flop

When the flop has a pair on it, a full house is possible. If it's a loose or very loose game, three-of-a-kind is a real possibility. The time to be very careful with these kinds of flops is when it makes your two pair but your pair is lower than the pair on the board. For example, if the flop is 9♥9♦6♣ and you have A♠6♠, you could easily be in trouble. If someone has a 9, then you have almost no way to win. If the ranks are reversed and the flop is 6♥6♦9♣ and you have A♠9♠, then the situation is different. Now, if someone has a 6, you still have some chance of winning by catching one of the two 9s still out. It's a long-shot chance, but still a chance. It's enough of a chance that when you combine it with the chance that no one actually has a 6, it's probably worth playing.

Straight draws and flush draws are usually not worth playing when the flop has a pair. This is especially true for straight draws because for you to have a straight draw must mean that the ranks on the flop are close together—which increases the chance that someone has flopped a full house. A flop of Q♥Q♦J♠ is much more likely to make someone a full house then a flop like J♠4♥4♠.

Be careful when the flop has a pair.

6

The Last Two Cards

The time to give up on a hand in Hold 'Em is either before the flop or on the flop. If you still have an active hand by the turn, you're usually in for the duration.

The betting rounds for the last two cards are at double the bet size of the first two betting rounds. By the time you reach this point, your hand and the likely holdings of your opponents should be fairly well defined. At the first of these last betting rounds, six of your seven cards have been exposed. You only have one more card coming. At this point you generally either have the probable best hand, or you have a draw to the probable best hand.

Most of the time, if your hand was good enough to stay for the turn card, then it's good enough to stay for the river card. Not always though. An example of when it might not be right to stay past the turn card is when the pot was offering you enough odds to draw one card for an inside straight, but when the bet doubles on the turn round, the pot is not twice the size and you're no longer getting good enough odds to call.

Generally, if your draw on the flop was strong enough for an automatic call, then it'll still be good enough to call on the turn. If your call on the flop depended on a close analysis of pot odds, then it's probably not good enough to call the larger turn bet.

There are two different general situations to consider: first, when you are playing a made hand, such as top pair, and second, when you're playing a draw, such as a flush draw.

MADE HANDS ON THE TURN

Pairs

If you had a hand such as top pair on the flop, you should usually just continue betting on the turn. You should usually bet even when the turn card is a scare card to you, such as an overcard to what had been the top pair. One overcard to your pair should not usually give you cause to slow down with a hand that's probably still best.

Two Pair

Two pair should also usually be bet on the turn. An exception is when the turn card made your two pair and you had been calling on the flop rather than betting or raising. In that case you should often consider checking and raising. For example, you have A♦7♦ and the flop was Q♥7♣4♦, and someone in late position bet after you checked. Now the turn card is an Ace, making the board Q♥7♣4♦A♥.

You should strongly consider a check and raise here. The flop bettor probably either has a Queen or a 7. If the flop bettor had not raised before the flop, then it's unlikely he has an Ace and a Queen. If you check, then he'll probably bet and you can raise. If he had raised before the flop, you should probably not check-raise here. The risk of his holding something like A♠Q♠ is just too great and you should just check and call.

Trips

If the turn card made trips for you, with a pair on the board, then whether to bet or check-raise depends on how aggressive the flop bettor is. For example, with the same hand and same flop as discussed earlier, suppose the turn card was a 7 rather than an Ace, making the board on the turn look like Q♥7♣4♦7♥. Now an aggressive player who had bet the flop will not likely be slowed down by the pair on the board, but if the flop bettor is a passive player, he might be concerned about the possibility that you've made trips and check behind you if you check. Check and raise if you think someone else will bet. If you're not fairly sure that someone else will bet, then go ahead and bet it yourself.

Overcards

If you called "on the flop" (i.e., the betting round after the flop is displayed) with overcards and didn't hit one on the flop, you should usually fold if someone bets. The bet size is now double the size of the bet you called on the flop, and you're not getting the pot odds to make another call in most situations.

Picking Up a Draw

There will be times when you called on the flop with, for example, an inside straight draw, and won't be getting the correct odds to continue to call on the turn bet. If you miss a draw like that, always check and make sure that you didn't pick up a flush draw with the turn card. If you now have a four-flush in addition to the inside straight draw, you almost surely have a good enough draw to call and take off the last card.

Letting Them Bluff

There are two exceptions when it's often better to check and call than to bet. That's when the turn card is an Ace or is the third card to a flush on the board. The reason is that those two cards present a bluffing opportunity to your opponent. Checking gives them a chance to bluff. The risk of checking is that they may check also, getting a free look at the river card.

The risk of betting is that they may fold a weak hand that they would have bluffed with had you checked; the benefit of checking is that it may induce a bluff; and the benefit of betting is they may make a mistake and fold even though they are getting sufficient pot odds to call. If they do call, then you still benefit because you're getting more money in the pot when you're probably favored to win. To decide which action is best, consider your opponents, weigh the potential risks and benefits in light of how you expect your opponents to react, and take the action.

KNOWING YOUR PLAYERS

With the doubled bet, the turn is when many players try to get tricky. If you get raised on the turn, it becomes important to distinguish between different kinds of players. You need to be able to distinguish between a player who is raising because he's got the best hand or best draw, a player who is raising for information, and a player who is raising just cause he thinks it's fun.

Each of those situations calls for a different response—basically, fold, raise, and call, respectively. The effort invested in learning the habits and tendencies of your opponents will almost always pay off.

7

Some Overrated Concepts

There are two mistakes that are common to almost every beginning poker player. They tend to bluff too much and they tend to slow play too much, but those aren't the only common mistakes. Another mistake that most players develop at some point is playing too aggressively. Beginners also have a tendency to call "just one more bet" to "see what the next card is."

Bluffing is betting when you don't have the best hand, hoping that you will not be called. Slow playing is not betting (or not raising) when you do have the best hand, hoping that you'll entice others to bet or call.

Both bluffing and slow playing are forms of deception, and they are both an important part of a poker player's arsenal. Both are easy to overuse, often to the point that they become so predictable that they lose all hope of deception.

Playing aggressively isn't really an overrated concept, but I decided to put a discussion of overaggressive play in this chapter just because it seems to fit as a common mistake. Aggression in poker, and especially in Hold 'Em, is generally a good thing. Betting and raising will win much more money over time then calling—but it can be overdone.

BLUFFING

Most beginning poker players bluff too much and call too frequently because "he might be bluffing." Both are mistakes.

Why Do You Bluff?

Most beginners tend to bluff when they think it's the only way they can win the pot. The mental focus is on winning this pot, but winning pots isn't what poker is all about. As I pointed out earlier in the book, the players who win the most pots are seldom the players who win the most money. In fact, most don't win any money at all.

Sometimes you are just beaten. You don't have the best hand. You're not going to win this pot. Bluffing might be your only chance to win in these situations, but it's often such a small chance that a bluff is just futile. Do not bluff just because it's your only chance to win. That doesn't mean don't bluff. You should bluff. In some games, against some opponents, you should bluff frequently—but have a good reason. "It's the only way I could win" is not a good reason. You should bluff when you have a reason to think that your opponent will not call. If the pot is large you often don't need much of a reason. You don't need to be successful with a bluff very often if the pots are large in order to make a profit, but a hope that your opponent will not call is not a reason.

Reasons to Bluff

As I said, bluff when you have reason to think your opponent won't call. Most of those reasons require you to be able to read your opponent.

Snapping Off a Bluff

There are two ways to catch bluffs—reading a player's body language and behavior and reading cards. In reading body language or behavior, the general rule is that strong means weak. That means that players will often intentionally behave in ways to attempt to convey deceptive information. If they are putting on an obvious act of heavy aggression, then they often actually have a weak hand. They are trying to use behavior to intimidate you into folding.

Reading cards requires an analysis of the entire play of the hand. To identify bluffs by reading hands, you need to determine the answer to the question: Is everything he's done up to now consistent with his holding the hand he's currently representing? If the answer is no, then suspect a bluff.

Either of these two approaches to catching bluffs requires experience and good poker judgment. If you're new to the game, you probably haven't acquired enough of either of those to be a reliable reader of either people or cards. There are some situations where many players do have a tendency to bluff. When you run across one of those situations, you should usually suspect a bluff.

One common bluff occurs when an Ace falls. In Hold 'Em, many players will habitually bet as a bluff when an Ace falls on the board as the river card. Whenever an Ace falls, and an opponent who has been playing passively up to then bets, suspect a bluff. It's not always a bluff, but it occurs often enough that you should be aware of it. Often, if you'll think about the play of the entire round (especially the early betting rounds), you can conclude not only that it's unlikely that the bettor has an Ace but also that they have a reason to think you don't have one either.

The main thing to look for when considering whether an opponent is bluffing is consistency of play.

An example is a hand I played recently. In a typical game, with a little loose and mostly weak, predictable opponents, I had Q♦J♦ on the button. Everyone folded to a late-position player who is usually fairly aggressive. He limped in. I raised. The small blind called, the limper called the raise. The flop missed me completely, that is, A♠9♦4♣, but I suspected this flop missed everyone. The small blind checked and the original limper bet. What did he have? This was a fairly aggressive player, and he had just limped before the flop. From late position, with any Ace this player would have opened with a raise. Because he hadn't, I guessed that the best hand he could have was a 9. I called. The small blind folded. The turn brought a second Ace. Now I'm almost certain he doesn't have an Ace. Anytime two of a rank are on the board, the statistical chances that another player holds one of that rank are reduced. He checked. Now I don't even think he has a 9. I bet. He folded. Apparently his bet on the flop had been a bluff attempt to win the pot right then.

Just looking at the cards, my call on the flop might appear to be a weak call. I had two overcards to second pair. Generally my hand didn't have a lot going for it. Why did I call? Because his play hadn't been consistent with what I knew of his playing habits. With callers in front of him, this player would have raised before the flop with any Ace. So, even though his bet now might suggest he has an Ace, I'm pretty sure he doesn't. It just didn't fit, and I suspected a bluff, calling just to see what happened next.

Whenever your opponent's past actions aren't consistent with the hand he appears to be trying to represent now, suspect a bluff. An important concept in that part of your game involves protecting yourself against bluffs. Look for inconsistencies, and when you find one, exploit the probable weakness of the player displaying them. Whenever you see a player who usually plays consistently doing otherwise, exploit it. It really is valuable to learn your opponents' habits. In the example I gave, the only habit I needed to have observed was the player's tendency to be aggressive.

SLOW PLAYING

I think most players slow play too much in Hold 'Em. There are at least three problems with slow play. One is that your hand is often not as strong as you think. For example, people will often slow play hands like the bottom two pair and the bottom set, even when the board is two-suited. These plays are clearly almost always wrong against typical players.

When I first started playing poker in cardrooms, an old man in a Reno Stud game gave me some advice. After one hand I played, he said, "The problem with slow playing the nuts is that there might be somebody else slow playing a hand they only think is the nuts."

He was right. Most players slow play too much, and it can cost them dearly at times. A slow play is just a deceptive play where you play a strong hand weakly. The idea is to allow someone else to get a cheap draw to a second-best hand, but there are many ways a slow play can go wrong.

One way is the case the old man in Reno was talking about. That's when you don't need to let someone draw cheaply to get a second-best hand. It's when they already have one, but they don't know it's second best and are slow playing themselves. This situation can cost you a lot of missed bets. Another way slow play can cost you money is when your hand isn't really as good as you think, and the free card you give can give someone a better hand, not a second-best hand. This is, of course, the worst possible outcome from a slow play, costing you both extra bets and the entire pot.

There are times when slow play is the right thing, but not as many as most players seem to think. If you've got any doubt whether slow play is the right move—you should probably just bet. The other reason to avoid slow play is that it's not as deceptive as you might think.

OVERAGGRESSION

Raising to Get Information

A lot of players will raise with mediocre hands to "define the hand," which is an attempt to get information about the strength of your hand. The cost of doing this is almost always greater than the value of any information you might get.

Raising to Intimidate

Many players will try to bully their way into winning a pot. They raise because they think you're weak and can be intimidated into folding.

CALLING TOO MUCH

Many beginning poker players seem intent on losing their chips just one bet at a time. These kind of leaks can add up quickly. If you don't have any reason to think you have the best hand and you don't have a good draw, then give it up. Fold and move on to the next hand.

PART TWO

Advanced Concepts

This part of the book contains more advanced material on identifying good games, weak opponents, and typical mistakes of your opponents, as well as exploiting the advantages that you can get from picking good games and weak opponents.

Two chapters focus on strategy considerations important in picking a table and picking a particular seat. Picking a good game is the first step toward beating the game. Even if you've picked a good game, you can often make a good game better by picking a good seat. Where you sit relative to the other players can often have a big influence on your ability to avoid trap situations or to manipulate the betting to your advantage.

Most poker books take a prescriptive approach to teaching about the game. They tend to pick what the writer considers a typical game, with some particular mix of players and a particular betting structure, and proceed to tell you what hands to play and how to play them. I don't take that approach in this book. Rather than try to tell you how to play, I try to teach you how to think about poker in a way that will lead you to the correct decision in most situations. This isn't the easiest way to learn to play Hold 'Em—but it's the only way to learn to play well. Three chapters cover the various theoretical perspectives useful in thinking about poker in general and Hold 'Em in particular. Hold 'Em poker in particular is a very complex game. It's not a difficult game to learn, but it can be difficult to learn to play well. To be able to analyze the game in a way that makes sense, we need theories and models to help us cut to the core issues that are relevant in a particular situation.

The first of the three chapters discusses the general concept of a theory and presents some different poker theories that are helpful in analyzing different situations; the other two chapters discuss some general theoretical ideas about hand value and betting.

If you're a beginning player, you might want to read through the chapters on theoretical concepts quickly and reread them again after you've finished the book.

An optimal playing stratagy for a tight-passive Hold 'Em table will usually not take the money if the game condition shifts to a loose-aggresive table. Hold 'Em requires playing strategy and tactics that specifically exploit the current conditions of the current game. The need to do this is probably more dramatic in Hold 'Em than in any other form of poker. The chapters on theortical considerations discuss this process of adjusting for game conditions. A chapter on anticipation of changing game conditions is included.

You need to be constantly adjusting your viewpoint to exploit the current conditions of the game. You also need to keep a focus on individual players, and you often need to make large tactical and strategic changes to reflect the habits of particular players. Three chapters address different player considerations.

8

Pick the Right Table

Nuances of pre-flop hand selection or playing variations on the later betting rounds can add a few dollars to your expected win. Decisions about where to sit can double or triple your expected win.

It's common among poker players to think of a 10/20 game as potentially more profitable than a 3/6 game simply because the 10/20 betting structure is so much larger, but if the players aren't putting a lot of bets into the pot, then it's entirely possible for a 3/6 game consisting of loose and aggressive players to be a larger game, with more money flowing around the table than a 10/20 game of tight, passive players. The game with the larger betting limits is not always the larger game, and it's not always the better game.

IMPORTANCE OF GAME SELECTION

If you don't limit your play to games you can beat, then you aren't likely to beat the game. Game selection is the most important element of poker. I've seen some estimates that it's 80 percent of what makes a winning player.

Your winnings from poker don't come from your excellent play. If everyone played perfectly, then the money would just be passed back and forth among the players, with the house skimming a small amount every time money was passed. Everybody would be a net loser. That's not what happens, though. Some players are net winners, and some are net losers. Some of the losers are actually better players than some of the winners. The difference isn't because of luck—it lies in who their opponents are. Losers play with people who play better than they do, and winners play with people who don't play as well. This does not mean that you need to be the best player at the table. You don't. In fact, if most of the other players play only slightly better than you, then one really bad player is probably enough to make the game worth playing.

Let's suppose for minute that I'm one of the ten worst poker players in the world, and let's suppose you're among the ten best. If I always play with nine players worse than me and you always play with nine players better than you, then I'll be a consistent winner, and you'll be a consistent loser.

What does that tell you about what's important for becoming a winning poker player? Many winning poker players develop a reputation as lucky. They accumulate larger wins more often than do other players who seem just as skilled. Often these players are highly skilled at identifying exploitable situations. They seem lucky because they pick those opportunities to get lucky. We'll talk more about this later in the book. Almost always these lucky players are those who choose good games. Once they are in the game, they identify individual player characteristics that can be exploited. The focus of this chapter is on selecting a good game. We discuss individual player characteristics in Chapter 9, and we give examples of exploitable situations throughout the book.

Your profits come from your opponents' mistakes. I'm going to repeat that frequently. Even if you don't play well, as long as you play with players who make more mistakes than you, you'll win.

For most players it's not enough to pick a game with weak players. You also need to pick a game you'll enjoy. Poker is not an armed conflict, it's a game. The whole point of playing any game is to have fun, and poker is no exception.

Every game has a kind of personality of its own. Your long-term success depends on matching the personality of the game to your own personality. You'll win more money if you're having fun.

WHAT TO LOOK FOR

Experienced players look at many factors when choosing a game to play. That's because they have a good handle on their own technical skills and have learned to recognize the characteristics of a game that are profitable for them. I do very well in wild and crazy games. I'm an expert at those types of games, and I enjoy them. I do well at other games, but I don't get as much enjoyment. So I look for a lot of chips on the table, seven or more players seeing the flop, players cold calling raises before the flop, a lot of laughing. When I see this at a Hold 'Em table, I know I'm going to like that game. The limit might be 1-5, 3/6/12, or it might be 20/40; it doesn't matter to me. The action and the players' attitudes attract me to the table.

Many players don't do well in that type of game; they've developed a playing style that just doesn't work for wild games. So they avoid them and look for games that are better matches to their style.

Beginners haven't developed that self-knowledge of their own playing style or personality, so game selection can be tougher, but you can still do it. In fact you should do it. You can evaluate a game based on two scales: a tight-loose scale and a passive-aggressive scale.

You'll want to play in loose games. Not only are the players in a loose game making a mistake by playing too many weak hands (we'll talk more about hand selection later in the book), but playing a lot of hands gives them many opportunities to make even more mistakes. Don't forget that your profits come from your opponents' mistakes.

Whether you will prefer a loose-passive game or a loose-aggressive game depends to some degree on your own preferences and personality. Most beginners should opt for a passive game. This is because in a passive game you won't be presented with as many situations where you have to make a critical decision. Once you get some experience at making these heat-of-the-moment decisions, you'll find the loose-aggressive games much more profitable.

CATEGORIZE A GAME

To make a judgment of the characteristics of a game you should watch the game for about ten hands. The longer you can watch the game, the better, but ten hands is usually enough. That will take about twenty to thirty minutes, maybe less. You're looking for two things: how many players see the flop and how often someone raises. The criteria I use in this chapter assume a full game—nine or ten players. Evaluation of a short-handed game requires a different approach. I discuss this later in this chapter.

Tight Table

A tight table is one with few players involved in each pot. You'll see some tables where there are seldom more than two players involved in a pot. If you see most flops involving two players, never more than three, that's a tight table. If you see a table where sometimes everyone folds to a single raise, that's a very tight table.

Loose Table

A loose table is one with many players playing each hand. If you see five or more players involved in most flops, that's a loose table. If most flops have seven or more active hands, that's a very loose table.

Passive Table

A passive table is one with very little raising. If, out of ten hands, you see no more than two hands with raises before the flop, consider that a passive game.

Aggressive Table

An aggressive table is one with frequent raises. If five or more of the ten pots have been raised, that's an aggressive game. A very aggressive game is one that is raised almost every pot. It's a very aggressive game if eight or more of the pots have been raised and at least two of them involved the maximum number of raises.

The first table on page 92 shows the playing characteristics of twenty different combinations of game characteristics. Twenty seems like a lot of different game types to remember, but it's really not. With just a little practice, you'll learn to identify these game types automatically. Except for very loose games, the aggressive and very aggressive games are often unprofitable, and the most important piece of strategy advice for those games is to avoid them.

The second table shows the various combinations of tight-loose and passive-aggressive scales with an assessment of how often they tend to be profitable.

The most profitable game is one that's very loose and very aggressive. However, I'm talking about potential profitability. There is no guarantee that you will realize that potential. Very loose, very aggressive games also tend to be very difficult to play. What seems to be a good hand is often beaten by a long-shot hand. Losing a pot to a player who is playing a hand that had very little chance of beating you is called a "bad beat." Sometimes players who suffer bad beats have an emotional response. An extreme emotional response is called "going on tilt," a phrase borrowed from pinball machines. A player who is on tilt is one who is not thinking clearly, tends to be reacting to past events rather than the current situation, and makes a lot of mistakes. The potential is there in the very loose, very aggressive games, although actually getting the money is something else again. Unless you're an experienced player, with good hand- reading skills, and don't become tilted by a bad beat, then you should avoid these games. Beginners, in particular, should avoid very aggressive games of all kinds.

GAME CONDITIONS

	Passive	Typical	Aggressive	Very aggressive
Very tight	1-2	1-2	1-2	1-2
	<15%	15–50%	50–80%	>80%
Tight	2-3	2-3	2-3	2-3
	<15%	15–50%	50–80%	>80%
Typical	3-5	3-5	3-5	3-5
	<15%	15–50%	50–80%	>80%
Loose	5-6	5-6	5-6	5-6
	<15%	15–50%	50–80%	>80%
Very loose	7+	7+	7+	7+
	<15%	15–50%	50–80%	>80%

Legend: number of players seeing the flop
          percent of hands with pre-flop raise

GAME CONDITION PROFITABLITY

	Passive	Typical	Aggressive	Very aggressive
Very tight	+	+ -	+ -	—
Tight	+	-	—	—
Typical	+	+-	+ -	—
Loose	++	+	++	+-
Very loose	+++	++	+++	+++

+++   very profitable
 ++   profitable
  +   marginally profitable
 +-   marginal
 —   tough game
 —   very tough game

Note that the chart is not entirely symmetric but that profitable games tend to be grouped in the direction of loose and passive games. For a beginner the focus should be on the passive. Even on a bad passive table, the game won't cost much.

RISK VS. REWARD

Almost every decision you make in life involves some sort of trade-off between risk and reward. Decisions in poker are no exception. In poker the more money your opponents are putting in the pot, the larger your potential reward—but the risk is larger, too. There are two ways your opponents can be putting a lot of money in the pot—by being loose or by being aggressive. Either of these creates risk for you. These two sources of risk affect the game in different ways.

Risk from Loose Players

Against many loose players, you might have five or six players calling every bet, giving you great odds. Even if you start with the best hand, having five or six players drawing to beat you creates a large probability one of them *will* beat you. Sometimes the chance of being beaten is enough to affect your decision by not playing a hand you might otherwise play. We'll discover some of these situations later in the book. At a loose table, it's not unusual for the best hand at the flop to end up second best by the time the hand is over. In poker you'll generally want to try to start out with the best hand. However, the disappointment and frustration that result from an opponent's long-shot draw can have a devastating effect on some players' temperaments. If you're one of those players, you might want to avoid very loose games. A better approach might be to learn some coping skills.

Risk from Aggressive Players

Aggressive opponents are putting a lot of money in the pot by frequent raises and reraises—but that means you'll also be putting in a lot. The more money you have to put in the pot, the greater

the risk. With a lot of raises, you'll be faced with frequent decisions, increasing the risk that you might make a mistake.

MATCHING THE GAME WITH YOUR PERSONALITY

Some table compositions are just more fun than others. Of course,
what's fun for me might not be fun for you. Picking the table that's
right for you is a personal choice that only you can make. The best
I can do is give you some guidelines about what to expect from different conditions.

Personality and Tight Games

Tight games can bring their own form of frustration. Even if
the game is fast paced, with players acting quickly, the money will
be moving slowly. Your won-lost column won't show quick entries.
If you are the type of person who likes to see quick results, you
can very easily try to push things when confronted with a tight
game. Because most tight tables tend to be populated by pretty
good poker players, this can be disastrous to your bankroll.

Personality and Passive Games

For some types of personalities, passive games can bring their
own form of frustration—boredom. Thrill seekers are not often
happy at passive tables. Passive players are often easily distracted;
they tend not to pay a lot of attention to the game, and they don't
have any strong reactions to what's going on around them. If you
are the type of person who is bothered by this lack of interaction,
you might find yourself easily bored in a passive game, and you
might begin to try to grab people's attention by excessive aggression with your chips. That can be costly.

Personality and Aggressive Games

Aggressive games can sometimes bring on too much mental
stimulation. Aggressive games are for thrill seekers. Frequent raises

by the other players mean frequent decisions on your part. When a passive player checks, it almost always means they have a poor hand; when an aggressive player checks, you don't know what to think. He may intend to fold and, if you bet, he may intend to raise. If an aggressive player raises, it may be because he has a strong hand, or it may be that he just thinks you have a weak hand. This need to make frequent decisions based on often contradictory information can tire and frustrate some people.

SHORT-HANDED GAMES

A winning short-handed strategy is significantly different from a winning strategy at a full table. We'll discuss these strategy differences much later in the book, but for now it's just important to realize that there is a difference and that many players don't realize this. Your profits will come from players who make mistakes. Game selection is the key to finding those players. In short-handed games, the key to identifying weak players is usually just the time of day.

Evening

Cardrooms are usually the busiest in the evening. If you find a short-handed game in the evening, you can almost be certain it's not a good game. A busy cardroom will have players in it who are looking for a good game and are skilled at finding them. If a game is short-handed, and the cardroom is busy, that's a game that other players don't think is worth playing in. Follow their lead. Avoid it.

Late Night or Early Mornings

Late in the evening, or very early in the morning, the situation has changed. Now even if the cardroom appears busy, the room is losing players. More people are going home then coming in. Any game that's short-handed has probably only recently become short-handed. The players who are playing are players who usually play in the evening when it's rare for a game to be short-handed. Most of them probably don't have a lot of experience playing short-handed. Add to this the fact that they've probably been playing for hours and are tired, and you have the potential for a very good game. It's almost always worth playing a short-handed game very late at night or very early in the morning.

Midmorning

At most cardrooms, the regular daytime players start coming in about 10 A.M. A short-handed game in the midmorning is almost always a game that has just recently started. These players tend to play every day, and the ones who are willing to start a short-handed game are usually players who play well short-handed. Don't bother to sit down. Avoid this game.

Afternoon

Games are often started short-handed in the afternoon by players who play in the evenings but come to the cardroom a little earlier than the usual afternoon crowd. A short-handed game in the afternoon that has just started is usually worth playing, and a short-handed game in the afternoon that's been going all day is usually not worth playing.

Overall

Evaluation of a short-handed game usually involves an evaluation of individual players rather than an overall evaluation of the table. Until you get to know some of the individual players, you won't be able to do this. However, making an assessment based on the time of day will usually lead you in the right direction.

SELECTION

By far the most important skill is table selection. It doesn't matter how well you play if you are always picking the games full of tough players where even an expert can't beat the rake. Most of your income will come from a few very bad players. If you play fairly well, you won't lose much to the better players, nor win much from the slightly inferior players; it's the really bad players that count. You'll have to first understand yourself before you can pick the table characteristics that are right for you. Think hard about what kind of mental stimulation you're looking for from poker, and pick a table accordingly.

HOW TO CHANGE TABLES

Often you'll find yourself at a table that just isn't working for you. Maybe some of the more passive players have left and been replaced by aggressive ones—maybe vice versa. It might be time to change tables. The floorman or brush maintains two types of lists: waiting lists and change lists.

Waiting Lists

Each limit has its own waiting list. They don't maintain a waiting list for Hold 'Em, they maintain a list for 3/6 Hold 'Em, a separate waiting list for 10/20 Hold 'Em, and so on. It's a good idea to keep your name on the waiting list for all limits for which you have enough of a playing bankroll. If your name comes up on a list for a different limit than you're playing, you can just decline if you think your table has a better game. If you have your name on the waiting list for other limits, it's important to keep an eye on the other games, constantly evaluating their potential. When your name is called, you will have to move or decline. You won't be given time to watch the game for a while before you decide.

Change Lists

Changing to another table at the same limit is an entirely different procedure. When they have more than one table at the same limit, cardrooms keep a list of players who want to change tables, but the actual procedures for doing this vary widely. In some cardrooms one of the tables is designated as a "must move" table. If Table Two is a must move table, then whenever a seat opens at Table One, the player who has been on Table Two the longest must move. New players are always seated at Table Two. If the cardroom you play at designates must move tables, then you'll probably have to negotiate something with the other players if you want to move before your turn.

In cardrooms that don't designate must move tables, changing to another table at the same limit is still not a standardized procedure. Some rooms keep a formal change list to allow players already seated in a game the option of taking a new seat when one opens up. In most cardrooms, however, the brush will rely on his memory to maintain a change list. Especially if they are busy enough to have more than one table at the same limit, you can count on the brush's memory being faulty. You'll have to maintain some vigilance of your own to make sure you are allowed to move to an open seat—once a new player has been seated it'll be too late. One of the benefits of playing in large cardrooms is that there are often other tables available for a change. When you're seated at a table, always ask the brush to put your name on the change list. You should keep yourself on the list for other limits within the range you're comfortable with. Pick a good table, and be prepared to change when the conditions change.

9

Picking a Seat

Besides finding a table that matches your personality and your style and skill level, you'll want to pick a seat that gives you an advantage. Some seats are more advantageous than others. I'm not talking about a lucky seat, but one that puts you in an advantageous position relative to other players with certain characteristics.

LOCATION, LOCATION, LOCATION

Your location in the betting sequence makes a difference. *Your position matters.* Some positions allow you to gather more information before you act than other seats do. The more information you have, the better decisions you can make. The later in the betting sequence before you have to act, the better. Position rotates with each deal, so your positional advantage is transitory and gets spread equally among all players. However, with a careful choice of seat you can sometimes find an advantage that is uniquely yours for every deal. This involves your position relative to certain other players.

There are two different kinds of advantages you can get from picking a good seat. In some cases you can gain an information advantage; in other cases you can gain a strategic advantage.

Ideally, before you have to make a decision about your own hand, you'd like to have as much information as you can. To get this information, you prefer to have two kinds of players act before you: loose players and aggressive players. When other players act before you, you gain information. Even having a player fold gives you information, but you gain even more information when a player calls (loose player) or raises (aggressive player). In other cases the strategic advantages you can get late in the hand from having a certain player on your left overshadows an early information advantage you might get from having them on your right.

PRIMARY PLAYER CHARACTERISTICS

The objective in choosing a seat is to put yourself in a position relative to certain players which enables you to exploit mistakes made by those players. Information gathering is one thing that can help you exploit opponents' mistakes, but it's not the only one and it's often not even the most important.

Picking a good seat is part of an overall strategy of being a lucky player—not because you pick a lucky seat, but because you pick a seat that will give you opportunities. The way your seat can give you opportunities depends on your opponents' habits and the kinds of mistakes they tend to make.

Loose Players

A loose player doesn't just play a lot of hands—he tends to get involved with a lot of pots. Loose players play many hands and continue to play into the later betting rounds. Because they play many hands, you get frequent information from them.

Playing a lot of hands means they often play weak hands, so you won't really know a lot about the strength of their hands, but you will know more about the size of the pot and whether you will be getting odds to play such speculative hands as J♠T♠. We'll talk about this more in later chapters.

Aggressive Players

An aggressive player is one who bets and raises a lot. If you bet into an aggressive player, he might fold or he might raise, but he is probably not going to just call. Because aggressive players raise a lot, their raise before you have to act means you can fold hands such as A♠6♠, which are moneymakers in multiway pots because of their flush potential, but you often don't want to call a raise with that hand. As you will frequently have to give up that hand on the flop, you would like to know you don't have to invest that money to call a raise.

Loose-Aggressive Players

Although you usually prefer a loose player on your right and an aggressive player on your right, if a player is both loose and aggressive, you're often better off with him on your left. A player who is too loose, but otherwise plays typically, is almost always making the mistake of playing too many hands; a player who plays too aggressively, but otherwise plays typically, is probably making the mistake of overplaying mediocre or marginal hands. These are different mistakes, but, as we'll see in a minute, you can usually best exploit either of these mistakes by sitting to the player's left.

A player who does not play typically at all, but plays both loose and aggressively, might not be making as many mistakes as you might think, depending on the particular game conditions. Whether a player who is both loose and aggressive is making many mistakes, you can usually do better with him on your left than on your right. This is because such a player gives you more opportunities for tactical maneuvers in later betting rounds.

Tight Players

A tight player isn't going to give up much money. The exception is a tight player who folds too often on the river, but you won't find many of those. Most tight players are tight in terms of their initial hand selection. They don't play many hands, but, typically, once they decide to play a hand, they're often committed to it. A tight player is one who doesn't get involved in many pots. He's very selective. Tight players make tight tables. Sometimes tight players will become overcommitted to a hand. Sometimes they give up easily to a bet on the flop or turn, or fail to bet good hands strongly.

Generally you'd prefer a tight player to be on your left. There are two reasons for this. First, although knowing that a tight player is playing a hand does give you some information about the strength of his hand, he seldom plays so you do better with information gathering by having room on your right for loose players and aggressive players. Second, if you're at a tight table, you'll get frequent opportunities to open from late position with a raise and steal a tight player's blinds if he's on your left.

Passive Players

A passive player doesn't bet or raise on most hands but will tend to call. A player who will almost always call and almost never raise is called a "calling station." You should avoid being a calling station, but you should look for calling stations at your table. It's usually best to have passive players on your left. Because they don't raise much, the information value from acting after them before the flop is fairly small.

Maniacal Players

A maniac is similar to a player with Fancy Play Syndrome, but a little more extreme. A player with FPS tends to make bets or raises in an attempt to be tricky, and he does it in situations where it's probably inappropriate and not to his advantage to do so. A maniac often raises just because it's fun. A maniac is not just a loose-aggressive player. He's much more than that. He's a loose-aggressive player with FPS and an itch to gamble. He's loose in that he plays too many hands; he's aggressive in that he tends to raise a lot, but he also tends to raise often in inappropriate situations. He check-raises too much, semi-bluffs too much, and bets marginal draws too much. The bottom line is that a maniac likes to play and likes to bet. Maniacs seldom fold, seldom call, and raise a lot—at the slightest provocation. It's best to avoid tables with maniacs if you're a novice. If you're an experienced player, maniacs can be a major source of income. Seat choice relative to the maniac can be very important and usually depends on the composition of the rest of the table.

One characteristic of maniacal players is that you can depend on them to bet or raise with weak hands frequently. Because of that a maniac is a certain type of loose-aggressive player that is sometimes best to sit four or five seats on either side of you. This would be the case at a table of generally loose players. When a player has an extreme loose-aggressive style, you can usually count on the probability that they will raise before the flop, and you can often gain a very large advantage by keying your playing tactics on the flop to a maniac.

When you sit to the right of a maniac, just raise when you want to be reraised, forcing other players to call two bets cold or to fold. If you want to trap other players into calling a raise, check and let the maniac bet so you can raise after other players have called his bet. The ability to manipulate the betting in this way is a huge advantage at a loose table. Let the maniac do the raising for you when you just call with your better hands, and by all means fold anything marginal. Try to get rational aggressive players on your right, and very loose, very aggressive ones on your left.

Players Who Bluff Too Much

Anytime you have a player who habitually makes the same mistake, such as bluffing too much, you want to be able to encourage them to continue to make the mistake. If a player bluffs too much, you want to encourage them to bluff. Nothing encourages a bluff as much as a check. Especially if you're in a game where the bet size doubles on the river, you want habitual bluffers on your left. The reason is, of course, you can pick up many extra bets by checking and calling if a habitual bluffer is acting after you.

Drunks

Drunks are almost always loose players: sometimes passive, sometimes aggressive, always loose. So if you have to play at a table with a drunk, sit on their left, but the best strategy for a table with a drunk is often to just move to another table—don't play. They can be counted on to lose their money, but they slow the game down to a snail's pace and tend to be quick to anger—neither of which is good for the game. Avoid drunks, but sit on their left if you can't.

GETTING A GOOD VIEW

If you've identified more than one good seat (or can't identify one), one way to break the tie is to pick a seat at the end of the table. Either the number 2, 3, 7, or 8 seats at a ten-handed table are the seats on the end of the table which allow you to watch everyone for tells, all at the same time. If you are in the middle and decide to watch the players on your left, then Murphy's Law dictates that the tell you needed to see will be on your right, or vice versa.

VIEW OF THE TABLE

When you first sit down at the table, you won't often have a choice of seats—usually only one seat will be available, that is, the one you're going to take. When you do have a choice, there are some clues that you can use to help pick a seat.

A loose player often just looks loose. He sits or sprawls loosely in his chair. His chips are haphazardly spread in front of him or stacked unevenly. Similarly a tight player just looks tight. He sits upright, firmly in the chair. His chips are neatly stacked by denomination, probably arranged in a triangle formation. Passive or aggressive players aren't as easy to identify, but they sometimes give off some clues also. Passive players can sometimes be identified by a blank look on their face. They tend to not appear to be alert. Aggressive players sometimes tend to look not just alert, but hyper-alert. The characteristics of a maniac are twitching eyes, continuously scanning the table or even the room, and fidgeting hands.

When you have a choice of where to sit, the first step is to quickly scan the table, trying to identify player types. This initial identification won't always be right—but you'll make accurate assessments often enough to make the few seconds it takes well worth the time. An ideal initial seat selection would be to sit as close to the right of the loosest looking, most aggressive looking player at the table as possible. Another good choice would be to sit to the right of the tightest, most passive looking player at the table. You will want to make sure the table has players who are easy to beat, that is, weak players, and does not have many players who are difficult to beat, that is, strong players.

SEAT VALUE AND TABLE CONDITIONS

The relative importance of the various factors involved in selecting a seat can change as the table conditions change. For example, the effect of a maniac sitting in a tight, passive game is very different from the effect of the same player taking a seat at a table that's already very loose and aggressive. As you're playing, try to identify seats that you think might be better seats than the one you have. When a player in a seat that you think you'd like to move to looks like he's getting ready to move, don't hesitate to speak up and announce that you want that seat. There are no rules for who gets first claim on an empty seat—it's first come, first served.

When you do move seats, there is sometimes a penalty of having to post an extra blind. It depends on where you've moved to in relationship to your current seat and current position of the blinds. But don't let this influence your decision. Having to post an extra blind is a trivial expense compared with the value of a good seat.

10

Theories of Poker

Poker theory is a topic that takes much more than a chapter in a book to cover completely. At least two books devoted almost entirely to poker theory have been written, and neither attempts to cover the topic fully. The point of this chapter isn't to give a complete review of poker theory, but to provide a summary of how poker theory provides direction to strategic and tactical thinking in poker.

One problem in poker theory is that many poker analysts who write books or magazine articles about poker don't seem to really understand how theory influences thinking about the strategy and tactics of the game. Most analysts have a favorite theory about the game, and whenever they are confronted with a situation for analysis, they immediately view the situation through their favorite perspective. There are many alternative theories of poker, and a complete analysis of the game requires a frequent shifting of theoretical perspective.

In most fields it's not unusual for researchers or analysts to blur the distinction between the theory of some phenomena and a model based on the theory. That's particularly true in the poker literature. A theory of poker and a model of poker, however, are really distinct things, and I think it's important to understand that distinction when you're thinking and learning about poker.

WHAT IS A THEORY?

A theory has three characteristics: descriptive, explanatory, and predictive. None of these characteristics are necessarily explicit or even complete in any particular theory. A good theory is usually one that can be simply stated in one or more straightforward declarative sentences which have desirable implications for describing, explaining, or predicting observed behavior of the phenomena under study. A good theory doesn't need to do all three of these things. A good theory, however, does need to have some strong explanatory power. A theory that doesn't help us understand the game doesn't really help all that much.

An example of a simply stated theory of poker is *poker is a struggle among the players for the rights to the ante*. This theory doesn't lend much toward describing poker. It doesn't tell us how the betting is structured to facilitate the struggle among the players. It doesn't tell us how to determine which player ends up with the pot.

The theory does have some explanatory power for the first round of betting. It explains why it's usually best to limit your opening hands to those hands with self-contained power rather than those that have value through drawing power. Because it does not address the pot growth that comes from multiple betting rounds, it adds nothing to an explanation of the value of such hands as Jack, 10 suited in Hold 'Em.

The theory has some predictive power, but not much. A theoretical prediction for poker should provide us with a prescription for play—it should tell us something about the best way to play the game. For poker variants with multiple betting rounds, such as Hold 'Em, it just doesn't do that. It does help us predict things like a tight range of likely hands which a knowledgeable player who opened from early position might have.

An example of a theory with a different kind of predictive power is *money flows from bad players to good players*. This theory doesn't have much descriptive power; it doesn't tell us who the good and bad players are. Assuming we have some other method to identify good and bad players, it does help us predict the outcome of a poker session. In fact I used a simple mathematical model of that theory to develop the recommendations in Chapter 8 for when a single really bad player in a game can make an otherwise unprofitable game profitable.

WHAT IS A MODEL?

A model is a structured representation of a theory. It's descriptive of the theory, not necessarily descriptive of the phenomena. Often we can use a model to derive the predictive elements of a theory. A model might be in the form of an explicit mathematical statement, or it might just be a conceptual structuring.

An example is a game-theory model of the *poker-is-a-struggle-for-the-ante theory*. You can use a game-theory model to derive a list of opening hands by position. In relatively tight games, where it's typically heads-up after the first round of betting, we can use that same game-theory model to determine the hands with which we should be willing to call an opening bet. We can extend the use of the same model to determine when to bet, call, or bluff on the river.

For a game such as draw poker, where in most games the players tend to be relatively tight and you only have two rounds of betting, you can use a game-theory model to almost completely specify a winning playing strategy. That approach, however, just doesn't extend for a game with more than two betting rounds. It doesn't help all that much for a game such as Hold 'Em.

Although a game-theory model does help us analyze some situations, a game like Hold 'Em requires a different approach to the game. Hold 'Em is very complex, and it's doubtful that we could formulate a complete model of the game—even if we could do so, the mathematics of solving it would very likely be intractable. We can, however, develop theories related to particular aspects of the game, and use the models that those theories suggest to analyze tightly defined situations.

The game-theory model suggested by the *ante theory* is one such use. As I've already mentioned, that model can be used productively to analyze opening hand requirements in tight game conditions.

Another model is suggested by the theory that *poker is a struggle between made hands and drawing hands*. This theory suggests the use of a multinomial-probability model to analyze the play of drawing hands. By "multinomial" I mean a model that assumes multiple discrete outcomes, such as win large pot, win small pot, lose small pot, lose large pot. Multinomial is like flipping a coin with more than two sides. A dice game is an example of a multinomial game.

The theory that *money flows from bad players to good players* suggests a conceptual model of the game which implies that table selection involves looking for a table with large pots. This step from theory to model is not always an obvious one—but it's an important one in an analysis of the game.

VARIABLES IN THEORY

Implicit in a theory of poker is the concept of a variable. This is something that might change value or might even be a constant with an indeterminate value. By indeterminate I mean we won't know its value until the hand is over, for example, the hand we are dealt is a variable. It's a special kind of variable in that it's random, but it's not indeterminate—we know our hand as soon as we look at it.

The hand our opponent is dealt is also a variable, in the same way our hand is, but it's indeterminate, we won't know his hand until the showdown. By the way my description of the hand you've been dealt as a random variable is something of an example of what I talked about earlier in the blur in the distinction between a theory and a model. In the extreme it's not really correct to call the deal random—once you've specified the initial order of the cards, tracked the exact shuffle, and cut the deck, it is perfectly deterministic and predictable. Of course we don't keep track of things like the exact shuffle, so it makes sense to just think of them as occurring as the result of randomness. Randomness is a model of the shuffling process, not a theory of shuffling.

STRATEGY AND TACTICS

Although it's not directly relevant to theories and models, I think here is a good place to differentiate between strategy and tactics. Strategy is about the metagame. An optimal strategy is one that maximized your expected playing result over some period of time, maybe a playing session of a few hours, maybe a longer period such as months or years. Tactics are about the individual decisions that make up the play of the hand. An optimal tactic is one that maximizes the expected result of the particular situation.

The topics we've already discussed, game and seat selection, are strategic issues. There is no expectation of an immediate payoff from picking a good game or a good seat. In fact, there is no possibility of an immediate payoff. No one is going to toss you a few chips as soon as you sit down.

Playing poker as a string of tactically optimal plays does not generally lead to an optimal strategy. However, an optimal-playing strategy will lead to optimal-playing tactics. The reason for this is that a focus on strategic issues tends to maximize the opportunity for profit. Without maximizing opportunity, you can't maximize profit. For example, if you consistently play in a game where the other players just aren't going to lose much money, then no amount of tactical superiority will win as much money as you would win by playing in a game where the other players will always just play until they go broke. Strategic issues, such as game selection, come first. Only then can you rationally deal with tactical issues such as a choice of what hands to play. In poker it's usually the case that strategy focuses on the other players, and tactics focus on the cards. The distinction isn't really that sharp, but you won't go far wrong by thinking of strategy and tactics in these terms.

USES OF POKER THEORY

Poker theories help us gain a deeper understanding of inherent elements of the game. They help us develop a perspective of the game. Some of the current poker theories are given in the theoretical table.

As you can see, each of these different theoretical perspectives essentially focuses on the key variable of some particular facet of the game. No one of these theoretical perspectives provides a complete theory of poker, but each of them has its uses in developing a complete understanding of the game.

THEORETICAL PERSPECTIVES AND GAME CONDITIONS

Perspective	Game Conditions
Poker is a struggle among the players for the rights to the ante.	Very tight, tight
Money flows from bad players to good players.	All game types
Poker is a game of money and odds.	Loose and very loose games
Poker is a game of partial information.	Very tight, tight, typical, loose, aggressive
Poker is a game of strategy and deception.	Very tight, tight, typical, aggressive
Poker is a contest between a made hand and a drawing hand.	Tight or typical
Poker is a game of kickers and hand domination.	Tight or very tight
Poker is a game of manipulation and pressure.	Typical, loose, very loose

---

USES OF POKER MODELS

A poker model helps us explore the implications of a particular theory. It's through the analysis of either a formal mathematical model or a conceptual model of a theory that we can uncover the strengths and weaknesses of a particular theoretical perspective. A good poker model isn't going to try to reflect every nuance and quirk of a poker game. We can use explicit poker models, inspired by the appropriate theoretical perspective, to analyze the effects of a wide range of decisions—from deciding whether to play in a particular game or deciding whether to raise with an A,A.

A GENERAL THEORY OF POKER

We don't have a general theory of poker. By a general theory I mean a unified theoretical view that encompasses most, if not all, of the commonly accepted theoretical perspectives of the game. All these theoretical perspectives are useful. No one of them is better than the others. Each is useful in a different aspect of the game. At different parts of this book, we look at poker through different perspectives. You've already seen two examples of this.

In Chapter 8, on game selection, we looked at poker through the perspective that *money flows from bad players to good players*. We used that perspective to identify games that involve many players putting a lot of money into the pot as profitable games.

Some poker players argue that the best games are those when the players are passive, preferably loose-passive, but also tight-passive. The reason they come to that conclusion is that they are looking at poker through a perspective of *strategy and deception*. A weak game of passive players does afford you more opportunity at using advanced strategies and deceptive plays, but that's not the most important source of profit in poker.

It's not a question of which perspective is superior to the other. It's a question of which perspective is more useful in helping to answer the question at hand. In the case of game selection, the key variable is the amount of money available. The *money-flow* perspective focuses on this key variable, and it is the preferable perspective to use when considering selection of a game.

In Chapter 9, on seat selection, we looked at the game with a different perspective. There the focus was on the point of view suggested by a strategy and deception perspective. Most poker writers seem to look at seat selection through a prism of a *partial information* perspective.

One major difference in seat selection strategy which results from these different perspectives is in the case of maniacs. A common recommendation is to sit with the maniac to your immediate right. I suggest the opposite, sit with him either on your immediate left or halfway across the table from you. What is the reason for the difference? It's because of the difference in focus from the two different theoretical perspectives. If you use a partial information perspective, you'll want him on your right to ensure you have as much information as you can get before you have to act. There is nothing wrong with that except that we are talking about a maniac, someone who plays almost every hand and raises at every opportunity. How much more information can you have? You get very little extra information from having a maniac on your right, but having him on your left expands your tactical playing options tremendously.

Poker is a struggle among the players for the rights to the ante.

This perspective has relevance in the early parts of the first betting round. In Hold 'Em we use blinds rather than antes, but the point of the perspective is that the game begins as a struggle for the initial money in the pot. It's a useful perspective in determining opening hand requirements, particularly in somewhat tight games and from early position.

Money flows from bad players to good players.

The premise of the *ante-theory* is that without some initial seed money in the pot, you have no game. The point of view of the *bad-player* perspective refutes that, however, with the observation that some players play so badly that they'd be willing to play even if the pot had no money to start with at all.

Poker is a contest between a made hand and a drawing hand.

This is a perspective of a simple two-player confrontation where one of them has the best hand and the other has a possibility of becoming the best hand. It's a useful perspective to use when analyzing situations where you're fairly certain that you either have the best hand or are fairly certain what the best hand is. This perspective is not useful, and in fact can lead you far astray, once you have more than two or three players competing for the pot.

Poker is a game of strategy and deception.

This perspective has a focus on making advertising plays to establish a false image, outwitting your opponents by bluffs and semi-bluffs, and using position to steal pots.

Poker is a game of partial information.

This perspective views poker as a mathematical game. The focus is on evaluation of information about your hand and the probable hands of your opponents. The idea of partial information games is derived from game theory.

Poker is a game of money and odds.

This perspective is a view of poker where pot size and drawing odds are the important variables. It's a particularly valuable perspective for play in loose games and in some aggressive games.

Poker is a game of manipulation and pressure.

This perspective is similar to the *strategy and deception* perspective. The difference is primarily more of an emphasis on false image than on tactical uses of position. Players who view the game primarily through this perspective tend to use a lot of table talk to manipulate and confuse opponents. Amarillo Slim was a master of this. Others who view the game through this perspective tend to apply pressure by playing in a fast, aggressive style. The current master of the techniques suggested by this perspective is probably Mike Caro.

Poker is a game of kickers and hand domination.

This is an important perspective in tight games or in any games where tight players have entered the pot. The emphasis is on the added value of having two high cards rather than one. Of course two high cards have value because of the increased probability of flopping the top pair, but the *domination* perspective focuses on the card that does not have a match on the board—the kicker.

WHAT IT ALL MEANS

Which theoretical perspective you use to analyze a situation just depends on the situation and the game-condition context of the situation. Before you finish this book, you'll see examples of using all the theoretical perspectives to analyze the game. That's the key to developing a dynamic approach to the game. Developing the ability to quickly shift your point of view is the first step in being able to adjust to changes in game conditions—the key to winning poker.

11

Betting Theory: The Odds

Before you bet, check, call, or raise, you should have a reason. Often, if you ask a player why they bet in a certain situation, they'll say something like, "I thought I had the best hand." Although that's probably the most common reason people bet, it's almost never a good enough reason to bet.

Your reason for betting should be about the expected result from betting. What's going to happen when you bet? How does that result compare with what will happen if you don't bet? The typical reason to bet or raise is to simply get more money in the pot. The situations where you want to get more money in the pot depend on the odds—both of the odds of your hand winning and of the money odds. If the odds of your hand winning are greater than the money odds from a bet, then you'll profit by betting. Before we get into the ideas and theories of betting, I need to discuss the different kinds of odds you need to consider when thinking about a bet.

MONEY ODDS

The concept of money odds is often confusing to beginning poker players. It's really not that difficult: At any given point in the play of the hand, there are three sources of money, and each needs to be considered separately. There's money that's already in the pot.

That's called "pot odds." There's money that's going into the pot in the current betting round. I call that "bet odds." And there's money that will be going into the pot on future betting rounds which is called "implied odds."

Past	*pot odds*
Current	*bet odds*
Future	*implied odds*

All these money sources are important, but their importance needs to be considered in different ways.

Pot Odds

Pot odds are an important consideration when you're deciding whether to call with a hand that's probably not the best hand. Pot odds are just the ratio of the amount of the current bet to the amount of money already in the pot. For example, if five people called before the flop, on the flop one person has bet and one has called, then there are seven bets in the pot, and you are getting 7-1 odds to call. You also need to keep in mind that if a player behind you raises, then your pot odds will be cut almost in half.

Let's say your hand is 8♠7♠, and the flop is 9♣5♥2♦. Should you call?

This is an example of when pot odds are important. You've got an inside-straight draw on the flop. Any 6 will make you a straight, and the flop does not have two of any one suit so it's not possible for a 6 to make someone else a flush.

There are forty-seven unseen cards, and the next card is equally likely to be any one of them. You have four "outs," which is just another way of saying that four out of the forty-seven will make your straight, forty-three don't help you. So the odds against making a straight on the next card are 43-4, or about 11-1. For every time you make the straight, there will be about eleven times you don't make it. With 7-1 pot odds, the pot is probably not large enough for a call. If the pot had eleven bets in it and you're reasonably sure that you won't be raised after you call, you should call a bet to draw one card to an inside straight.

To evaluate your hand in terms of pot odds, you need to keep track of the size of the pot. When you're keeping track of the money going into the pot, it's usually easier to just count the number of bets and calls rather than the total amount of money. If ten bets have been put into the pot and you're now considering calling a bet and a raise (two bets), then you're getting pot odds of 5-1. At the turn, when the bet size doubles, just divide the count of the number of bets in the pot by two to put the pot-odds calculations in terms of the new bet size.

Pot odds are important anytime you're considering a call, not just when you're on a draw and have more cards to come. Pot odds should also be taken into consideration whenever you have a mediocre hand, and someone bets on the river. By this point in the betting, the pot odds are often very large, and you need to compare the pot odds with your estimate that a player is bluffing or is betting a mediocre hand slightly worse than your hand. In many cases the pot will be large enough to be worth a call even if the chances of a bluff are very small.

Bet Odds

The odds on the current bet are important when deciding to bet or raise. It just depends on the number of callers. It's much more difficult to estimate than pot odds because you need to anticipate the number of callers. Raises from players still to act don't cut down your bet odds, however, except to the extent that a raise might cause a potential caller to fold.

Bet odds are an often ignored part of poker theory. Most books just suggest you should bet or raise whenever you probably have the best hand, but if that's the only time you bet or raise, then you're missing out on a lot of potential profit. You should bet or raise whenever the odds your getting on the bet (the number of callers) is greater than the odds your hand will end up the best hand. Throughout the rest of the book, I'll show you how to determine this in various situations.

Implied Odds

Implied odds are an important consideration anytime you have action to take—whether it's calling or betting. Implied odds can be very difficult to estimate, however, because it involves estimating what will happen on future betting rounds.

In the inside-straight draw example I used when discussing pot odds, the existence of implied odds suggests you can call with a draw to hands like an inside straight even though the pot isn't offering you sufficient odds. In the example the pot was giving you 7-1 odds and you were 11-1 against making your hand on the next card, but if you make your hand on the next card, you'll likely win more than just what's in the pot now. If you know, for example, that the bettor will bet again on the turn, will call a raise, and will call a bet on the river, then you're getting implied odds of 6-1 (bets on the turn and river are twice the size of the bet you have to call on the flop). That would mean you'd only need pot odds of about 5-1 to combine with your implied odds to give you good enough odds to draw to an inside straight. Of course there is also some chance that you'll make your straight and still lose, so I'd usually want the pot to be giving me something like 9-1 to compensate for those times.

It's also important to consider the implied odds that other players likely have. Drawing hands have high implied odds because they will win extra bets if the hand is made but will not lose any extra bets if the hand misses.

However, you need to be careful not to overestimate your implied odds by counting on future calls that might not materialize. Flush draws are an example of hands that often don't have as high implied odds as you might think. Many players will slow down and check when a third flush card hits the board, but they'll bet when a third card to a straight shows. The flush is just more obvious, and you often should not count on being able to raise. Luckily you are usually getting sufficient pot odds to draw to a flush and don't need to count on implied odds. As a general rule, it's often right to accept pot odds just a notch or two less than ignoring implied odds would suggest.

REASONS TO BET

Before you take any action on a hand, have a reason. Make a plan. There are generally two situations when you want to bet—one is when you have the probable best hand and the other is when you have a good draw. These are situations where you'll probably want to bet, but they aren't the reason to bet. The reasons to bet involve the odds, either pot odds, bet odds, or implied odds, depending on the particular situation.

The Probable Best Hand

There is no universal way to determine the likelihood that you have the best hand. For purposes of this discussion, we can just think of the top pair as the probable best hand. Top pair is when one of the cards in your hand matches the highest card on the board.

Whenever you bet or raise with the best hand, you're reducing the pot odds your opponent is getting. For example, let's say you have A♠A♣, and your opponent has K♥Q♥ with a flop of K♠T♣6♦. Your opponent will likely bet, thinking he has the best hand. Let's say the pot has five bets in it before your opponent bets. Now, if you call, then your opponent is getting 6-1 odds to try to outdraw you. The 6-1 comes from 5-1 on the pot odds and even money on your call of his bet.

If you raise, however, your opponent's odds are cut from 6-1 down to 3.5-1 (or 7-2, five bets already in the pot plus your two bets, compared with the two bets he has to put in the pot).

The odds of him getting a King or a Queen on the next card to improve to a better hand than your pair of Aces are 8-1 (that's rounded off a little—six of the forty-five unknown cards will improve his hand). The astute reader might notice that I'm ignoring flush and straight possibilities. I'm doing that for convenience only; although slight, those chances should be included in a complete analysis.

Whenever the money odds your opponent is getting are less than the odds he has of improving, he is losing money. That means you gain money. You would profit in this situation if you only called. His bet was a mistake and you profit from it, but you profit even more by raising and reducing his money odds. Note that you're not raising because you have the best hand. Although you do have the best hand, you're raising because you profit from reducing your opponent's money odds.

The Dreaded Free Card

One of the things you want to avoid is giving your opponents a free chance to beat you. That's equivalent to giving infinite odds. Let's say you have J♠J♦ and the flop is 9♥7♥3♣. You probably have the best hand and there are some important reasons to bet here. What if your opponent has two hearts? Or T♦9♦? Or A♣7♣ or 8♣6♣? A player with any of these holdings has to draw to beat you. Make them pay to try. If you bet, they are probably getting the correct odds to call, but if you don't bet, you're giving them infinite odds. You can't give away gifts like that very often and expect to be a winning poker player.

Note, however, that we're talking about a single opponent. When you have four or five opponents who call, you may not have such a good hand. Later we look at an example of this hand, this flop, and four opponents. When you might not profit from a bet, you should consider folding if someone else bets, and a couple of other players are calling or raising. The perspective you need to take when evaluating a hand on the flop is different when you have multiple opponents than when you have a single opponent.

Betting to keep from giving up a free card can be even more important when you're not sure you have the best hand. For example, let's say you're on the big blind with a hand like 9♥4♦, and no one raised before the flop. The flop is Q♣4♥2♦. What should you do?

You should probably bet. You might not have the best hand. Someone may have a Queen, but you're not sure, and the danger of that is not nearly as large as the danger of giving someone with a hand like 10♠8♠ or 7♠6♠ a free chance to beat you. If you do have the best hand and check, then a lot of cards could come on the turn that will give someone a better pair than your measly pair of 4s. Also by betting you might get someone with a better hand, like 8♥8♦, to fold.

In the same flop, but with a hand like Q♦7♥, it's not nearly as important to bet. In fact, with that hand you probably shouldn't bet. The reason is that with this hand you still might not have the best hand but, if you do, then it isn't likely that the next card can hurt you. By checking you are giving your opponents a chance of a free card that will make them a second best hand, not a best hand. You also may encourage someone with a hand like 8♥8♦ to bet, and you aren't risking a raise in case your hand isn't best.

Think about these two examples. In the second one we are more likely to have the best hand, but it's the first case, when we aren't sure at all that we have the best hand, that it's important to bet. The free card concept is a much more important concept in deciding whether to bet than whether you have the best hand.

Check-raising

Because the nature of fixed-limit Hold 'Em makes calling one bet often correct for very weak hands, it's difficult to protect your hand. A major weapon you have to protect your hand is check-raising; however, you must be conscious of where you think the bettor will be. Typically, if you had a made (but vulnerable) hand, you would check in early position if you thought there would be a bet in late position. You then raise, and the players in between face two bets plus a risk of a reraise by the late position player, making it difficult for them to call. If you have an invulnerable hand that you want to make everyone pay you through the nose for, then you would check in early position if you thought there would be an early position bet, and then you would raise after everyone trailed in calling behind. The downside of check-raising is that you risk giving a free card if no one bets. The consideration of who the likely bettor will be is a very important concept when considering a check-raise, especially so in loose games.

Raising to Thin the Field

There is a popular misconception that a primary purpose of raising before the flop is to drive other players out of the pot—to limit the field. It's an idea that just keeps getting repeated over and over again in poker books—a mantra to soothe the soul. It's an idea that's just wrong.

So far I haven't found a single Hold 'Em book that doesn't suggest someplace in the book that you should raise with a hand like A♣A♠ if your raise will cause others to fold. The idea they all express is that if you can reduce the number of opponents, you'll increase your chances of winning the pot.

Well, that idea is right. Fewer opponents do mean you have a greater chance of winning the pot. That's true whether your hand is A♣A♠ or 7♦2♥. Poker isn't about winning pots—it's about winning money. With a very strong hand such as A♣A♠, you'll win the most money when you have as many callers as you can get.

Semi-bluffs

In most cases, aggressive play is winning play. You should constantly be applying pressure to the other players to give them tough decisions to make. You may reraise when you think you're either beaten badly or your opponent is bluffing. Bluffing and semi-bluffing are important to keep yourself unpredictable, and because you're keeping track of the ranges of plausible hands, it's quite likely you'll often know where your opponent stands.

Cold bluffing is usually restricted to the river, where you might bet into one or two opponents (who might fold) if you have no chance of winning the pot at a showdown. Semi-bluffing is betting with a hand that is not likely best but has some big outs. Your opponent may fold immediately, and, if not, you may hit your out and your opponent may seriously misread you. There is an important balance here. You must have sufficiently tight hand selection criteria such that when you do bet your opponent is positively terrified that you may have a big hand like an overpair. Semi-bluffing is very powerful, because you've been so careful in choosing your starting hands that even if you aren't there yet, you are likely to get there.

Value Bets

"Value bet" is a term used for betting when you just think you have the best hand, but "best hand" is a broad concept with a definition that's dependent on the situation.

Value Bets on the River

Once all the cards have been dealt, it's easy to fall into the trap of thinking that all that matters now is who has ended up with the best hand. Even here, having the best hand is not a reason to bet. Let's say you have a small pair, maybe a hand like A♥4♥, and the board is Q♥T♥5♠7♣4♣.

It's possible you have the best hand—maybe your opponent might have a K♠J♠ and have been drawing to a straight, for example. Even if you're 90 percent sure that's the hand he has, you probably shouldn't bet. The relevant question isn't whether you have the best hand, it's whether you have the best hand if he calls. If so, then a bet by you would be a value bet.

Value Bets with the Best Hand on Intermediate Rounds

On the river, the only consideration about the hand is the likelihood that your opponent has a worse hand than yours and will call (or a better hand and will fold). On intermediate rounds, when there are more cards to come, it gets a little more complicated. You have to consider not just the current strength of the hands, but the drawing power of both your hand and your opponents' hands.

Value Betting Draws

It's common in Hold 'Em to have multiway situations on the flop where the hand that is getting value from bets is the best draw, not the best hand.

For example, consider a four-handed situation where the players hold

Player 1	K♥Q♥
Player 2	A♥9♠
Player 3	J♣J♠
Player 4	T♣8♣

and the flop is 9♥7♥3♣.

The best hand is held by player 3, with a pair of Jacks, but the only hand that will profit from a bet is player 1—the flush draw. Any Heart, King, or Queen will make player 1 the best hand. That's fourteen cards if we look at all the hands. With three callers, any hand that has a greater then 25 percent chance of developing into the winning hand will profit from a bet or raise. In the four-handed scenario as illustrated, the flush draw with the two overcards is the only hand that has a winning potential higher than 25 percent.

The winning potentials are

Player 1	45%
Player 2	18%
Player 3	20%
Player 4	17%

We discuss this hand in a little more detail in the chapter on the theory of flop play. For now, just realize that having the best hand does not mean you have the best hand. By that I mean the best poker hand on the flop is not always favored to end up the best poker hand by the river. What is most important is that *the best hand is not always favored to win the most money*.

12

A Theory of Starting Hand Value

A CRITICAL DECISION

In most Hold 'Em games, the most critical decision you will make in the play of the hand is whether you will play the hand. Some hands, if played at every opportunity, will be long-term winners. Such a hand is A♠A♣. Others will be long-term losers if you play them. Examples of such hands are 7♠2♣ or 8♠3♣. Some hands, such as T♥9♥, are speculative hands, which will be profitable if played in the right situations.

You want to pick hands that are either powerful in their own right or have multiple ways to improve and win. Hands such as A♠A♣ or K♥K♦ are powerful on their own, often winning without any further improvement. An example of a powerful multiway hand is A♠K♠. It can win by pairing either card or by making a flush; it has straight potential, and, if you get really lucky, it can even win just on high-card value. Other hands, such as 7♦7♥, have speculative value, although they generally have only one way to win. If a third 7 falls on the flop, you'll have a very powerful holding, but that seldom happens so you'll usually have to give up such a hand on the flop. Not always though—even small pocket pairs can sometimes win unimproved.

A WINNING STYLE

As a general rule, a winning poker style requires that you only play your very best hands, folding most hands early, but in Hold 'Em it's not always clear how to determine which hands are best. There is no magic list of playable hands. Determining what kinds of hands have value in what kinds of situations is one of the skills you need to develop to become a winning poker player.

STRUGGLE FOR THE ANTE

In poker theory, poker games begin with *a struggle for the antes or blinds*. Theoretically a bet is a declaration of the form, "I have the best hand, give me the pot." As I pointed out in the last chapter, there are important reasons to bet other than because you have the best hand. Also there are reasons to play a hand other than it's probably the best hand.

In fairly tight games, this theoretical principle of playing the best hand is the guiding principle—it's how you'll make the most money for that game. As the game becomes looser, however, this principle based on the *ante theory* becomes less important, and theories based on *bad players* or *odds* become more important.

As the game conditions become loose, hand values derived from the drawing potential of the hand begin to become more important than value derived from the hand being best right now. Potential value from betting that will occur on future rounds becomes important. This is the implied odds we talked about in the last chapter. Also, as always, the mistakes that your opponents tend to make add value to hands. Different kinds of player mistakes can give value to different hands. When you're evaluating a hand to play, you need to think in terms of potential value, not in terms of rank.

CHANGING HAND RANKS

First let's look at why it's a mistake to even attempt to list hands in rank order. A complete poker hand requires five cards. In Hold 'Em you must make a decision whether to play after seeing only two cards. This is not enough to get a definition of what your five-card hand will be or to be able to provide any firm rules about how good a starting hand it is. Some hands are better than others and we can formulate some general guidelines, but we can't formulate a universal ranking.

In other popular forms of poker, you don't have to commit to a bet until you have more cards: three cards in Seven-Stud, four cards in Omaha, and in Hold 'Em you cannot determine a fixed ranking of the initial two-card hand. You simply don't know which is best. Any ranking you might attempt will be intransitive.

Transitive is a mathematical concept that says that if A beats B and B beats C then A will beat C. This is a property of numbers, for example. It's a property we are all familiar with, even if we aren't familiar with the term transitive. Intransitive means that the things we are dealing with don't have that transitive property. Not every group of entities can be treated as if they are numbers. Two-card Hold 'Em hands are an example.

For instance, in a two-player showdown (where both players will stay to the end), most of the time

$$A\spadesuit K\clubsuit \text{ beats } J\spadesuit T\clubsuit$$
$$J\spadesuit T\clubsuit \text{ beats } 2\heartsuit 2\diamondsuit$$
$$2\heartsuit 2\diamondsuit \text{ beats } A\spadesuit K\clubsuit$$

So, which is the best hand? It's going to be the one that wins the most money, and that depends on the game conditions—the nature, caliber, and habits of your opponents.

Two-card Hold 'Em hands just don't have stable ranks. You cannot just list all the hands, draw a line, and say play all the hands above this line. It just doesn't work.

I'm saying this more than once, because it's important. Many players seem to be looking for some magic formula to make them a winning player. There is no Holy Grail.

Different writers have tried to categorize hands. They come up with slightly different rankings because the different writers are considering games with either different betting structures or different playing conditions. The various hand rankings you'll find in poker books are all correct—and they are all incorrect. Hand rankings don't really exist except within very specifically defined situations. The value of a hand is determined by the playing characteristics of the game you're in and the betting structure. The differences you might find between different books are just a reflection of the differences in the particular situation for which they are trying to value the hands. There is no right or wrong except in the idea of what composes a typical game or typical opponent.

The only thing that's settled about Hold 'Em hand rankings is that there is no such thing as stable hand rankings. You can say with certainty that A♠A♣ is a better hand than K♠K♣, but you can't say with certainty that A♠K♦ is a better hand than J♦J♣ except within the context of a specific situation.

What we've shown here is that, even when you consider the value of a starting hand only in terms of its probability of winning the pot, hands can't be ranked, but poker hands have value from sources other than just the poker hand value. Some hands have increased value from a late position in the betting sequence because the position itself is likely to give you more opportunity to make tactical plays such as bluffing.

Another source of value for a hand is the kind of mistakes your opponents tend to make. An example is a player who in a loose game tends to overplay hands like the top pair. There are at least five sources of value for a poker hand:

Characteristics of the hand that make it likely to be the best hand at the moment

Characteristics of the hand that make it likely it will develop into the best hand

Characteristics of your position that give you tactical opportunities

Characteristics of the game that make it likely the hand can win a large pot should it develop

Characteristics of certain kinds of common errors that your opponents tend to make

When you're thinking about a starting hand in Hold 'Em, it's very important to *think of the hand in terms of value—not in terms of hand rank*. Hands just can't be ranked and most of the value of a hand comes from sources other than the characteristics of the hand itself. Think about value.

HAND TYPES

Hands can be grouped into types, such as pocket pairs like A♠A♦, suited connectors like 7♥6♥, or suited Aces like A♣6♣. In most situations (not all), hands can be ranked within these types. Some of a hand's value comes from features that are intrinsic to the hand, but less of a hand's value is intrinsic than most players think.

Pairs

Large and even medium-sized pairs can be powerful hands. Power hands tend to play well anytime. There is no situation where you should refrain from betting with big pairs. A decent-sized pair in Hold 'Em is valuable on its own, in almost any situation.

Smaller pairs are more speculative. The small pairs pretty much will need to flop a set to do well. They play well only with the right kind of flop, a flop of low cards, or against the right opponent. If that single opponent is a tough player, these medium-sized pairs tend not to do so well without flopping a set and having many players in the pot. The smaller pairs need either a particularly weak opponent or the money odds from having many opponents.

Suited Connectors

The large-suited connectors can flop the top pair, or a flush draw, or a straight draw. Of course, the midsized-suited connectors are looking to flop a draw. Except for the few times that they will flop two pair, the very small-suited connectors have little potential value as pairs, and they have few straight capabilities. The straight draws they will likely flop will tend to be draws to second-best straights.

The gapped-suited connectors, cards with a single gap between the ranks, such as T♠8♠, are called one-gap connectors. Hands like T♠7♠ are called two-gap connectors, and hands like T♠6♠ are three-gap connectors. These hands all have some potential straight value, but not enough to make them generally good hands. They do, however, often flop straight draws that aren't obvious draws and so do have some deceptive value.

Suited Aces

A single Ace is not a strong hand in Hold 'Em, even when matched with another card of the same suit. The exception is when the second card is a big card, like a King or Queen. In many multiplayer situations, flushes and potential flushes can win large pots. Because of this potential of making the best possible flush, suited Aces sometimes have significant value.

Unsuited Aces

An Ace matched with a card of a different suit has very little potential to make a flush, and although a single Ace is not generally a strong hand in Hold 'Em, in short-handed situations just the presence of an Ace in a hand does give it some value.

Suited Kings

A single King is much weaker than many players seem to think. Even a hand like K♠Q♠ can be deceptive. It looks strong when you peek at your hand and see those two connected face cards, and it is a pretty good hand. It's just not as strong as most players seem to think it is. It does, however, gain a lot of value in loose games. Suited Kings usually need multiple callers to have much value.

Other Hands

Pretty much all other hands can be considered weak holdings. At least weak on their own, they may gain value from position or mistakes of the opposition. Two suited cards, in particular, often gain value from a table of players who play way too loose.

CHARACTERISTICS OF POSITION

The first step in playing winning poker is simply *to not play too many hands*. You should only select hands that figure to be the best, stick with situations where you have an edge. This need to restrict your play to only those hands in which you have an advantage means you won't be able to play many hands when you're one of the early players to act. Generally you just don't have enough information. The more information you have about the strength, or lack of strength, of other players' hands, the better an evaluation you can make about the strength of your own hand. Remember though, hand strength doesn't just come from being the strongest hand at the moment, it often comes from being the best draw. Which is the more important source of strength depends entirely on game conditions. In all poker games, and Hold 'Em in particular, your hand selection should depend on your position in the betting.

What Is Position?

At every betting round, players act in turn. The first to act is at a large disadvantage because his action takes place before he has any information about the strength of other players' hands. That is what we mean by positional value. The first player to act has a reduced hand value because of his lack of information, and the last player to act has an increased hand value because he has more information available before he has to act. Every time another player acts (folds, calls, bets, or raises) you get information about the value of his hand, and, accordingly, the value of your hand. Accurately evaluating that information is, of course, another story.

Risks of Early Position

The first player to act has to do so with no information about the hands the other players hold. In a typical ten-handed game, the under-the-gun player has to decide whether to bet or fold while facing a field of nine other players who have given no indication of the strength of their hands.

The table on page 135 summarizes the effects of this lack of information on the decision to open the betting. Note that the percent of hands you can safely open with goes up meaningfully only after four or five players have folded.

You should play only very strong hands from early position. It takes a powerful hand to beat nine other players. Speculative hands without high card value should generally not be played from early position. You want to see the flop as cheaply as possible with speculative hands and playing them from early position puts you at too much of a risk of a raise. The exception is when the game conditions are consistently loose or very loose, and you know that there will be many callers with weak holdings.

When your position is more toward the middle or late position of the field, you can loosen up somewhat. If four players ahead of you have folded, and no one has yet bet, you only need to beat

Hands to Open the Betting with a Raise

Percent of hands that are usually playable under a struggle for ante perspective by number of players left to act

Number of players who haven't acted	Percent of hands that you can open with a raise
9	6%
8	7%
7	8%
6	9%
5	11%
4	13%
3	17%
2	24%
1	50%

NOTE: The percent was calculated based on a comparision between the odds you are getting from the blinds and the probablitiy that you can beat n random hands, where n is the number of players left to act.

five random hands and can probably open with much weaker holdings.

CHARACTERISTICS OF THE GAME

Tight games

Tight games are high-card games. Drawing hands such as suited cards, connected cards, or small pairs don't have much added value in a tight game. Two large cards, middle pocket pairs, and large pocket pairs have strong intrinsic value in a tight game. They can often win unimproved.

Loose Games

Loose games add value to a lot of different hand types. Suited cards, connected cards, and small pairs all have strong drawing value in a loose game. High cards have increased value also, even hands with only a single high card. Because in a loose game your opponents are often playing hands such as K♦4♦, a hand such as K♥9♠ has much more high-card value than it would in a tight game.

There is a popular misconception that unsuited hands go down in value in a loose game. This just isn't true. All hands gain value when your opponents are making mistakes. Suited hands do tend to gain more value than unsuited hands in loose games, but that does not mean that unsuited cards lose value.

Passive Games

A passive game usually means calling stations. These kinds of games tend to add value to high cards if the game is also loose because you will tend to be called by weaker hands when the game is loose, and won't be raised by stronger hands when the game is passive. Marginal draws also tend to be worth more in passive games because you will often be able to draw for free and will be called if you bet when the draw is made.

Aggressive Games

Aggressive games add value to very strong draws. This is a concept that is often not well understood. Pre-flop raises cut down on the implied odds of draws, but raises on the flop add value to good draws. Depending on how many outs your draw has and the number of callers on the flop, it's often a winning play to bet or raise for value with draws. Aggressive games make this easy to do. The looser the game is, the more draws that will profit from aggressive opponents, but even in a tight game, some draws profit from raises. For example, a flush draw with two overcards is a favorite against the top pair if neither of the overcards will make the top pair into two pair.

HOW MUCH IS A HAND WORTH?

That depends. The question really is what does hand value depend on? It depends on a lot of things, only one of which is the hand itself. More than any other factor, it depends on how well you play relative to the other players at the table and on the particular kinds of mistakes the other players at the table tend to make.

It's possible that it's correct to play tight and also correct to play loose. It's possible that there is no single, correct answer to the question being posed here.

All other things being equal, it's correct to play tight in a low-limit raked game. However, if the players are very loose calling stations, it might be correct to play looser pre-flop and tighter after the flop.

If you can see the flop cheaply, it might be right to play a lot of suited hands—but if the players are tight passive after the flop, you won't get paid off much, and it might not be right to do that.

Some of the questions to consider are:

1. How cheaply can you see the flop?
2. What kind of price are you getting to see the flop (number of callers)?
3. How weak are they pre-flop? (Will a raise by you buy the button, for example?)
4. How aggressive are they after the flop?
5. How loose are they after the flop?
6. How weak are they after the flop?

It's the answers to all those questions (plus a couple more I'm sure I left out), taken together, that help you select hands to play. Just because you can see the flop cheaply doesn't mean you should play 7♠5♠ and just because you're getting a good price doesn't mean you should play 4♦4♥, and just because they are aggressive after the flop doesn't mean you should play 7♠5♠.

Top Pair Value

High-card value is enhanced when both your cards are big cards. The high-card value of K♦Q♦ is much greater than the value of K♦8♦. There are two reasons. From an odds perspective, the K♦Q♦ just has more ways to flop the top pair. A Queen is much more likely to make the top pair than an 8. From a domination perspective, the K♦Q♦ will have a good kicker no matter which card pairs the board. In the case of K♦8♦, you'll only have a good kicker if the eight is paired by the board.

CARSON HAND GROUPS

It's common for poker writers to try to rank starting Hold 'Em hands. For reasons I've already discussed, I don't think that's a worthwhile endeavor and I'm not going to do that, but I'm going to give you some hand groups that should help you in thinking about the important playing characteristics of starting hands.

These hand groups are not intended to be a prescription for when to play certain hands. The groups are intended as a guide for how to think about hand values. Hands should be played when the conditions are right to give the hand value. Exactly what these conditions are tends to be sufficiently complex that it really isn't worthwhile to try to develop a specific rule-based hand selection system.

Power Hands

"Power hands" are hands that have sufficient starting strength to be worth playing in almost any game condition. There aren't many of these hands. Basically, by power hand I mean a hand with which it is almost always worth opening the pot. Just because they are

Carson Hand Groups

Pairs	Suited Aces	Suited Kings	Suited Queens	Suited Jacks	Suited 10s	Suited 9s	Suited 8s	Suited 7s	Suited 6s	Suited 5s	Offsuit Aces	Offsuit Kings	Offsuit Queens	Offsuit Jacks
Power Hands														
9,9°	A♦Q♦°°				Dominating power hands							—		
8,8	A♦9♦	K♦10♦	Q♦10♦	J♦10♦	Dominated power hands						A♥K♦	—		
Drawing Hands														

Add these hands to the list of dominating power hands:

Pairs	Suited Aces	Suited Kings	Suited Queens	Suited Jacks	Suited 10s	Suited 9s	Suited 8s	Suited 7s	Suited 6s	Suited 5s	Offsuit Aces	Offsuit Kings	Offsuit Queens	Offsuit Jacks
6,6	A♦8♦	K♦9♦	Q♦10♦	J♦10♦	10♦9♦						A♥K♦			
Speculative Hands														

Add these hands to the list of drawing hands:

Pairs	Suited Aces	Suited Kings	Suited Queens	Suited Jacks	Suited 10s	Suited 9s	Suited 8s	Suited 7s	Suited 6s	Suited 5s	Offsuit Aces	Offsuit Kings	Offsuit Queens	Offsuit Jacks
4,4	A♦7♦	K♦7♦	Q♦8♦	J♦8♦	10♦8♦	9♦8♦	8♦7♦	7♦6♦	—	—	A♥10♦††	K♥J♦	—	
Gambling Hands														
2,2	A♦2♦	K♦2♦	Q♦5♦†	J♦7♦	10♦8♦	9♦7♦	8♦5♦	7♦4♦	6♦4♦	5♦3♦°°°	A♥9♦	K♥10♦	Q♥10♦	J♥10♦

° Means any pocket pair 9,9 or larger.

°° Means an Ace with a suited Queen or better. Queen or King.

°°°5,3 suited is the lowest suited one-gapper that's usually playable; 5,4 suited is the lowest suited connector that's usually playable.

† Aces and Kings have enough high card value that they are sometimes worth playing even with a suited 2 as a kicker. Queens don't quite have that much high card value and need a kicker that has at least some decent change of making second pair.

†† A,10 is often considered a weak hand, but in loose conditions you'll have many players playing weaker Aces and the value of an Ace with a marginal kicker goes up. It's a similar situation with K,J.

worth opening with, does not mean you should always play them. In particular, with some of these hands you should often not call an early position opener. You often need a stronger hand to call than you do to bet.

The reason for this is that when you're opening the pot you only need to consider your chances of beating random hands. Once another player has opened from an early position, his hand is no longer random—it's likely to be a fairly strong hand. Even players who play very poorly tend to be more selective about what hands they play from early position.

So I've divided the hands I consider power hands into two groups—I call them dominating power hands and dominated power hands. You should generally open the pot with hands from either of these groups, but you should usually not call an early position opener with the dominated power hands.

The power hands include any above-average pair, 8s or larger; suited Aces, with a 9 or larger; suited Kings, with a 10 or larger; suited Queens, with a 10 or larger; suited Jacks, with a 10 or larger; and unsuited Aces, Queen, or larger.

Dominating Power Hands

By a "dominating power hand," I mean a hand that is likely to be a better hand than the hand a typical player will open with from an early position. Medium and large pairs, 9s or above, seem to do well even against an early position opener. The only other hands that seem to consistently do well are suited Ace, King or suited Ace, Queen.

Dominated Power Hands

In the poker literature, a "dominated hand" is one that when it makes a pair it is often against either a better pair or the same pair with a better kicker. A hand like Q♥T♥ is an example of a hand that is likely to be dominated. When I use the term "dominated power hands," I don't mean the term in exactly the same way, although I include those hands that are typically considered dominated hands. I also consider other hands such as A♠K♦, which would not typically be considered a dominated hand.

By a "dominated power hand," I simply mean hands that are usually good enough to open with but not good enough to call an early position opener. This group of hands contains a pair of 8s; Aces suited with a Jack, 10, or 9; any suited King; any suited Queen; any suited Jack; and unsuited Aces.

Note that with the majority of the hands that you should open with, you should not call an opener with. There are two reasons you can open with more hands than you can call an opener with. First, when you're first to act, you're against a group of unknown, random hands. You should open with hands that tend to be better than a group of random hands. When someone else has opened, his hand is no longer random. Now you're against one fairly good hand plus a bunch of random hands. It's the information that one player has a fairly good hand that makes it correct to fold most hands you would have opened with yourself. Second, you can open with some marginal hands such as 8♠8♦ or A♥9♥ because most players tend to call an opener with worse hands than they would open with. That's a mistake on the part of your opponents, and it's one you can exploit by opening with hands that might not seem like strong hands. This is one of the situations where the kinds of mistakes your opponents tend to make have a large effect on the value of your hand.

Drawing Hands

"Drawing hands" are hands that aren't better hands than the opener, but they have enough potential for improvement that they should usually be played when at least one other player has called the opener, giving you at least two opponents. Once that has happened, you're getting much better pot odds on your call. Although the hand usually won't prevail, it will win often enough to make it worth playing.

Most of the dominated power hands, along with some slightly weaker hands, have value as drawing hands. As an example, let's look at a hand like K♦9♦.

If there is an early position opener, the chances of them having a hand like A♥K♠ or even K♠J♠ or 10♥10♠ will diminish the high card value of K♦9♦. There is also some chance that the early position opener has a hand like Q♥J♠, where your K♦9♦ would be in fairly good shape in a confrontation. By itself this chance isn't enough to be worthwhile, but adding the odds you're getting from just a couple of callers to flop a flush draw or even two pair will often make a hand like K♦9♦ well worth playing.

Note that with just a few callers giving you odds, you don't need much of a chance that your hand is best. You just need some chance, with fairly good drawing chances.

Drawing hands are usually playable when you have two to five other players in the pot. This gives you fairly good odds on a call. However, if the players in the pot are mostly players who tend to play fairly well after the flop, some of the drawing hands might not be profitably played. Exactly how many callers you will need depends on how poorly and how loose they play after the flop. Against good players, two callers probably won't yield enough odds, although two callers are probably enough against poor players. Depending on these factors, you can sometimes call a raise, or even raise yourself from a late position with a drawing hand.

Speculative Hands

"Speculative hands" are hands that likely will need to improve to win but have enough of a chance of improvement that they are profitable hands if you're getting 4-1 or so on a call before the flop. Generally these are hands you'll be playing when four to six players see the flop. Again, exactly how many callers you'll need depends on how poorly and how loosely they play after the flop.

An example of a speculative hand is a hand like 7♦6♦. This hand is certainly not going to be the best hand before the flop, but its chances of flopping the best draw are good. A good draw with this hand is likely to get plenty of action at good betting odds on the flop.

Without the right flop, you won't be taking speculative hands past the flop. That's going to be most of the time. But when you do hit a good flop, like A♦6♥5♦ or 8♦5♥3♣ then you'll want to play your draw very aggressively (I talk about that more later on). Because you'll be folding on most flops, you don't want to call many raises before the flop with these hands. Again the exception would be if you have more than just a few callers, and the callers are players who tend to be too loose and too willing to call raises after the flop.

Gambling Hands

"Gambling hands" are long-shot hands that do have some chance of hitting a flop that leads to a big pot. These hands, however, are sufficient long shots that you need to get very long odds on a call before the flop, something like 6-1 or better. Generally these are hands you'll be playing when five or more players see the flop. Because of dead money from the blinds, it's often the case that you only need five players to get 6-1 on your money.

A lot of unsuited hands are included in this group. This goes against the grain of popular thought that unsuited cards play best against few opponents. In tight games it's true that high-card value is the predominant consideration in hand value and that flush potential only becomes important as a secondary feature. In typical, loose, or very loose games, flush potential is almost always of primary importance. Hands without flush potential are generally only worth playing if you get very good odds on the pre-flop betting round to compensate for the lack of potential of the hands. Suited hands profit from extra callers; unsuited hands often need the extra callers to get the odds they need to be worth playing at all.

An example of a gambling hand is A♥9♦. This hand doesn't really have a lot of ways to win. It's not a bad hand, just not a hand that often wins a big pot. The 9♦ is a weak kicker to the Ace, and you don't want to call any raises before the flop with this hand. If the pot is unraised and there are many loose callers, however, the 9♦ may actually be the best kicker if another player also has an Ace. Play these hands carefully, and don't put a lot of money in the pot before the flop.

EXPLANATION FOR SOME OF THE CUTOFFS

For suited Aces, the minimum hand in the speculative group is A♠7♠ while the gambling group includes all suited Aces, A♠2♠ on up. Many poker players don't think there is much difference between those hands, because with either an A♠7♠ or A♠2♠, you are probably out-kicked if there is an Ace on the board, and they reason, a A♠2♠ has a chance at a straight, but there is a difference. The second-pair potential of a 6 or 7 is much greater than the straight potential of a 2. An A♠6♠ is a little marginal. An A♠7♠ is a pretty good hand in a loose-aggressive game though.

If you've got an A♠7♠, it's not always the 7♠ that's the kicker, it's often the A♠. In a loose game, a flop of Q♠7♥3♦ might very well involve you and a player with a J♦7♦. Even if some third player has a Queen, the fact that the J♦7♦ is calling gives you good enough odds to draw, and if the Jack kicker hits, you don't care. You still win if you hit your Ace, and if you don't hit, you were beaten anyway.

When the game gets loose, it's often a mistake to think of the game in terms of hand domination. It's better to think of the game in terms of *odds*, and what kinds of hands the players giving you the odds are likely playing. With the A♠7♠ you are more likely to benefit from other players with pair draws than you would with an A♠2♠. That's the reason for the difference.

ADJUSTING THE PLAY OF THE FIRST TWO CARDS

You will want to limit your play to only your best starting hands, those that are likely to give you an edge over the likely holdings of your opponents. The determination of the best starting hands, however, depends on the table conditions, on individual opponents at the table, and to a lesser degree on your table image. The only constant is that you should play fewer hands from an early position than from a late position. How many fewer hands, and which hands, depends on the table.

Let's review the characteristics of a hand that give it value:

High-pair potential
Flush potential
Straight potential
Three-of-a-kind potential

Large pocket pairs have both high-card value and the potential for three of a kind. They will often win unimproved and have a small chance of improving to a very powerful hand.

Two large-suited cards have high-pair potential, flush potential, and some straight potential. The straight potential is limited; with A♠K♠ you can only flop a gutshot straight draw, but it will be a draw to the highest possible straight and will include overcard pair draws.

Do you see a pattern here? The really powerful starting hands have multiple ways to win. This is another important factor involved in determining the value of a starting hand, not just its likelihood of winning, but its likelihood of winning a large pot.

That's why in a very loose, very aggressive game, pocket pairs can be valuable starting hands—not because they'll win a lot of pots, but because the pots they do win will be very large. In many very loose games, you need not fear a raise pre-flop, because the pots you win when you do win will be large enough to cover the cost of calling a few raises.

With small- or medium-sized pocket pairs, you'll probably have to hit three of a kind on the flop to win. That won't happen very often. In an aggressive game, the other players raise and reraise for you on those times that you do.

Often a poker game develops a particular dynamic where some aspects of the game seem to become routine, automatic, and very predictable. Player behavior before the flop is one such aspect. I don't mean that you can predict what an individual player is going to do (although sometimes you can), but you do often know what the result of individual actions are—you can often be very sure that four to six players will call to see the flop and that no one will raise, or two to three players will see the flop and someone will raise from an early or middle position. Whenever a table dynamic like that happens, you've got what I call a stable game condition, and you can make strategy adjustments to exploit this stability

Hand value changes dramatically as game conditions change. The popular belief is that there is a shift in relative hand values when game conditions change—for example, in a very loose game, suited cards go up in value, and in a tight game, high cards go up in value. That's true as far as it goes, but it's a simplistic view.

It's not just relative hand values that change with game conditions, it's how hands derive value and how hand value relates to other aspects of the game, such as position, that changes.

Game conditions dictate a theoretical perspective to take on the game.

A tight game is a *struggle for the antes*.

An aggressive game is a game of *strategy and deception*

A passive game is a game of *money flows from the bad players to the good players*.

A loose game is a game of *money and odds*.

TIGHT GAMES AND VERY TIGHT GAMES

Power Hands

In tight or very tight games, high-card values usually are the important pre-flop hand value.

Dominating Power Hands

For the most part, the dominating power hands are the key hands to focus on. These hands should be played strongly in all conditions of tight and very tight games.

Dominated Power Hands

The dominated power hands should be played judiciously in tight and very tight games. Other conditions matter with these hands, however. There is less danger with these hands at tight-passive or very tight-passive tables than at more aggressive tables. This is because you are likely to be called with worse hands and not raised with better hands if the game is passive. If you do catch a flop like Q♠7♥3♦ with a Q♥10♦ and get raised by a tight-passive player after you bet the flop, you can often fold if the pot is not very large, knowing that you are certainly beaten.

In a very aggressive game, however, it would be more difficult to be sure that the laydown would be right because a very aggressive player is likely to be raising with something like A♥3♥. Because of the likelihood of being confronted with that kind of tough decision in a very aggressive game, the dominated power hands should be avoided in a tight-very aggressive, very tight-aggressive, or very tight-very aggressive game.

Drawing Hands

Drawing hands don't have much value in tight or very tight games. Even in passive games, you won't make much money when the hands are best, and you will lose a lot of money when the hands aren't best. The odds just aren't there.

Speculative and Gambling Hands

The speculative and gambling hands rely on getting odds to have any value. They generally are not favorites but can still be profitable if you're getting good enough odds. In tight games you won't get enough pot odds for these hands, so they only tend to be playable in situations when the implied odds are large.

Tight-Passive Games and Speculative-Gambling Hands

Against passive players the big-little suited hands, such as A♦7♦ or even Q♥5♥, often have semi-bluff value, particularly from a late position. A semi-bluff with a hand like A♦7♦ and a flop like 10♦7♥3♠ often wins the pot against a tight-passive player, and even if it doesn't win, you'll frequently have the best hand anyway; even when you don't have the best hand, you have many cards that can improve your hand on the turn.

Tight-Aggressive Games and Speculative-Gambling Hands

At a more aggressive tight table, the big-little speculative and gambling hands should probably be avoided, but the small-suited connector hands of those categories do tend to play well. One tendency of very aggressive players at a tight table is to overplay big overcards. Against many of these kinds of players, your implied odds with a hand like 5♦4♦ are actually fairly large, even if you have to call a raise to see the flop. These very aggressive players are often willing to put in extra bets on the flop and turn with hands as weak as A♦Q♥ and a flop like 9♠6♦5♣.

Tight Games with Many Callers

Sometimes, even at a tight table, you'll have a situation where four or five players see the flop. When that happens, many of the drawing hands and speculative hands become playable from late position—not all of them, however.

When four or five tight players have entered the pot, the high card value of a hand such as K♠J♥ goes down dramatically. The chances that one of these players has a hand like K♦Q♥ or A♠J♦ are pretty good. The prospects of a K♠J♥ against either of those hands aren't very good.

The situation is different when you have four or five loose callers. We'll discuss that situation in the next section. When you have tight players in the pot, even four or five of them, you should be thinking about your hand value from a domination perspective first, then from an odds perspective. The difference between having a K♦J♦ and a K♠J♥ can be significant in this situation.

LOOSE AND VERY LOOSE GAMES

Dominating Power Hands

Of course, dominating power hands are strong hands under any game conditions, and should be played accordingly.

Dominated Power Hands

The dominated power hands gain some strength in loose and very loose games, but just as in tight games, these hands should only be played selectively if the game is aggressive or very aggressive. Even seemingly strong hands such as A♦K♠ should often be folded in early position if the game is very aggressive. Such hands do usually play well from late position, however.

Drawing Hands

The drawing hands often become very strong hands in loose and very loose games. They get the odds needed and aren't as likely to run into the problem of only getting action when they are dominated, which tends to happen in tighter games.

Speculative Hands

Speculative hands tend to have intrinsic value in loose and very loose games. The speculative hands depend on getting a good flop, and in a loose game you're usually getting the right kind of odds. This is especially true for the suited speculative hands in loose-aggressive, loose-very aggressive, and very loose-very aggressive games. That's because, when you do flop a strong draw with these hands in a loose game, then you're almost always getting good bet odds on the flop, so that aggression on the flop works in your favor.

With loose players it's not unusual to have four or five callers seeing the flop. In that situation some of the speculative hands, like K♥J♦, can have greater high-card value. This is because, unlike the previous sitution with four or five tight callers, loose callers are just as likely to be playing J♥8♠ as A♠J♥. A hand like K♥J♦ is not nearly as likely to be dominated by the hands of four or five loose callers as it is by four or five tight callers.

Gambling Hands

The gambling hands tend to need the odds of a very loose game to be worth playing. In fact, in most very loose games, gambling hands become worth a raise if you're certain that the raise won't cause you to lose any players.

The reason these hands are often worth a raise in a very loose game is that players in a very loose game tend to be playing hands like Q♠5♦. Compared with that kind of hand, a hand like K♥6♥, or even 9♦7♦, is a powerful hand when you're in late position.

When the game conditions are loose enough to be playing gambling hands, you're often getting the right price to raise with hands you normally wouldn't raise with. You want to raise with hands where the chances of winning are larger than the odds you're getting on the bet. For example, if a hand figures to win about 20 percent of the time, then you profit from a raise if you get more than four callers.

NUMBER OF VERY LOOSE CALLERS NEEDED TO RAISE ON THE BUTTON

Callers	Pairs	Axs	Kxs	Qxs	Jxs	10xs
4	7,7	A♠9♠	K♠10♠	Q♠T♠		
5	6,6	A♠2♠	K♠9♠	Q♠9♠	J♠9♠	10♠9♠
6	4,4	A♠2♠	K♠6♠	Q♠7♠	J♠7♠	10♠8♠
7	2,2	A♠2♠	K♠2♠	Q♠5♠	J♠6♠	10♠7♠

The table specifies the number of callers needed for a raise with gambling hands.

Loose Aggressive Games and Suited Aces

When a game is both very loose and very aggressive, suited cards tend to gain value. This is particularly true of hands like A♥6♥. This is the kind of hand that is best when it flops a draw, and in a loose game, the odds you will be getting on the flop are usually better than the odds of making your draw. So you profit from callers of each bet or raise that you make on the flop.

Sometimes it's easy to start thinking of a hand such as A♥2♥ as just as good as a hand such as A♥6♥. The 6 is a little bigger than the 2, but you might think that because both kickers are pretty small, the added value of possible straights makes A♥2♥ just as good, or maybe an even better, hand. Don't start thinking that. It's not true.

It is true that under some very specific conditions, A♥5♥ does, on the average, make a little more money than A♥6♥. This difference is attributable to the straight possibilities of the A♥5♥ and the only slight difference in high-card value between a 5 and a 6. The game conditions for this are when the game is very loose and very passive, and you're in late position. Under these conditions you'll get a cheap or free draw to an inside straight often enough to give a little extra value to A♥2♥ through A♥5♥. The value of an A♥5♥ is close enough to A♥6♥ in terms of pip value that the A♥5♥ does make a little more money because of potential straights when the conditions are right—but the difference is slight.

TYPICAL GAMES

In typical games position tends to be more of a dominant factor than in either tight or loose games. In early position you should stick to the dominating power hands. In later position play the dominated power hands in unraised pots and the drawing hands in multiplayer pots, raised or unraised.

WHEN TO ADJUST RAISE REQUIREMENTS

Tight Games

In tight games you should raise with most of the hands that you will be playing. With the very strong hands, you should often limp, intending to reraise. With the weaker hands, you should often limp with the intention of calling if you're raised.

Loose Games

In loose games you should raise less frequently with drawing, speculative, or gambling hands, but you should limp and reraise more often with these hands. These hands depend on volume pots. You should not raise initially because you don't want to discourage callers, but once you have enough callers, a reraise is usually a value raise.

Very Loose Games

In very loose games, the dominating power hands are also strong drawing hands. You should play them accordingly, limping to encourage callers and reraising to take the odds. The dominated power hands tend not to flop such good draws though, and with these hands you should usually raise initially. If a raise discourages one or two callers, it's not costing you that much.

IMPORTANCE OF IMPLIED ODDS

Much of the value from starting hands comes from implied odds. If the bet is small relative to future bets, then a lot of hands such as small pairs, suited connectors, or suited Aces have high implied odds and are big moneymakers.

You're more likely to get implied odds when you've got lots of callers seeing the flop. It increases your implied odds if those callers don't play well after the flop. Another thing that increases your implied odds is if some of the callers tend to be hyperaggressive after the flop, and two or three others tend to be willing to call raises with weak hands. *Your implied odds come from mistakes that your opponents will make.*

THOSE NO-FOLD 'EM HOLD 'EM GAMES

My favorite type of Hold 'Em game condition is a very loose, very aggressive game. By this I mean the kind of game where seven or eight players see every flop, and it's almost always raised before the flop; most of the time there are four bets pre-flop. The main characteristics are that the flop is almost never checked around, most flops are raised, and three-player showdowns are the norm.

In a tighter or more typical game, the most common mistake players make is playing too many hands. That's not the case in a really wild and woolly game. In this type of game, the most common mistake is playing top pair and overcards more aggressively than they should be played. Because of the looseness of the game, drawing hands can profit greatly from that kind of overaggressiveness. This is because the odds on the bets for a strong drawing hand are almost always greater than the odds of making the hand. This is a great source of profit. The value of suited cards, particularly suited connectors and suited Aces, goes way up in this type of extreme game. Play suited cards, and, as we discuss in the next chapter, if you flop a draw with them, play the draw very aggressively.

OPENING UTG

Game conditions should have a significant impact on your selection of starting hands. If the conditions tend to be stable and predictable, you should make significant adjustments to your early position hand selection.

UTG Opening Hands for Different Game Conditions

	Passive	Typical	Aggressive	Very aggresive
Very tight	7,7 A♠9♠ K♠J♠ Q♠J♠	7,7 A♠10♠ K♠Q♠	8,8 A♠J♠	9,9 A♠Q♠
Tight	6,6 A♠7♠ K♠9♠ Q♠10♠ J♠10♠	7,7 A♠7♠ K♠9♠ Q♠J♠	8,8 A♠9♠ K♠10♠	8,8 A♠J♠ K♠J♠
Typical	6,6 A♠7♠ K♠10♠ Q♠10♠ J♠9♠ 10♠9♠	7,7 A♠7♠ K♠9♠ Q♠10♠ J♠9♠ 10♠9♠	7,7 A♠8♠ K♠9♠ Q♠10♠ J♠10♠	7,7 A♠9♠ K♠10♠ Q♠10♠ J♠10♠
Loose	4,4 A♠7♠ K♠7♠ Q♠8♠ J♠8♠ 10♠8♠ 9♠8♠ 8♠7♠ 7♠6♠ A♠10♦ K♠J♦	5,5 A♠7♠ K♠7♠ Q♠8♠ J♠8♠ 10♠8♠ 9♠8♠ 8♠7♠ 7♠6♠ A♠10♦ K♠J♦	6,6 A♠7♠ K♠7♠ Q♠8♠ J♠8♠ 10♠8♠ 9♠8♠ 8♠7♠ 7♠6♠ A♠10♦ K♠J♦	6,6 A♠7♠ K♠9♠ Q♠8♠ J♠8♠ 10♠8♠ 9♠8♠ 8♠7♠ 7♠6♠ A♠10♦ K♠J♦
Very loose	2,2 A♠2♠ K♠2♠ Q♠5♠ J♠7♠ 10♠8♠ 9♠7♠ 8♠5♠ 7♠4♠ 6♠4♠ 5♠3♠ A♠9♦ K♠10♦ Q♠10♦	2,2 A♠2♠ K♠2♠ Q♠5♠ J♠7♠ 10♠8♠ 9♠7♠ 8♠5♠ 7♠5♠ 6♠4♠ 5♠4♠ A♠10♦ K♠10♦ Q♠10♦	4,4 A♠2♠ K♠2♠ Q♠5♠ J♠7♠ 10♠8♠ 9♠7♠ 8♠6♠ 7♠5♠ 6♠5♠ 5♠4♠ A♠J♦ K♠10♦ Q♠J♦	4,4 A♠2♠ K♠2♠ Q♠5♠ J♠8♠ 10♠8♠ 9♠7♠ 8♠6♠ 7♠5♠ 6♠5♠ 5♠4♠ A♠J♦ K♠J♦ Q♠J♦

Legend: 7,7 means any pocket pair, 7s or larger; A♠9♠ means any suited Ace, 9 kicker or larger; 7♠5♠ means any suited 7,5 kicker or larger, and so on.

154

The table gives some suggested opening hands when you're first to act and the game conditions are very stable and predictable.

The table also shows how you profit from raises and multiple opponents with A♣A♠. You *do* want to raise with this hand. It's a powerful hand and you're getting the best of it with every dollar that goes in the pot, but the purpose of the raise isn't to thin the field. *You want them to call.*

13

A Theory of Flop Play: Counting Outs and Evaluating Draws

A popular perspective on poker is that it's a contest between a made hand and a draw. Under many game conditions, this is a useful perspective, but, under loose game conditions, maintaining that perspective of the game can lead to frequent tactical errors. As game conditions become loose, involving more players actively competing for the pot, poker becomes more a game of *money* and *odds* and less a classic confrontation between a made hand and a draw.

Under the made-hand-versus-draw perspective, the made hand is in the lead and bets-raises to punish the draw, which is the hand that's chasing. Bets and raises are used to reduce the pot odds that the chasing hand is getting, to the benefit of the made hand. This line of thinking works fine in games where most hands become two- or three-player confrontations. In those kind of game conditions, ideas about *best hand* and *hand domination* are of paramount importance, but when the game typically involves four or five players contesting the pot on the flop, a different view of the game is needed.

WHO'S IN THE LEAD?

Let's look closely at an example I gave in a previous chapter.

                    Player 1: K♥Q♥
                    Player 2: A♥9♠
                    Player 3: J♠J♦
                    Player 4: T♣8♣
                    Flop: 9♥7♥3♣

We need to analyze this situation from the point of view of each of the four players.

The K♥Q♥

This player can be fairly confident that he does not have the best hand on the flop. Of course, without knowing the exact holdings of the other players, he can't be sure what the probability of ending up with the best hand is, but he can make a fairly reliable estimate. Any Heart (nine cards) will make a flush. Any King or Queen (six cards) will make a pair higher than the flopped top card. That's fifteen cards that will improve the hand to a possible, if not probable, best hand. In addition, a 10 or Jack will give him a gutshot straight draw. This kind of draw, where you need the last two cards to hit your hand, is called a "backdoor" draw. This draw is strong enough to raise with, even heads up. In a multiway pot, it's a very strong hand.

The A♥9♠

This player has the top pair with the top kicker—a good hand. In addition he's got the flush Ace, giving him both a backdoor flush draw and protection in that if he makes two pair it won't make someone else a flush. Again, this is a strong hand. This player has no particular reason to think he doesn't have the best hand, and, if it turns out he's beaten by two pair or a pocket over-pair, he's still got a draw to beat it. Even if someone makes a flush on the turn, this hand isn't dead; a fourth flush card makes an Ace-high flush. This player will probably raise.

The J♠J♦

This hand actually is the best hand on the flop—at least according to its poker hand rank—but it's a very vulnerable hand. This hand doesn't have much of a way to improve. Even if it catches a third Jack, things aren't looking all that great. One of the two Jacks it can catch will complete a Heart three-flush on the board. Any Jack makes a straight possible.

This player will probably raise, but against the particular lineup we're examining, that's a mistake. He loses money on each bet he puts into the pot. Of course, he can't know that, but he can know that this kind of situation is very common in multiway pots. Aggressive play by this player, in this kind of situation, can be very expensive. It's a huge mistake that is frequently made by players who consider themselves good players.

The T♣8♣

This player has a straight draw and a backdoor flush draw. Although this hand is the weakest of the four hands we're reviewing, it's actually stronger than many people think. It's not a hand that should be raising with this flop, but it has enough possibilities that it should be played, even when others are raising.

Often you'll see advice that straight draws when there is a possible flush draw should not be played if other players are raising on the flop. It's true that straight draws aren't strong draws, and the presence of a possible flush draw tends to make them even weaker. In this case, however, we've also got a little extra equity in the backdoor flush of our own. That's not much, but it is just enough to offset that risk of making your straight when someone else is making a flush.

VALUE OF DRAWS

This hand illustrates a concept that's become known as Morton's theorem, named after a poker player who died in a motorcycle accident shortly after he popularized the concept in the Internet newsgroup rec.gambling.poker. My version of his concept is slightly modified from his original idea: *When many hands with draws are competing on the flop against a semi-strong made hand, the primary beneficiary of flop bets is the best draw, not the best hand.*

This concept is not well known and often misunderstood. Many players seem to think that the implication is that you should play your big cards and big pairs very aggressively to drive out all the marginal draws. That's correct in tight games and some typical games, but that's not the correct interpretation when the game loosens up. In a loose game, the idea of starting with the best hand goes out the window, draws start getting value. That's the important concept of Morton's theorem.

This concept is illustrated by the table on page 160. For various numbers of callers, the table gives the combined outs, which collectively make the best pair an underdog to the field.

In all forms of poker, it's very important to get your money in the pot when your hand is best. The idea of "when your hand is best" needs to be extended beyond thinking of poker as a game of hand domination or a struggle between a made hand and a draw. *In Hold 'Em, your hand is best when the odds that you will win the pot are greater than the odds you are getting from the number of active hands that will call a bet.* Play on the flop is very much a game of *odds*. A manipulation perspective is also important, but in some situations you'll want to manipulate players to fold; in other situations you'll want to manipulate players to call. This is a fundamentally important concept in Hold 'Em, and the looser the game conditions, the more important the concept.

NUMBER OF OUTS

Number of collective outs to make an overpair a money underdog by number of opponents

Number of outs	Number of opponents
14 ´	1
20	2
24	3
26	4
28	5
29	6
31	7
32	8

EVALUATING THE FLOP

The first step in playing the flop is an evaluation of your prospects. Let's look at situations where the flop is:

- A virtually worthless hand
- A probable big winner
- A probable winner
- A probable best hand with large loss potential
- A strong draw
- A probable best hand with a strong draw
- A weak draw
- A steal opportunity

Let's focus on how to recognize and evaluate the hand you've just flopped. The skill to quickly assess how the flop has affected your hand's moneymaking potential rather than its poker hand value is an important skill. The actual value of various kinds of flops is highly dependent on the game conditions, that is, the loose-tight and passive-aggressive characteristics of your table.

Defining Your Hand

The flop defines your hand. Before the flop you have two cards that may or may not develop into a poker hand. Once the flop hits, you have a hand. You still have two more cards coming to complete your hand, but the possibilities are defined and limited by the flop.

Most poker books discuss your hand at this stage of the betting only in terms of its poker value. Poker value is, of course, important. We discussed that in the last chapter. In Hold 'Em, however, a hand's potential to win money isn't always related to its poker value. The phrase "texture of the flop" is often used to refer to how the flop cards combine with your hand and other players' cards to determine your moneymaking or money-losing potential. Here's an example: Say you start with A♥K♥. That's a very good starting hand. Its value as a starting hand comes from the wide range of possibilities of the hand. It can develop into a high pair, a nut flush, a nut straight, or nothing at all. Which possibility is realized won't be determined until you see the three cards on the flop. A list of example flops follows:

10♦9♦8♦
A♦K♦7♥
A♣10♣10♠
A♣9♠5♥
Q♥J♥5♠
A♣10♣5♥
J♣10♣7♥
9♥5♣2♦

Each of these flops makes A♥K♥ a very different hand. Before you proceed you might want to stop and determine into which of the eight categories of hands each of these flops fits best. Don't memorize the categories. The particular categories don't matter as much as the idea of looking at the hand's money potential rather than its poker rank.

Reading the Flop

When the flop hits the board, you should immediately be able to determine the strength of your hand. Let's look at the A♥K♥ example. As I said, that's a very good starting hand.

Virtually Worthless Hand

Unfortunately when a flop such as 10♦9♦8♦ falls, all of a sudden your hand is not looking good anymore. Any pocket pair; any 10; 9; 8; two Diamonds; Q, J; J, 7; or 7, 6 now has you beaten. Anyone with one Diamond, a Jack, or a 7 has a good draw to beat you. Any hand has at least a weak draw to beat you. (They can pair either card and win as long as you don't pair.) Because A♦ or K♦ would make a flush for anyone holding a single Diamond, you only have four cards left in the deck that could be a possible winning hand.

Probable Big Winner

With a flop of A♦K♦7♥, you're in pretty good shape; you probably have the best hand by far, and you will likely get action from other hands. Here, even if you're currently beaten by, for example, 7,7, you've still got outs of your own (an Ace, a King, or two running Hearts to complete your flush).

Part of the value of the hand comes from the potential draws other players might have. They need a reason to put money in the pot. With this hand you will likely get action from a flush draw, from another Ace, and possibly from someone with a gutshot draw. It's a good flop for you and a potential moneymaker.

Probable Best Hand with Large Loss Potential

With A♣T♣T♠, you might have the best hand *or* you might have a hand in trouble. This is an example of a hand that will win the small pots and lose the big ones. An opponent either has a 10 or not. With this flop there are not a lot of hands worse than A♥K♥ that will give you much action; however, hands better than yours will give you a lot of action. This situation is potentially troublesome for you, but even when you're beaten in this situation, you do have some outs. Playing with a pair on the board can be tricky.

Probable Winner

With A♣9♠5♥, you almost certainly have the best hand, but it is unlikely that you will make a lot of money from it. You will, of course, get action from another Ace, but it's unlikely an opponent will have a strong drawing hand.

A Strong Draw

With Q♥J♥5♠, you probably don't have the best hand in terms of its current poker ranking, but you probably do have the best hand in terms of potential to win a large pot. This is a premium draw, any Heart or 10 will give you a winning hand, and any Ace or King will give you a possible winner. You will get action from players who flopped a pair, a straight draw, or maybe even from someone drawing dead to a second-best flush.

Probable Best Hand with a Strong Draw

With A♣10♥5♥, you not only have the probable best hand, but you've also got a good chance at improvement. It's another example of a premium draw.

Weak Draw

With J♣10♣7♥, you have some outs, but it's a weak draw. A Queen, as long as it's not Q♣, will give you a winning hand, but that's only three cards. An Ace or King, as long as they aren't Clubs, will give you a possible winner, but the possibility of those cards helping another player even more means you still can't play the hand hard against many opponents. The hands that are large money winners are those that can be played hard against a large group of opponents. Many bets combined with many callers lead to very large pots.

Steal Opportunity

A flop such as 9♥5♣2♦ is not likely to have made anyone much money. A bet will likely win the pot. Even against very loose players, not many hands will fit this flop. In addition, with your A♥K♥, even if you're called by someone who paired you probably still have six outs. If the pot is small, even someone who flopped a nine may fold here if you've raised pre-flop, fearing you hold a large overpair.

Things to Consider

There are three things besides your own hand you need to consider when evaluating the flop:

1. What better hands others might have
2. What good draws others might have
3. What hands others might have that put them drawing dead

In the first flop discussed earlier, 10♦9♦8♦, there are a lot of hands that have you beaten. Even if that flop doesn't give anyone a pair, a flush, or a straight, it almost certainly gives them a draw to one of those hands.

However, A♦K♦7♥ not only gives you the probable best hand, it is also unlikely that anyone will improve to beat you. This is an example of a flop that might have another player drawing dead. If another player with an Ace makes two pair, he still loses to your higher two pair. It does give someone a draw to a Diamond flush, but you are a 2-1 favorite against anyone with that draw. This flop, to A♥K♥, could generate a large pot, which you will win over 60 percent of the time.

OUTS AND ODDS

With the flops we just reviewed, our evaluation was a little vague in some cases. Such a vague assessment is a good idea, just to get a sense of the situation. However, often you'll want to be more formal in the evaluation, considering an explicit count of outs and pot odds.

Counting Your Outs

An "out" is a card that will improve your currently losing hand into a winning hand. If you've got A♥K♥ and the flop comes 9♣7♥5♥, then any Heart is an out for you. It's possible that any Ace or King will also win for you.

So you've got between nine and fifteen outs. We aren't sure exactly how many because we only want to count a card as an out if we are sure it will give us a win. We're pretty sure a flush will win, although 9♥ might give someone a full house or 6♥ followed by 6♣ may also. We aren't sure at all that making a pair of Aces or Kings will give us a winner. In counting your outs, should you consider this a hand with nine outs? Or one with fifteen outs? Or even one with eight outs (the 9♥ might not make your hand a winner)?

The answer depends primarily on how many active opponents there are. The fewer opponents, the less likely a card that helps your hand will help someone else's even more. However, the effect of this is much smaller than most players think.

Still considering the A♥K♥ starting hand, let's look at our outs with the flop J♦10♦7♥. Any Queen makes us a nut straight, with the exception of the Q♦, which may make someone else a flush. Likewise, if we pair either of our cards, it makes us the top pair, but might make someone else a straight. So, we have three cards that make us the winning hand and seven cards that improve our hand but may improve someone else's hand even more. How many outs do we have? Three outs to win and ten outs to improve, but will just an improvement be enough to win? Take a look at the table and see.

With both the flops, the A♥K♥ has one characteristic that adds significant value. It's that the hand might actually be the best hand right now, without improvement. This is actually more likely with

Outs and Win Probabilities by Field Size
FOR SELECTED HANDS AND FLOPS

		Hand				
Odds°	No. of opponents seeing the flop	A♥K♥	A♥K♥	10♥9♥	10♥9♥	10♥9♥
				Flop		
		9♣7♥5♥	J♦10♦7♥	7♦6♦2♥	5♦3♥2♥	7♠6♦2♥
1-1 (.50)	1	.77	.56			
2-1 (.33)	2	.65	.40	.25†	.50	.29†
3-1 (.25)	3	.55	.31	.19†	.45	.25†
4-1 (.20)	4	.49	.25	.16†	.43	.21
5-1 (.17)	5	.46	.23	.15†	.40	.21
6-1 (.14)	6	.44	.22	.13†	.35	.20
7-1 (.13)	7	.42	.20	.12†	.33	.19
8-1 (.11)	8	.41	.19	.11	.32	
9-1 (.10)	9	.39	.18	.10		

NOTE: These win probabilities were estimated using Turbo Texas Hold 'Em simulations. Various lineups were used. The larger the number of opponents seeing the flop, the looser, in general, the lineup that was used. This was done primarily for convenience in getting estimates with a reasonable amount of computer time. The exact values will vary, depending on the particular playing characteristics of the simulated opponents.
° The odds are the odds resulting from the number of opponents calling. The values in parentheses are the win probabilities needed to profit from the odds.
† These scenarios were money losers for our hero.

the 9♣7♥5♥ flop than with the flop of J♦10♦7♥. This isn't obvious to most players. Most weak players would immediately be concerned that someone has flopped a straight with either flop, but that's generally unlikely. The biggest concern should be that someone has flopped a pair and has an Ace or King kicker. It is much more likely that someone is playing a K♠10♥ than someone is playing a K♠7♣. Even most very loose players won't call a raise pre-flop with a hand like K♠7♣.

Pot Odds Calculations

Be aware of pot odds. You can count the outs, comparing them with the money in the pot to estimate if calling has a positive expected value. Although it is a subjective estimate, *knowing whether the pot is giving you the right odds to take the risk of continued play is the difference between winning and losing poker*.

It is particularly important to keep track of pot odds in loose games. The reason loose games are so profitable is that you can play more hands profitably when you are getting the right price— so knowing the price is critical. It's a little less important when playing heads-up. There it is more important to outplay your opponent than outdraw him.

Figuring your pot odds is rather straightforward. Just count the money that's in the pot, comparing it with how much it will cost you to remain in the pot for the next card. As an example, four players each put $10 into the pot before the flop. At the flop, the first player bets $10, the other two fold. The pot has $50 and it costs you $10 to call, so you are getting 5-1 pot odds. If, in the example, you were second to act instead of last, then it gets a little more complicated. You are still getting 5-1, but the betting round is not yet over. If both other players call, you end up getting 7-1. If one of them gets in a raising war with the opening bettor, you will have to put $40 in the pot before it's over. The pot will be $120, so you will only get 3-1 pot odds.

Comparing your pot odds with your number of outs requires a little mathematical conversion. To convert the number of outs to your drawing odds, you just compare the number of outs (good cards) with the rest of the remaining cards (bad cards).

Let us take the case of a somewhat tight game (one or two opponents) where the flop is 9♣7♥5♥. We counted the outs as fifteen (when we held A♥K♥ as our first two cards). Because there are forty-seven unseen cards, your drawing odds are about 32-15. Rounded off, that's about 2-1. As long as these odds are better than the pot odds, we should play this hand.

How Callers Affect Your Outs

When you're on a draw, it's important to make sure you've got enough callers to keep your pot odds or bet odds high enough to pay for the draw. How many callers you need depends on how many outs will make a good hand. Sometimes, however, more callers mean your effective outs are reduced. It's hard to judge exactly how much your effective outs are reduced by more callers, but you can formulate some guidelines.

One example is when some of your outs come from an over-card Ace. Let's say you've got an A♥6♥, and the flop is J♥9♥5♦. You've got nine outs for your flush draw and maybe three outs for your Ace overcard. The Ace, however, is somewhat dangerous. If one of the other players has a hand like A♠J♣ or A♦9♦ or A♠5♠, then you'll just have a second-best hand if an Ace falls on the turn. In loose games many players often do play any hand with an Ace in it, and you should not give an Ace overcard in your hand full credit for outs. This is not a serious problem with the flush draw example, because with a flush draw, you'll probably be playing the hand strongly even without the Ace overcard. However, in some situations it matters a great deal.

An example is if you have A♦J♣, and the flop is K♥Q♠5♦. You have the Ace overcard and a gutshot straight draw, but, if you have more than one or two callers and they are betting aggressively on the flop, then it's probably a mistake to consider this hand as having seven outs. Normally I suggest raising three callers if you have seven outs, but not with these seven outs. The chances of an Ace making someone either two pair or a straight are just too high for you to consider the Ace overcard as three outs in this situation. The key to determining which of your outs are good and should be counted in evaluating your hand depends on an evaluation of the probable outs of your opponents.

Counting Their Outs

We've seen that the strength of a probable best hand like the top pair or an overpair depends on the collective number of outs that the opponents have, but how do we know how many that is? Of course, we usually don't know, but we can put a bound on it, a range for the number of outs that depends on the size of the field.

As an example, let's look at the hand we started the chapter with from the perspective of the overpair, the J♠J♦, and the flop of 9♥7♥3♣. If there is only one caller, he could have a hand like J♥9♦ or J♣7♣, where his number of effective outs is between two and four, or he could have a hand like A♣7♣ where his effective number of outs is seven. Other hands are possible, like a gut-shot straight draw or a straight draw. Of course a flush draw is possible, but it's unlikely that a flush draw with two overcards would only call. The range of outs that one caller might have varies between two and nine, with five the most likely number.

A second caller would likely add between five and nine outs. It's unlikely that you would have two callers whose kicker matches your pair. So the cumulative number of outs with two callers is likely between seven and fifteen. A third caller will probably add between four and five outs, bringing the total to a range of eleven to twenty. A fourth caller will probably add the same, bringing the total to a range of fifteen to twenty-five.

If there is a raise, you can probably add the possibility of a very strong draw such as a flush draw with two overcards, bringing the range to about fifteen to thirty outs with a raise and four opponents and a range of about fifteen to twenty outs with a raise from a single caller.

In this case, even if you know you currently have the best hand, it's probably best to just call if you're raised because of the likelihood that the total number of outs against you is large enough to make you a money underdog to the field. However, until you get that raise, you're probably a money favorite and should bet this hand. Just don't raise with it.

Comparing Outs

Some players seem to have trouble conceptualizing the idea that a hand with a flush draw and two overcards (fifteen outs) is a favorite in a heads-up confrontation with the top pair. The thinking is often that the draw has fifteen cards which can give it a win, but the thirty cards that don't hit the draw are wins for the top pair, so why isn't the top pair hand a 2-1 favorite? The reason is that there are two cards still to come.

The draw has two chances to hit one of his cards—the turn and the river. The top pair also has two chances for the draw to miss, but for the top pair to prevail, the draw must miss both times. For the draw to prevail, the draw only has to hit once.

ADJUSTING

One of the things we've been doing in this chapter is looking at the possible flops from a different perspective—from the view of how valuable your hand is in terms of its potential to win money rather than its value in terms of its poker-hand rank.

For many poker players, it's easiest to think of your hand in terms of its poker rank. That's the traditional approach, and that's the way most poker books present the material. *In Hold 'Em you need to adjust your thinking about poker hands away from its poker ranking and toward its money-winning potential.*

We've been showing you how to adjust your estimate of the drawing value of your hand to compensate for the number of opponents. By doing this you'll find yourself playing identical hands differently at different times, depending on both the pot size and the number of opponents. A side benefit of this dynamic strategy is that it adds the perception of deception to your play without you even having to try. Your more observant opponents will often notice that you don't always do the same thing twice with the same hand. It will confuse them. That's always to your long-term benefit.

There's more to adjusting your play than just looking at the number of opponents. It also matters what their playing habits are, how loose or tight they tend to be, and how aggressive they tend to be. Adjusting to game conditions in general is important, not just adjusting to the number of opponents.

Let's look further at adjusting to game conditions by an analysis of a hand. This is a hand that was played by an Internet poker acquaintance of mine and discussed on the Internet. Our hero was on the small blind and held Q♥J♥. The game was a loose and passive 10/20 game with a couple of very loose players and no real strong players. Six players limped in, and the player one seat before the button raised. Everyone called. It was a family pot with all ten players seeing the flop.

The flop was 10♣8♠3♥. The first few players checked. Someone bet. A couple of players called. Someone raised. The pre-flop raiser made it three bets. Now our hero is faced with $30 to call, and the pot has close to $300 in it. What should he do?

First I'll tell you what he did do, and why he did it. He folded. The reason he folded was that he thought that he was almost certainly against more than one two-pair hand or a hand that had flopped a set and that even if he caught one of the four cards for a straight someone else might still make a full house. So, he reasoned, the approximately 10-1 pot odds that he was getting would normally be enough to call for one more card to see if he caught his gutshot straight draw, but it wasn't enough in this case. He was wrong to fold. Not only were the odds he was getting more than enough, but his hand also was much better than he thought.

Most of the time Hold 'Em can be looked at as *a struggle between a made hand and a draw*. That's what our hero was doing. Because there were so many people competing for the pot, he upgraded his normal estimate of what the best hand, the hand he was drawing to beat, actually was. If someone actually did have two pair, then his hand really wasn't good, and folding was probably a good idea. That's the conclusion that looking at Hold 'Em as a struggle between a made hand and a draw leads to. That, however, is not always the right way to look at Hold 'Em. Sometimes you can come to more profitable conclusions by looking at the game as just *a game of money and odds*. That's especially true at loose tables. Although it's true that having many active hands does increase the chances that one of them has hit the flop very well, the chances of that happening really aren't that high. What is much more likely is that many players have picked up weak draws on the flop. Hands such as second pair or two overcards are much more likely on this flop than two pair or trips. Opponents with hands like 8♠6♦ are just more likely than opponents with hands like 10♥10♦ at a loose table.

The way to look at the situation in a loose game isn't in terms of what the likely best hand is, it's in terms of what the likely draws are, and with this flop, the likely draws are all fairly weak draws.

Our hero has a lot more than four outs with this hand. The backdoor flush draw adds the equivalent of about two outs, and there is no strong reason to think that the best hand is any better than a pair of 10s. Many players would raise a flop like that with a hand like J♠9♠ or even A♠3♠. A lot of hands could raise, but our hero could beat them by hitting one of his overcards. The overcards add somewhere between zero and six outs to a total of between six and twelve outs. That's a strong draw and is almost certainly the best draw at the table with this flop. Our hero should be thinking about betting and raising, not folding or calling.

In a tight game, *bet the best hand*. In a loose game, *bet the best draw*. That's the primary secret to adjusting the play on the flop to table conditions.

VALUE BETTING DRAWS

Draws are key to playing the flop in Hold 'Em, under almost all table conditions. The differences are that under some conditions you should be betting when your opponent has a draw. With other conditions, you should be betting when you have a draw. In some cases you should be checking and calling when others have a good draw. Different draws need to be approached in different ways.

A draw on the flop has value if the chances of the draw making and winning are larger than its fair share. By "fair share" I mean what the percentage win rate would be if winning was just random. If four players are competing on the flop, then a fair share is 25 percent (one out of four). If your chances of winning are larger than 25 percent, and you have three or more opponents who will call, then you should be betting or raising for value. This is not pot odds. It's a value bet on a draw where the value comes from having enough callers to give you bet odds larger than your fair share.

FLUSH DRAWS

There are four categories of flush cards and they all play a little differently. There are suited Aces, suited big-little (such as K♠5♠ or Q♠5♠), suited connectors, and other suited cards. The strongest of these are the suited Aces and the suited connectors. The suited Aces are, of course, draws to the best possible flush. That's not really their primary strength, because suited Aces and suited connectors tend to have other drawing features when they flop flush draws. The Ace is an overcard, adding three outs to the hand, and suited connectors often flop a straight draw, or a gutshot straight draw to combine with the flush draw. These extra three or four outs are what make them premium draws.

A flush draw is about a 4-1 underdog to make in one card. It's about a 2-1 underdog to make in two cards. When you have a flush draw, you know that you will need 4-1 pot odds to call a bet on the turn. If the game is only a little loose, you also know the pot will be big enough to give you those odds. That means that when you evaluate a flush draw on the flop, you can think about the odds of making it in two cards but don't have to worry about the cost of those two cards. The pot will pay for the second card. The current betting round is what pays for the first card. If the pot is large enough on the turn to give you 4-1 pot odds, then you only need two callers on the flop to give you sufficient odds to bet or raise an Ace-high flush draw for value.

This makes flush draws very strong on the flop in a loose or very loose game because you don't need pot odds to call on the flop. It's even stronger in a very loose, very aggressive game because you only need 3-1 bet odds to profit significantly from a bet or raise. If you're in that situation where you have three or four callers, and one of them raises for you, then that's just free money.

If you don't see any solid tells that would indicate that you're drawing to a second-best flush, then you will want to play a flush draw at a loose table very aggressively. You want as many callers as you can get, but you also want to put as many bets in the pot as you can.

As we mentioned before, a flush draw is a 2-1 underdog on the flop if you'll take the hand to the river. You'll make the flush once for every two times you miss. That means, if you're getting 3-1 on your bets on the flop, you'll make money if you know your flush will be good. Because we're never quite sure about that, you want to get 4-1. If you get four callers on the flop whenever you bet a flush draw, you will make a lot of money on flushes.

So, on the flop you want to bet or check-raise in such a way as to trap players, not to thin the field. If you think a player to your left will bet, then you should check-raise. If you think a player on the button will raise, then you should bet from UTG, and reraise him if three players besides him have called. You aren't semi-bluffing; you aren't trying to thin the field; you're trying to get as much money, from as many players, as you can.

If your table is very loose and at least somewhat aggressive, you can exploit that by playing a lot of flush cards. The reason for this is that you'll be paid off. Getting paid off with a flush involves more than just getting called when you make the flush. It also involves getting extra bets in the pot when you've got a draw. In a loose, somewhat aggressive game, this can be a major source of winnings.

STRAIGHT DRAWS

Straight draws are not played as automatically as flush draws. There are a couple of reasons for this: one is that straights are harder to make than flushes; the other reason is that straights are often vulnerable to being beaten by a flush.

Look for Something Extra

The more players there are who are active in the pot, the less likely it is that you should play a draw to a straight. In many cases you shouldn't draw at all unless you have a little something extra in your draw.

You should tend to draw to a straight if:

1. There is no flush draw on board.
2. Your draw is to the nut straight.
3. Your draw includes overcards.
4. Your draw includes a three-flush.
5. Your draw includes a pair.

Suited connectors frequently have to be given up on the flop. You aren't going to hit a whole lot of flops with these hands, and when you do hit a flop, you still need to be fairly selective about going past the flop with these hands. For example, if you flop the second pair, you might want to call a bet on the flop if you've also got a three-flush, but without that three-flush you might not want to call. You might not want to call if you flop a draw to the low end of a straight, but if you've also got a three-flush, you might want to go ahead and take a card off.

The looser the game, and the more aggressive the game, the fewer straight draws you should be playing. Let's look at some situations. Suppose you have 8♦7♦. Some flops that give you a draw are:

A♦5♠6♥
A♦5♠6♠
Q♥10♥9♥

A♦5♠6♥

This is a nut-straight draw. There is no possible flush draw on the board. You have a backdoor flush draw. The backdoor flush draw is worth the equivalent of about two outs. With no flush draw out on the board, the nut-straight draw has eight outs. This flop gives you ten outs, which is better than a flush draw. You should raise with this draw if you can get two callers.

A♦5♠6♥

This flop is almost the same, but there is the possibility of a spade-flush draw on the board. The backdoor flush is worth two outs and the straight draw six outs, so this flop gives you about eight outs. You should still raise with this hand, but you need three or more callers.

Q♥10♥9♥

This is a terrible flop. You've got a straight draw, but the Jack won't make you a best hand. A 6♥ is not likely to help you. You may already be beaten by a flush, and if not, you only have three outs. Fold if someone bets.

A PAIR ON THE BOARD

In tight games, a pair on the board does not automatically present a significant risk that someone has three of a kind. In fact, depending on the rank of the pair, there might not be much risk at all. In a tight game, there is a big difference between a flop of Q♥Q♦7♠ and a flop of Q♥7♦7♠. That's because players are more likely to have played a hand with a Queen in it than a hand with a 7 in it.

This is not true in a loose game. In a loose or very loose game, the risk that a pair on the board has given someone three of a kind is significant. Tread cautiously.

MADE HANDS

There are three kinds of made hands:

1. A strong hand that might improve. Top pair or a large overpair are examples.
2. A very strong hand that can improve. Examples are a set or a straight with a flush draw.

3. A very strong hand that won't improve. A flopped straight or flush are examples.

A Strong Hand That Might Improve

In most game conditions, this kind of hand, which is probably the best hand, should be played aggressively on the flop. You want to bet or raise in order to reduce the pot odds that players calling with draws are getting.

When the game gets loose, however, and especially when the game gets very loose, the situation changes. Now, if the flop contains draws, in particular a flush draw but sometimes also a straight draw, the idea of Morton's theorem kicks in and the best hand is not always the one to benefit from bets and raises on the flop. In loose or very loose game conditions, usually you should bet top pair or an overpair, but you usually should not raise with it.

In very loose-aggressive games, often you should not even bet top pair. The chances of being raised by a draw and getting many callers are just too great, and you won't benefit from those bets on the flop if there are many loose callers. The benefit will go to the best draw, not the best hand. When you add the possibility that you might not actually have the best hand, then it pays to be careful in very loose-aggressive games with hands that you would be betting very aggressively in tighter or more passive games. The looser the game, the more often the best thing to do is to wait until the turn to get aggressive with strong hands.

Examples of what I mean by strong hands that might improve are A♦A♣ with a flop of 10♥9♥3♠ or the same flop with a hand of A♦10♦. In both case you probably have the best hand. With the overpair, if you're not best now then you probably have about five outs—another Ace or a 3 will probably be good enough. With the top pair and a good kicker, you might only have the three Aces as outs, because if you're not best, then it's likely that another 10 makes a full house for someone.

In either of these examples you should usually play the hand very strongly on the flop. The exception comes when the game is both very loose and very aggressive. Then you're likely to have players with good draws raising and reraising. As I showed earlier, if the field is large and their combined outs are large, then you won't benefit from bets and raises on the flop, even though you probably have the best hand.

Just a small change in these hands, however, can make a big difference. If you had A♦A♥ or A♠10♠ to give you a three-flush backdoor draw, then that would add about the equivalent of two outs to the hands. Those extra outs, combined with the value as the probable best hand, are usually enough to play the hand very aggressively, even against a large loose and aggressive field. In close situations look for a little extra. If you don't have it, you should slow down.

A Very Strong Hand That Can Improve

In a tight game, you might sometimes want to slow play very strong hands to give others a chance to catch up. The bet size on the turn is larger, and a slow play might gain a caller if you wait until they've had a chance to catch up with you.

In more typical games, it usually doesn't pay to slow play. Even when you have a very strong hand, the chances are pretty good that others have flopped some kind of hand and will likely call bets both on the flop and the turn. You usually don't need to give anyone a chance to catch up.

In looser games or in very aggressive games, slow play almost never pays. You have the best of both worlds with a very strong hand that has good improvement chances when you're in a very loose, very aggressive game. You probably have the best hand, many of the callers will be drawing almost dead, and about one-third of the time your hand will get even better. Play these kinds of hands very aggressively in the wilder type games. You'll be paid off handsomely.

Examples of very strong hands that can improve are A♦A♥ with a flop of A♠K♥Q♦ or J♠J♥ with a flop of A♥J♦10♦ or 10♠9♠ with a flop of 10♥9♦3♠.

A Very Strong Hand That Won't Improve

By this kind of hand, I mean a flopped straight, flush, or full house.

Playing a Straight

One example of when straightforward aggressive play is the best course to follow is when you have a straight. When you have a straight, there is some chance another player has two pair. That's because the cards that make your straight are connected cards, the kind of hands Hold 'Em players like to play. Other draws to beat you are likely out there also, draws to better straights and flushes. Therefore straights should usually be played aggressively, but not always.

If there are a lot of draws out to beat your straight, and this is not uncommon, then you are in a similar situation to the top pair or the pocket Jacks in the hand we discussed earlier in this chapter. In that case you should slow down on the flop. This is particularly true if the flop is two-suited, containing a flush draw, and the game is very loose and aggressive. For example, let's say you have a 8♦6♦ in late position in a very loose and aggressive game. The flop is 10♥9♥7♠.

If the action is hot and heavy before it gets to you, you might want to think about folding this straight. You might have the best hand right now, but you might not. If your hand is not best now, then you have no chance to win this pot and will end up putting a lot more money in it. Even if you are best, you have to worry about any Heart, an 8, a Jack, a 10, a 9, or a 7. There are many cards that have the possibility of beating your hand even if it is best now. I'm not saying you should always fold it, but you should consider folding in a very loose and aggressive game if there has been action like a bet, a call, then two raises before the action reaches you. There is a good chance you are beaten, and if you aren't, there is a good chance you will be before it's all over.

The situation is a little different if you have, for example, a 10♦8♦ and the flop is 9♥7♥6♠. Now you know you have the best hand. There's no folding this hand. If the game is very loose and aggressive, and the action is similar to what I described earlier, you probably don't want to put in the last raise unless you think raising will limit the callers to two or three players. Any more callers than that and the collective outs they have are very likely to combine in such a way that your hand won't profit that much from the bets on the flop. If the turn card doesn't help any of the possible draws (maybe a black Ace falls on the turn), then raise away with this hand. Play it aggressively on the turn, but only if the turn card doesn't complete any of the draws that could beat you.

In a tighter game, both these hands play a little differently. With either, if you only have two or three other active players on the flop, a straight is still very vulnerable. With few opponents, flopping a straight probably gives you the best hand. Flops like those already discussed do present risks however, and in a tight or typical game, the hand should be played very aggressively while it's still the best hand.

Playing a Flush
When you flop something less than the top flush, you're again in a situation that's similar to the top pair or an overpair. How aggressively you play this hand depends on how many callers you're getting and how aggressive they are. If you're getting three or more callers, you should slow down with a flopped flush that isn't headed by the Ace or King. There will be draws to a bigger flush than yours, and they will benefit from the bets and raises, not you.

With only one or two other active hands, a flopped flush should usually be played very aggressively. In a tight game, it's very unlikely that anyone else has also flopped a flush, so even if you don't have an Ace-high flush, you don't have much to be concerned about.

In a loose game, there is more of a chance that you're not the only player who has flopped a flush. Even if you have four or five other active hands, the chances of someone besides youself having a flush are still fairly small. If you have a flush on the flop, then five of the thirteen flush cards are accounted for. For someone else to have a flush, they must have two of only eight cards unaccounted for. This is unlikely even in the loosest of games.

Of all the possible beginning Hold 'Em hands, less than about one-third of them are suited. So if you're at a loose table where players are seeing the flop 60 percent of the time or more, they probably don't have suited cards at all, even suited in suits other than the flush. Don't think the worst if you flop a low flush. Your hand is probably by far the best hand, and you should play it as such.

Also, in a loose game don't let a lot of action on the flop convince you that someone else has a flush. A hand that was discussed on the Internet newsgroup rec.gambling.poker illustrates this. Our hero in this hand was dealt a 8♦6♦. He saw the flop along with six other players, and the betting was capped at four bets before the flop—a large pot. The flop was A♦10♦2♦. He flopped a small flush. He was third to act on the flop and the first player to bet. This player had been one of the raisers before the flop. The second player raised and our hero reraised. Everyone called, and the original raiser put in the last raise. At this point our hero became convinced that he was beaten, that someone, probably the player doing the raising, had a larger flush then he did. One of the factors that helped convince our hero that he was beaten was that the raiser was what he considered a solid player.

Let's analyze this. How likely is it that the raiser on the flop has a flush? To determine that, we need to do an inventory of the possible hands he might have, hands that would be consistent with the way that he's played both before the flop and on the flop. First, what hands would he play this aggressively (raising twice) on the flop? A flush for sure, but probably he'd also play a set or two pair that aggressively. He might also play that aggressively with the K♦ and a second card that gave him a pair or a gutshot straight draw, and a hand like A♥K♦ or K♦Q♥. Which of these hands might he actually have? Before the flop the raiser had been on the big blind and the bet had been raised twice when the action got to him, and

RAISER'S HAND

Likely hands of the flop raiser in our example hand.

Ax Ay

K♦ Kx

Ax K♦

Ax 10x

10x 10y

K♦ Qx

K♦ Jx

Any two ♦ with one over an 8

Any two ♦ with none over an 8

---

he called. With seven players seeing the flop, he would likely have called with any of the hands listed in the table.

There are about forty-eight hands that a solid player might have which he'd be playing aggressively on the flop. Of those hands, twenty-one of them would have our hand beat, twenty-seven would not. Of the twenty-seven, twenty-one are hands that have draws to beat our small flush. So if a solid player is playing a single-suited flop aggressively, and we have a small flush, we probably are not beaten. He does, however, probably have a draw to beat our flush. In this case the best tactic to take is to play aggressively on the flop and turn. This is because, although a draw to a bigger flush has a good enough draw to profit from the odds he'll probably get from the flop bets, the other draws are pretty much drawing dead, and the made flush benefits also from the bets on the flop. In this situation the best draw and the best hand both benefit from bets and raises on the flop, as long as two or three other players with pairs or worse flush draws are calling.

Of course, in our example there were many other callers who might have beaten us, but it's not likely they'd passively call in this situation unless they had relatively weak draws such as Q♦Q♥ or J♦10♥.

What did the other players have in our example hand with a flop of A♦10♦2♦? The aggressive raiser had A♥K♦, and one of the other players had Q♦Q♥. The others didn't show their hands but probably had some mix of weak draws or pairs.

KICKER PROBLEMS

Hold 'Em is often a game of kickers. When a hand flops the top pair and gets action that reaches a showdown, the result is often based on which hand has the best kicker with its top pair. For example, if you have a hand like K♥6♣, get a free ride to see the flop from the big blind, and get a flop of K♦8♠3♥, you have to consider the value of that 6♣ when compared with the likely kicker of any other player that might have a King. This kind of hand is potentially in big trouble. The conventional approach to playing this kind of situation is based on a *hand-domination* perspective. The conventional recommendation is to check the hand and call if someone bets. This does two things—it minimizes your losses when you are beaten by another King with a better kicker while improving your profits by inciting other players to bet as a bluff.

In a tight game, the hand-domination perspective does lead you to the best course of action. You should check and call if someone bets. You should probably not call if there is a bet and a raise, although it actually turns out that checking and calling a raise rather than folding to a raise is not a large error. It only costs you a few pennies on average.

In very loose games, this popular wisdom just doesn't hold up. In a very loose game, betting the hand straightforwardly, and calling if anyone raises, makes almost twice as much money in the long run as checking and calling. This is not the popular wisdom. Most players would feel very uncomfortable if they bet this top pair with a weak kicker and got raised when the flop had no draws that someone may be raising on. Betting and calling is the right thing to do against a field of loose or very loose players.

The reason for this is that in very loose games you are more likely to have other players with 3s and 8s than Kings in their hands. In a loose game, your opponents are more likely to have two kinds of hands than are likely in a tight game. A hand such as K♠2♠ is much more likely to be played by an opponent in a loose game, and a hand such as 8♦6♥ is also much more likely to be played. You'll get action, maybe even a raise from hands like that, if you bet out your top pair with a weak kicker in a loose game. In a tight game, players aren't likely to be holding those kinds of hands on the flop. Of course, even in a loose game, you are probably beaten if you get raised, but the chances are good enough that you are not beaten to make it worth calling a raise. The pot will be large enough to hold onto that hand because there are enough worse hands that loose players might raise with to make it pay off. Don't expect to win most of the pots by doing this, but do expect to win most of the money eventually.

In more typical games, the two plays, betting versus checking and calling, are about equivalent in terms of the amount of money made. The best play is to probably check and call in a typical game. It makes about the same money as betting and does so with a little less risk.

The general lesson here is to play your top pairs more aggressively in loose games while playing top pairs with weak kickers more passively in tight games. This is a major difference in how a common situation should be played differently under different game conditions. I think it illustrates how important it is to think in terms of the game conditions and the kinds of hands your opponents are likely to have rather than thinking in terms of only your own hand.

SECOND PAIR FROM THE BLINDS

Let's look at that K♥6♣ on the big blind again, but this time let's think about a flop like Q♦6♥2♠. You've flopped the second pair with a pretty good kicker. Someone may have a Queen, but if they do, you still have five outs that will improve enough to win.

How should you play this hand? Again, it depends on the kinds of hands that the other active players are likely to have, with which kinds of hands they'll be likely to call or raise if you bet, and with what kinds of hands they'll bet if you check. It turns out that you should probably play this hand very similarly to how you'd play the hand if you'd flopped top pair.

In the loosest games, you should bet and call if anyone raises. In the tighter or more typical games, you should check and call if someone bets but fold if there is a bet and a raise.

This is again contrary to popular wisdom. Popular wisdom suggests that you should check and fold this hand in the loosest games and bet in most game conditions. The argument for betting is that it will cause overcards to your 6 (hands with cards between a 6 and a Queen) to fold, improving your chances of winning the pot. This idea of betting to thin the field is very common, but it's frequently emphasized more than its value. Most of the time you thin the field of hands that you would profit from if they called. You aren't really accomplishing anything of value.

In this situation of the second pair with a flop that has no potential draws, you just aren't going to get called by hands that you can beat. A bet might well win the pot for you, but if it doesn't win it for you right now, in a tight or typical game you are not going to be in good shape if anyone calls or raises. The best thing to do in a tight or typical game is to check and call. By checking you are likely to induce players from late position, or because of the ragged flop even from early position, to bluff at the pot with maybe something like a single Ace or King overcard. Letting another player bet a single King overcard is the best possible result for you. You not only have the best hand, the long-shot card they are hoping for is a King, a card that still leaves your card best.

In a very loose game, however, you should go ahead and bet because, like when you flopped the top pair with a weak kicker, you're more likely to get calls from players with hands like 5♦2♦. These are calls you will profit from.

Again, be more aggressive in very loose games with marginal hands. The loose players play hands even more marginal than your hands, and you will be paid off. In tight games, however, you'll usually do best by checking and calling with marginal hands. If you bet, you won't get called by hands that figure to be worse than yours, and by checking you may induce a bluff from a hand that would not have called your bet.

COMMENTS ON WEAK PAIRS

One caveat exists for both these situations. I'm not trying to give you hard and fast rules here. How to play these hands depends entirely on the kinds of hands your opponents are likely to have and how they are likely to play them.

The top pair with a weak kicker or the second pair can be major money leaks in your game. They do have to be played carefully, and often it is best just to fold them. What I've tried to illustrate is that these hands can be moneymakers if you're careful and adjust your strategy to the specific game conditions.

I've tried to give you some general guidelines for how to adjust your play of weak pairs with ragged flops. In general you should be more passive in tight games and more aggressive in loose games.

Before you decide what to do in the game, you need to analyze your game. What kinds of hands do the players in your game play? How do they play those hands? It's common to think that a weak pair is probably beaten if there is a large field of active hands. That's true if the game is fairly tight and there just happens to be many active hands this hand, but if the game is just generally loose, then you're likely to be called by all kinds of hands that can't beat even your weak pair. Plan your play accordingly.

OVERPAIRS

Before I finish this chapter, I want to look at one more example situation. Let's look at everybody's favorite hand, a pocket pair of Aces when the flop looks a little scary. Suppose you have A♣A♦, and the flop is 10♥9♥6♠. This is not the flop you wanted to see with your pair of Aces. The odds are that you've got the best hand, but with this flop you can't be sure. If you're not best, then it's going to be expensive for you, and even if you are best, there are a lot of cards that can fall on the next two rounds that will beat yours. It's not a good situation. So what should you do?

In most cases you should play this very aggressively. You should almost always bet or raise if someone else has bet first. You should almost never slow play in this kind of situation. Giving a free card, or a cheap card, can be a disaster here. You probably have the best hand, and you should bet or raise to cut down on the odds that the probable draws are getting.

If the field is small, only one or two other active hands, then you should be particularly aggressive. Do not just bet and raise, but put in the last bet. Even many passive players will raise with a flop like this if they have a decent draw, but if there are only one or two callers, they probably are not getting the right odds to be raising against your overpair. Reraise. There is one exception to this. That's when the game conditions are very loose and very aggressive. In that case you should still bet and raise if someone else has bet first, but if you bet and are raised, you should probably not reraise. The reason for this is that if there are four or five active hands, the collective draws they have are likely to put your overpair at a disadvantage to the field. Against an aggressive field, the chance of being reraised by very good draws is just too large to risk putting in extra bets.

This is an example where you should almost always play the hand the same way. Bet it, raise it, reraise it. The only exception is that you should slow down if it's a very loose and very aggressive table and you are raised. In this example it's not as important to think in terms of what kinds of hands the other players are likely to play as it is important to think of how they are likely to play those hands.

14

The Dynamics
of Game Conditions

Game conditions are generally derived from the behavior of the players. Loose players make loose games and tight players make tight games, etc., etc., but it really isn't that simple. Players interact to create the game conditions, and they interact not just with each other but with the environment. Sometimes it's like that butterfly who flaps its wings in France and creates a storm in Thailand. Little things can have big effects on the game conditions.

You'll seldom see tight tables suddenly become loose or passive tables suddenly become aggressive unless there is a change in two or three players. Even replacing one tight-passive player with a maniac isn't enough to change the overall character of the table.

The main changes that you'll sometimes see occur abruptly are a loose table turning tight or an aggressive table turning passive. Those changes can occur at a table with lightning speed, seemingly without warning, and if you play a strategy geared toward a particular game condition, it's those fast, unanticipated changes that can cost you a lot of money if you don't quickly realize that the change has occurred and adjust accordingly. The way to guard against this is to be aware of clues that suggest that a swift, dramatic change in game conditions may occur. There are some events, some external to the table, some part of the game, which should heighten your vigilance about game conditions.

EVENTS THAT CAN TIGHTEN UP A TABLE

Fun games tend to be loose games. Most people play poker because it's fun, and when they're having fun, they tend to play a lot of hands. Such games tend to have a lot of table banter, joking back and forth among the players. Anything that is likely to interject a note of seriousness or discord into this banter will likely cause many of the players to tighten up, at least temporarily.

Often the table banter is being driven by a single, jovial, fun-loving player. Everyone may be joining in the fun, but it's that one player who's been driving it. In such a situation, game conditions can change immediately if the jovial player leaves the game. He doesn't actually have to leave for this to happen. Anything that might cause a change in his mood tends to cause a change in mood for the table. Things like a particularly bad beat or another player slow-rolling him on the river might cause it. Even a business-related phone call on his cell phone might cause it.

There is a good chance the table will tighten up if one of the more loose-aggressive players at the table is distracted, maybe eating, maybe talking to a cocktail waitress, he just got a call on his cell phone, a friend of his walked up to the table, or any one of a number of possible distractions. This is because loose players tend to be attracted to pots that have a loose-aggressive player active in the pot. Even loose players who don't do much raising often seem to enjoy competing in a pot where they know someone will be raising with probably weak hands. If that player is distracted and not involved temporarily, the other loose players will tend to pass.

EVENTS THAT CAN TURN A TABLE PASSIVE

Aggression at the poker table takes a lot of energy. Often this energy tends to feed on itself, with each hand being played slightly more aggressively than the previous one. When that starts happening, look for the aggression to reach a climax and quickly dissipate.

One climatic event that frequently occurs is when an aggressively contested, very large pot is won by a player who was aggressively betting a draw and there is a multiplayer showdown. It often brings a temporary halt to aggressive conditions. Even players who weren't involved in the pot often feel the climax and will play passively for a few hands after that.

Aggressive games tend to be fast-paced. If the pace of the games slows, the aggression will often dissipate. A change in dealers is one thing that frequently causes this. Don't assume that an aggressive game will continue to be aggressive for the first few hands of a new dealer.

THINGS THAT SUGGEST THE TABLE
CONDITIONS HAVE CHANGED

One common characteristic of players at a loose-aggressive table is that, once they've called a bet on the current betting round, they've committed to seeing the next card—they'll call raises. When you see a player call a bet in middle position, then fold when there has been a raise and reraise, you can usually count on a change in game conditions to occur soon.

EXTERNAL EVENTS

Many events that don't directly involve your table can cause a change in conditions. Any kind of commotion or activity in the poker room might tend to distract the players' attention, causing them to play both tighter and more passively.

A large pot at a nearby table might be enough to cause a distraction. A dealer shift change, when for a short period there are twice as many dealers in the room, may cause a distraction. Many seemingly unimportant events might cause a distraction to the players. Watch for it.

15

Table Image

A lot has been written in poker books about establishing a table image—creating a false view of your playing style and habits in other players. It's a major topic of debate among poker players, writers, theorists, and analysts. Until now there have been two sides to the debate. One side says you should establish a tight, tough image because that gives you more opportunity to steal pots. The other side says you should establish a loose, weak image because that will induce players to call you, creating larger pots when you win. I'm going to introduce a third side to this debate: It doesn't matter. What matters is that you know what image other players do have of you and adjust accordingly. Creating an image just isn't the point. It usually doesn't work, and it often costs money to try. Just go with what you have.

IMAGE DEBATE

Advantages of a Tight Image

Some writers think it's important for your opponents to think of you as a tight player because it will give you more opportunity to buy small pots with a bluff. A tough image also tends to discourage players from bluffing when you're in the pot, making fewer situations where you have a tough decision to make. Mason Malmuth is a popular writer who espouses this view.

However, a tight image is not always the same thing as a tough image. Many times players perceived as tight are also perceived as weak, with a tendency to fold too easily. If that's the kind of tight image you have, then it may be true that you can sometimes use that image to steal a pot or two, but players will also attempt many steals from you. If you really are a tough player, then that's a good thing. If you're not really that tough, then a tight image may not work to your advantage as much as you think.

Advantages of a Loose Image

Others think it's important to establish a loose image because it entices players to call you more often, increasing the size of the pots you win. It also induces them to bluff more often, under the assumption that you always have a weak hand. The basic idea here is that you're getting other players to put more money in the pot in those situations where you have the best of it. Mike Caro is a popular writer who's associated with this view. By the way, this is the only area of poker I can think of where I disagree with Mike Caro.

Disadvantages of Both Views

I disagree with both sides of the debate. I don't think that it's worthwhile to go out of your way to do anything to try to manipulate the image that others have of you. Your energy is much better spent making sure you know what that image is, whatever it might be, and adjusting to it.

IMAGE OF A DYNAMIC, AGGRESSIVE PLAYER

What image are other players likely to have of you if you play a dynamic, aggressive game? (The kind of game this book suggests you play.) Many of them will likely think you're a near maniac: a loose, aggressive, weak player. Others will think you're a tough, tricky player. The reason for this is that most players think of playing in terms of the cards. They will look at the cards you play and how you play them, but they will not pay much attention to the situation.

For example, do you raise on the flop with a flush draw? Sometimes you will, sometimes you won't. You will raise if you are on the button, the UTG player bets, and three or four players call. You might raise if you are on the button and the UTG player bets and everyone else folds. If you are UTG, you might bet a flush draw, but if you think that the player on your left will bet, then you'll check and raise after three or four players have called his bet. If you check and you were wrong about who was going to bet and it's checked to the player on the button, then you'll probably just call with your flush draw, not wanting to drive other players out.

Most of your opponents will only notice that sometimes you raise with a flush draw and sometimes you don't. They usually will not notice the situation. They'll look for such things as, Does he only raise when he's got an Ace-high flush draw? Does he only raise when he's on the button? They'll likely conclude that you're unpredictable and that you play your cards almost randomly.

Another example of the kind of thing your opponents might notice and not fully understand is that they might see you raise on the button with a 6♠6♦ but then not raise on the button with a 7♠7♦. They won't notice that when you raise with the pair of 6s you already had six players in the pot, but when you only called with the pair of 7s, there were only three players in the pot. They'll focus on your cards, not on the situation.

Even though your play might be highly predictable, they just won't notice it. Maybe they'll conclude you're a lucky maniac, maybe they'll conclude you're a tricky player. It doesn't really matter that much. You can profit dramatically from either of these images. What's important is knowing what image each player at the table has of you. They won't all have the same image, and you will often have to modify your play to exploit the particular image that active players have of you.

EXPLOITING YOUR IMAGE

You have to know what image your opponents have of you. It's not difficult to determine. They'll tell you. Some time during the course of a session you'll have some players offering advice to you. They'll tell you how terrible your play of a hand was and how lucky you were to win that pot. These are players who have decided that you're a loose-aggressive maniac. Other players at the same table will say something to the effect that they just can't put you on a hand, "You're too tricky," they'll say. These players think you're a tough player.

It's really that simple. They'll almost never mislead you about this. They'll just tell you.

When They Think You're a Maniac

If they think you're a maniac, they'll raise and reraise you with weak holdings. If they bet and you raise, they'll reraise you with hands like top pair and a weak kicker. Discount any raises these players make. Because they'll always think you are bluffing, they'll tend to slow play when they have a better hand than you.

When They Think You're Tough and Tricky

You can bluff more often when these players are in the pot. They will almost always think that you have a better hand than you really do. If the flush card hits the river and you bet, they will sometimes even fold top two pair, convinced that you must have the flush.

MATCHING AN IMAGE TO AN OPPONENT

If they are weak-tight, you want to be perceived as tight-aggressive.

If they are loose-aggressive, you want to be perceived as weak-tight.

If they are tight-aggressive, you want to be perceived as loose.
If they are loose-passive, you want to be perceived as loose-
wild.

THE IMPORTANT IMAGE

One thing you can do is just be nice. Players appreciate it. A nice
guy image is probably the most important image you can have,
and it is one you can cultivate.

The people you're playing with get enjoyment from playing
poker. If your behavior does a little something to enhance their
enjoyment of the game, they might actually start enjoying playing
at your table. And it's players who are playing for fun that you want
at your table. Most losers don't mind losing, but they really don't
like to give their money to surly, rude people most of the time.

16

Player Stereotypes

A common proverb holds that there are three kinds of people:

1. Those who watch things happen
2. Those who make things happen
3. Those who wonder what happened

Those who watch things happen are called passive players, those who make things happen we call aggressive, and those who wonder what happened, we call clueless. Most tables will have a selection of all three of these kinds of players. Even within these groups, there are different kinds of players. This is particularly true among aggressive players. Aggression is a characteristic of a good poker player, but not all aggressive players are good players. Some of them play pretty badly, and some of them tend to play well under certain game conditions and don't seem to be able to adjust when the conditions change.

AN INITIAL ASSESSMENT

The first step in evaluating a player is to categorize him. Players can be generally categorized along two scales: passive-aggressive and loose-tight. The extremes of these scales are readily recognizable. Someone who is extremely loose and aggressive is called a "maniac" because he will bet or raise on just about anything. Someone who is extremely tight and passive is called a "rock" because he will only play sure hands, and even then he will play them conservatively and rarely raise. Someone who is extremely loose and passive is called a "calling station" because he will nearly always call someone else's bet but will rarely raise or bet himself. The last extreme type is both tight and aggressive and is called a "stone killer" because he is the one who waits for his opportunities and then pounces on them, making the most money. Most players do not fit into these extreme types, but you will recognize these four characteristics to a greater or lesser extent in every player at a poker table. In addition to the basic four characteristics, you may want to further categorize players along two other scales: weak-tough and straightforward-tricky.

In order to categorize a player, watch what he does, how he plays, when he calls, when he bets, and when he raises. If you're new to the game, you can also get an assessment of what type of player you are dealing with by watching how other players, the ones who presumably know something about him, react to him. Let us examine the scales and see how various players fit into their respective categories.

The Tight-Loose Player Scale

A tight player is one who doesn't get involved in many pots. He's very selective. A loose player plays a lot of hands and continues to play the hand into the later betting rounds

The Passive-Aggressive Scale

A passive player doesn't bet or raise on most hands but will tend to call your bets. An aggressive player is one who bets and raises a lot. If you bet into an aggressive player, he might fold or he might raise, but he's not likely to call.

The Weak-Tough Scale

A weak player is one who always fears the worst. If three flush cards are on the board, he fears a flush. If you bet, he might call, but he won't raise with his straight. A tough player will try to figure out whether you actually have a flush. If he doesn't think you have one, he'll raise with his straight. If he does think you have one, he might call or he might fold, depending on how big the pot is. Tough players tend to be hard to read, whereas weak players tend to be easy to read.

The Straightforward-Tricky Scale

Some players always bet their good hands, always check and call with good draws, and always fold their weak hands and weak draws. You always have a good idea what kind of hand this player holds.

Other players try to get tricky. They'll bet when they don't have much, check and call the flop, then raise on the turn when they have a good hand or a great hand. They'll semi-bluff and raise a lot. These players are sometimes more difficult to read, but often they overdo the tricky attempts so much that you can read them even more easily than you can a straightforward player. It's just that the clues are backward.

NARROWING DOWN THE HANDS

By just getting a general category of the player, you can often narrow the range of hands he might have. For example, suppose a tight-aggressive player just calls pre-flop in early position, the flop is Q♠7♥2♦, and he suddenly goes berserk by reraising, you then have to think what hands are likely.

The hands that are consistent with the play on the flop might be A♦Q♦, K♦Q♦, Q♦7♦, 7♠2♠, Q♥2♥, 7♠7♦, or 2♠2♥. Most players would slow play Q♥Q♦ here. Even a straightforward player will tend to slow play a really big hand. You can eliminate most of those hands based on what kinds of hands the type of player would have limped into the pot with from early position.

We can look at these hands and see which are reasonable to just call, pre-flop, in early position. The hands A♦Q♦ and K♦Q♦ are often raised in early position, but at least some of the time they just call, so they are still consistent. The hands Q♦7♦, 7♠2♠ and Q♥2♥ are not reasonable calls from an early position, except for the loosest of players, and 7♠7♦ and 2♠2♥ are candidates for early position play from all but tough or tight players. So that leaves A♦Q♦, K♦Q♦, 7♠7♦, and 2♠2♥ as his possible hands, and, for most players, you can eliminate the 2♠2♥. This narrows down the field of possibilities quite a bit.

Be aware also of how other players may interpret your betting. If you have an image as a very loose player, then the reraiser might have any Queen if he's an aggressive player.

This is just an example of the kind of thinking you need to go through when trying to put a player on a hand. Think about their habits, and use stereotypical thinking if you haven't played with them long enough to know their individual habits. Think about what they think your habits are. A raise from a passive, straightforward player who thinks you're tricky likely has a very different meaning than a raise from a tricky, aggressive player who thinks you're a maniac.

GATHERING INFORMATION

As play goes along, give yourself a running commentary of the events, "she open-raises, he folds, he cold-calls." Don't do it out loud. You must make a lot of mental notes based on this, and you must do this even when you're not in a hand, because in addition to being useful during a hand, it's useful for later hands. You want to see the frequency with which a player sees the flop, the frequency with which a player defends his blinds from raises, and the hands a player open-raises with, raises with, cold-calls with, and just calls with. In conjunction with the narrowing down of the hands discussed, this will often give you a good idea of what's going on even when there is no showdown. Stereotype each player, as well as note particular idiosyncrasies of the individuals for use not only now but in future sessions.

It's useful to get an idea, for each player, what kinds of hands he'll tend to play, and how he'll play them in various situations. Getting this kind of information can take some time, but you should do it for those players with whom you play regularly. Write a book on them. Examples of the kind of information you should look for about specific hands are:

1. Will he play pocket pairs less than 6,6, and from what position?
2. When he plays an A,xs from UTG, will he limp or raise? What's his cutoff for an open-raise?
3. If he's on the button, will he raise with A,xs?
4. Will he raise with less than a nut flush when the flush card hits?
5. Will he raise and reraise with a flush draw when heads up?
6. If he raises with two big cards pre-flop, will he continue betting to the river with just overcards?

You'll have to answer dozens more questions about each player to get that book written, but these questions should be a good start. Once you've answered some of these questions about a player, you can sometimes infer the answers to others.

INFERENCES

Most players are generally consistent in different kinds of situations. The situations don't have to be the same, but the theoretical perspective that the player is using will probably not vary much from situation to situation, so that you can often make a lot of inferences. For example, if a player tends to frequently raise pre-flop with speculative hands, then you can also expect that player to play draws very aggressively. A player who flops a middle-sized flush and checks and calls to the river will probably not play draws aggressively. Such a player will also probably not draw to a straight if the board shows a flush draw and will not often draw to a flush if the board is paired. Knowing what kinds of hands a player probably does not have can often be just as valuable as knowing what kinds of hands he does have.

WHY DO THEY PLAY?

Earlier in the book I talked about a hunting analogy. Some people enjoy the hunt itself more than the kill. Some people don't see much reason to hunt if you don't kill something. Others just like having the neatest gun. Poker is the same thing. Some play because they want to win money. That's the book players. Some play because they enjoy the gamble. They want to win also, but they want to create a gamble even more. That's the loose maniac crowd. There is a third group that doesn't really care if they win, just so long as they "play right." They probably think they want to win, but they really don't care. These are the players who are always quoting what they've read in a book to the winners, telling them what they did wrong.

Many poker players play simply for the thrill of the gamble. There's a large subset of aggressive players who fall into this category. These players want high-risk games, and they'll create them by frequent raises. High-risk games come about because that's what the players want—they made them high risk on purpose. Risk is the point. That does not mean those players are unskilled. Some of them are, of course, but some of them are very skilled. They just use their skills to meet their needs, not yours.

Before you categorize a player beyond the simple dichotomous scales, identify the reason they play—determine their motivating force.

AGGRESSIVE PLAYERS

Tough players tend to be aggressive players, but most aggressive players aren't tough players. Most of them are fairly transparent, and tend not to have very good table judgment.

Macho Players

There is a class of aggressive player who just enjoys dominating the game. These players are often tight and aggressive *and* tricky. There is a certain kind of tight-aggressive-tricky player on tilt who will almost always raise pre-flop with two big cards and limp with big pairs. This certain kind of player will not give up overcards and will be aggressive with them, but will tend to try to trap you with a big pocket pair.

The term tilt comes from a pinball tilt. A player on "tilt" is one who's playing very badly as a result of some emotional trauma.

If a player like that raises before the flop and I can get heads-up with them, I'll always call with small-suited connectors. With a player like that, I'll know whether I'm likely best. He'll raise me on the flop when I'm best, and if I call or check then call on the turn, he'll call a raise on the river with his Ace King. That's implied odds.

An FPS Player on Tilt

One of the most aggressive players you'll run across is a Fancy Play Syndrome player on tilt. They can get more inappropriately aggressive than a table maniac. Players with FPS tend to attempt to steal-raise (i.e., a player in late position who open-raises in the hope that everyone will fold and that he can steal the blinds) before the flop too often. They tend to always slow play big hands, like checking a flopped full house. Players with FPS seem to tilt easily. They think of themselves as tough, tricky players, and when their tricks don't work, it angers them. The frequent result is that they start getting more tricky, not less tricky. They make more mistakes, not fewer.

Book Players

Players who tend to play strictly according the recommendations of their favorite poker book tend to self-identify. They talk about playable hands and correct play. They tend to talk about hand groups a lot and use phrases such as pot odds, implied odds, or dominated hands at the table. They also tend to categorize other players based on how their pre-flop play matches their favorite hand groups. In loose games they tend to overplay pairs on the flop and underplay draws. These players tend to read about the game a lot. They subscribe to *Card Player* and *Poker Digest* magazines. They tend to devote a lot of energy to memorizing the things they read and not much energy to just thinking about the game. They believe they think about the game a lot, but they really don't. They are not good players, but they tend to play fairly tight and are aggressive in passive games. Because of this they do tend to be consistent but small winners in a typical passive game.

Book players tend to select their starting hands from a list, rather than according to the game and the opponents. That tends to make them rather easy to read. Such players also tend to be somewhat timid about betting less than the nuts when the board is somewhat scary.

Specifically, if this kind of player finds himself in a very loose or a loose-aggressive game, he tends to become a fish. If it's a double bet on the end game (3/6/12 or 10/20/40), he approaches the characteristics of a huge fish. When he does think about the game, he tends to think in terms of a contest between a *made hand* and *a draw*—sort of a fuzzy two-player game theory perspective. That's a perspective that doesn't work well in a very loose or loose-aggressive game. Also, reverse tells tend to work well against this kind of player—especially if you have been labeled a maniac because you were seen as you limp reraise six callers from UTG with A♥5♥.

When an Aggressive Player Calls

I'm an aggressive player. I raise often and I don't often slow play. You don't have to play with me for very long to realize that I'm an aggressive player, but having that information doesn't help you much if you don't use it.

I recently played a hand that illustrates the importance of using information when you have it. I had K♠J♠ on the big blind. Two players limped in from middle position, the small blind called. I thought about raising, but decided not to. The reason I didn't was that one of the players who had limped in was an aggressive-tricky player who frequently limped and reraised with very good hands. The flop was A♠4♠10♣. This was a very good flop for me—nut flush draw and a gutshot draw to a nut straight.

The small blind was first and bet. When I saw the flop I decided that I was going to play this hand aggressively, but there were two players behind me who hadn't acted yet and there was a good chance one of them would raise if I just called. So I just called, hoping for a raise so I could reraise. My plan failed when both players folded. The turn card was 9♥. Now, to my surprise, the small blind checked. He must be on a draw, I thought. I bet. He called. The river card was 2♦. I missed my draws, but when the small blind checked, I knew he had missed his, too. So I bet. He folded. I got the money.

There is a lesson in the play of this hand. Not from my play, I didn't do anything out of the ordinary, and I probably didn't steal that pot. With my King for high, there is a good chance that I had the best hand. The lesson comes from the mistake made by the small blind—he could have easily won that pot. I have no idea what his hand was, but I hadn't shown any aggression at all. He knew I was a very aggressive player, and all I did was call before the flop and on the flop. There was no reason for him to think I had much of a hand at all. In fact my play should have suggested that my hand was very weak. Why did he check the turn after taking the lead on the flop? I don't know, but I do know it was a mistake. If he had just continued betting I would have just quietly folded on the river when I missed my draw. The money would have gone to him.

This was a very loose table, and few pots were won by a single bet on the flop. It was unusual for the two players behind me to fold. So his bet on the flop only makes sense if he followed through and continued to bet on the next round. If he had used the information he had about my normal playing style and combined that with the way I was playing that hand, then the natural thing for him to do was just keep betting. He didn't think it through. He didn't really have any kind of plan for the hand, and he didn't really pay much attention to what I was or was not doing. It cost him a pot.

WEAK WHEN STRONG AND STRONG WHEN WEAK

A frequent and very consistent pattern you'll note in players who have a *deception* perspective on the game is the weak-when-strong and strong-when-weak pattern. If such players have a hand in early position like 8♦7♦ and the flop is Q♥8♠8♣, they will always check-raise. They might check-raise on the flop, or they might wait until the turn, but their initial reaction will be to check. They have a strong hand, their initial impulse is to disguise that by checking, and they will follow that impulse. From your perspective the beauty of that pattern is that if they bet when the flop looks like that and you have a hand like A♥Q♦, then you can be almost certain that you have the best hand.

TARGETING PLAYERS

It's important to evaluate the table as a unit rather than individual players. Once you sit down at a table, you need to be concerned with individual players, but in picking a table, a focus on individuals can easily steer you away from a good table or even steer you toward a bad table. The presence of a few very good players at a table is not enough of a reason to avoid that table. You don't need to avoid players who are better than you, as long as there are a few players at the table who play very badly. Money doesn't flow from all the players straight to the best player at the table. It flows from bad players to all the players who play better than them, even if only slightly better. The bad players at a table will lose to everyone, even to other bad players. Don't avoid a table just because it has a few very good players.

By the same token, don't sit at a table just because it has a single very bad player. Unless the limit is very high (30/60 or above), a single bad player will not lose enough money to provide more than a mediocre win to a table full of good players. Most of the losses of a single bad player will be soaked up by the rake.

You need at least two bad players at a table to provide enough losses to cover the rake and have enough left over for the rest of the table to book a meaningful win. The key points are that one very bad player isn't enough and that the more bad players there are, the less each one is losing, even though the wins of the good players are increasing. This illustrates two things about loose games (bad players are always loose players): not only will you win more by playing in very loose games, but also the losers won't go broke as quickly, making loose games longer lasting.

When There Is One Really Bad Player at the Table

Once you've been playing in a cardroom for a while and have gotten to know the players, you'll sometimes run across a player who plays very badly and is almost certain to lose all his money. Usually that alone is enough to make it worthwhile to sit in the game, but not always. First you need to make certain that player isn't already close to losing all his money. If he only has a few chips left, then it probably isn't worth sitting in the game unless the game has other characteristics that would make it profitable. Once you've ascertained that the really bad player still has plenty of chips, you need to consider how your skills compare with the other players at the table. As a general guideline:

1. If seven or eight of the other players are all better players than you, then you should pass the game.
2. If six of them are better than you, you can probably still play if the other two players are worse players than you.
3. If five of the players are better than you, then you can probably still play if at least one of the other three players is worse than you, and the other two are no better than you.
4. If no more than four of the players are better than you, then play.

Target Seats and Flush Draws

As I've mentioned before, in loose games you'll make a large portion of your money from flushes if you play your draws aggressively in a way that keeps many players in on the flop. Seat selection can help you do this.

In a typical lineup of a loose-aggressive game, you'll often have at least one near maniac player, a player who plays a lot of hands and raises with most of them. You'll also often have a player with some FPS symptoms, in particular you'll find players who like to check-raise a lot. When you have a flush draw on the flop, particularly a flush draw with overcards, you want to get as many players calling as many bets as you can. If you have these two players (a maniac and an FPS player) in the right seats, you can do this easily.

If you can sit in between the maniac and the FPS player, with the maniac on your left and the FPS player on your right, then you have a perfect situation to get a maximum number of players to call four bets on the flop. In fact, if you can arrange that seating, the implied odds you get from potential flushes will be large enough to make any two suited cards worth playing in a loose game. The way to play a flush draw in this situation is to check.

The maniac will bet, and he'll get a lot of callers because they know he'll beat almost any hand. The FPS player will raise, you can call, the maniac will reraise, everyone who already has one bet in the pot will call. Now, if the FPS player doesn't put in the last raise, you can do it. When you can get this kind of ideal seat in the right kind of game, this really works—and it's very profitable.

PICKING UP TELLS

One of the things that can help in your game is picking up tells of other flush draws by keeping track of the habits of your opponents. What hands do they play from early position? With some tight players, for example, if you have the Queen of a suit, the board has the King, and the player limped in from early position, he does not have a flush draw. That's because he wouldn't have come in from early position without at least an Ace, King, or Queen, or a pair, and he would have raised with any of the hands with an Ace that he would play from that position.

Pay attention to hands players open with from various positions and start building a Turbo Texas Hold 'Em profile of the players who play in your game regularly.

EVALUATING PLAYERS

Poker is about the exploitation of weakness. To exploit a weakness, you've first got to identify it. You have to study your opponents.

17

Women and Poker

There was a time that poker was a man's game. Of course that's not true anymore—poker has very much become a co-ed game. There are many women poker players today, and they're welcome every place I've ever played. Still, the majority of poker players are men, and men are still men. This works to the advantage of women who understand it and can exploit it. If you're a man, you should be aware of this and take defensive measures.

The majority of successful women poker players are more aggressive than their male counterparts. All successful poker players are aggressive players, but successful women tend to be almost hyperaggressive. They seem to have found success in adapting this style because it usually works well against almost any male poker player. Aggression tends to work well for women because of the way most men perceive and react to hyperaggressive women. You can categorize men poker players according to the way they to react to women at the table.

CHAUVINISTS

There are chauvinistic men who tend to think all women are weak, predictable, tight players. Nothing they see at the table will sway them from this view. They think all women are bad poker players

210

and that they are easy to read. They assume that a bet or raise from a woman simply means that the woman has a very good hand because they think no woman would have the nerve to bet or raise without a near cinch hand. The result is that chauvinistic men tend to fold marginal hands whenever a hyperaggressive woman player bets or raises.

At the same time, chauvinistic players do not think that women have good judgment. Therefore, if he starts out thinking he has a good hand, he isn't likely to change that assessment of his own hand based on anything a woman player does. One interesting characteristic of chauvinistic players is that they also tend to be tight players. This combination of tight and chauvinistic does make it easy for an alert aggressive woman to profit from his reaction to her aggression.

MACHO MAN

Macho men can't stand to let a woman win or take control of the betting. This kind of man can't stand to lose, and especially can't stand to lose to a woman. He'll tend to develop an acute case of FPS trying to outplay an aggressive woman. He's usually doomed.

MR. FLIRT

Flirtatious men like women to think of them as nice guys. They will often just call a raise from a woman with a hand that they would reraise if the raise had come from a man. They'll fold marginal hands when a woman bets. Generally they play too passively against an aggressive woman.

YOU ARE?

There is a fourth group of men who simply treat women as just another poker player. There aren't really very many men in this category. Probably, if you're a man, you belong to one of the three groups I described. Be honest with yourself. Which group are you in? You don't have to tell me, but you need to know. Once you know what group you're in, the adjustment to a hyperaggressive woman is easy. Just don't engage in that kind of behavior.

EXAMPLES

Playing Chauvinistic Men

When faced with an aggressive woman player, chauvinistic men tend to react with hyperaggression of their own when they fear their hand is second best. They try to win by psychological domination and intimidation. When they think they do have the best hand, they'll often play aggressively, but not hyperaggressively. They go on tilt and react predictably, overextending themselves with second-best hands.

For example, say a tight, chauvinistic player has opened with a raise from an early position. You should raise with most hands. Even a hand like 8♠5♦ is worth raising with. The reason for the raise is to begin a determination of whether he has a big pair or two big cards. Because he opened with a raise from an early position he almost surely has one of those two hands. Either something like A♥A♦ or A♦K♠. Whatever your hand is, just raise. He'll reraise.

If the flop comes something like A♠10♦2♣ and he bets, you should probably give it up right there. Just fold. If the flop comes something like J♦8♣4♥ and he bets, you should raise.

If he reraises then you can be pretty sure he has two overcards and you have the best hand, but you should just call. The reason you should just call is to encourage him to bet again on the turn and the river. Unless an Ace or King comes on one of the last two cards you can be fairly sure your pair of 8s is the best hand. If no big cards come by the river, you can sometimes even raise for value on the river. He'll call you with an A♦K♠.

If he just calls your raise, you should worry that he has a large overpair, but the good thing that will probably happen now is that he'll check on the turn, thinking you'll bet and he can check-raise. Disappoint him. Check. If you don't improve to three of a kind or two pair, then you should probably fold when he bets on the river.

This kind of behavior is very predictable with a chauvinistic player when he's playing against an aggressive woman.

Playing Macho Man

You should play against a macho player in a similar way that you'd play against a chauvinist, but you need to be more careful. The macho player is not as likely to try to play deceptively when he has as big a hand as the chauvinistic player. He's more likely to just play any hand he has aggressively. With the chauvinist player, you can often be sure you have the best hand, even when your hand is weak. That's not the case with the macho player. With him you need to be much more selective with which hands you get involved.

You probably don't want to get heads-up in a pot with a macho player with a hand like 8♠5♦, but you might want to with a hand like 8♦7♦. With that hand you're more likely to have a few extra outs like a three-flush or a three-straight, just in case he actually has you beat. Usually though, if the flop is like the second flop discussed, he won't have you beat and he'll just keep raising anyway.

Playing Mr. Flirt

The primary benefit from playing with a flirtatious player is that he isn't likely to raise. If he has a really good hand, he'll usually just tell you. For example, let's say you've got A♦J♠, and the flop is J♥8♥4♦. If you bet and he calls, you can sometimes just ask him, "Do you have a flush draw?" He'll tell you. If the next card is a Heart, ask him, "Did you make a flush?" Again, he'll tell you. This can save you a lot of bets.

Even if you don't ask him and he did make a flush, you can still bet without fear of a raise. If by chance he does raise, he'll do so apologetically, saying something like, "I really don't like to raise, but with this hand I really have to." If something like that happens, you can just fold.

18

Spread-Limit Games

Spread-limit games don't have fixed bet sizes. They are structured with a maximum bet, and you can bet any amount from $1 to the maximum for the betting round. The first thing to keep in mind when playing spread-limit games is that you should almost always bet or raise the maximum amount. An exception is when you're just calling, then call whatever the bet is.

Sometimes spread-limit games are structured to allow the same betting range at every betting round. An example of that is 1-5. Some spread-limit games double the maximum allowable bet on the turn. An example of that is 1-4-8-8.

No matter how the spread-limits are structured, spread-limit games tend to have two things in common:

1. The blinds are small compared with the maximum bet.
2. The initial pre-flop bet is small compared with bets on future rounds.

The small blinds and small initial bets mean that it's sometimes correct to play very tight in these games. It's sometimes correct to play very loose. Which you choose depends on the particular game conditions.

TIGHT VERSUS LOOSE PLAY

Pot Odds and Tight Play

In most spread-limit games, there isn't much money in the pot to start with. In many 1-5 games, for example, you only have one blind, $1. The rake is going to be larger than that if there is any action, so you're not competing for much money at all. The competing-for-the-ante-perspective suggests you should play very, very tight if no one else has entered the pot.

Implied Odds and Loose Play

At the same time, the initial bet size tends to be very small compared with the later bet size. So, the implied odds are good, and a money-and-odds perspective suggests that loose play really is correct.

A MIXED STRATEGY

What should you do? Play tight? Play loose? Well, as you might guess, the answer is that it depends on game conditions, but generally you should do both. You should play tight and you should play loose. Before the flop you should usually play tighter than normal from early position. This is because there simply isn't enough initial money in the pot to compensate for your chances of a raise, but if someone else has opened, you should call much more liberally than normal from late position. This is because you're getting large implied odds to try to outdraw an early position opener.

Passive Games

In a passive game, you should see a lot of flops. You can do so cheaply compared with the size of future bets, and you're getting good implied odds to play drawing hands, even if the game is tight.

If the game is loose, you should play most of the speculative and gambling hands.

You should fold most hands on the flop. If you don't flop a very good hand or a very good draw, just give it up and try another one. If there was no raise before the flop, then you won't be getting any pot odds for a draw. Loose pre-flop and tight on the flop is the way to play a passive spread-limit game.

Aggressive Games

Pre-flop raises in spread-limit games tend to destroy any implied odds you might get. You should play very tightly before the flop in an aggressive game. However, if there is some raising before the flop, the pot is likely large enough to loosen up some on the flop, and you can play a few more marginal draws. Often the maximum bet doubles on either the turn or the river in spread-limit games. In these games you should especially loosen up some on the flop. In an aggressive spread-limit game, you should usually play tighter pre-flop and looser after the flop.

Loose Games

In a loose game, it takes a fairly strong hand to open the pot if you're first to act from an early position. If the game is very passive and you don't have much reason to fear a raise, you can sometimes call an early position raiser with drawing hands or speculative hands. This is because the situation of two or three early position callers often tends to draw in late players with weak holdings.

The drawing hands, speculative hands, and gambling hands require progressively higher odds to be profitably playable. Most of those higher odds come from implied odds—from bets on future betting rounds. In loose spread-limit games where the initial bet is very small compared with bets on later rounds, these implied odds are often large.

Tight Games

In tight games, when you're in late position and an early position player has called, you should usually only call with the dominating power hands. When you only have one or two opponents, you need to play hands that have a fairly good chance of starting out as better hands. That's because you're getting weak odds to begin with, and your implied odds with few callers are also low.

LOOSE-WEAK PLAYERS IN SPREAD-LIMIT GAMES

We often think of the hands that need implied odds as playable if a certain number of callers have entered the pot, but that's not really correct in spread-limit games. Often these games will be populated by loose players before the flop who play much tighter on the later betting rounds.

Your implied odds do tend to go up as the number of callers increases, but it's not an exact relationship. When you have a game where a lot of players see the flop, but only the best one or two hands go past the flop, your implied odds are not very high. You see this frequently in spread-limit games.

When you have this kind of loose player in the game, you don't really have very high implied odds because you won't have more than one or two players calling bets on the flop and after. In this kind of spread-limit game, you should make your pre-flop hand selections more as if it's a tight game.

As the number of callers goes up, many of the speculative and gambling hands become playable. More important than the number of callers is who those callers are. It's important to catalog the kinds of mistakes your opponents make.

19

Double Bet
on the End Games

In some areas of the country, primarily in the South, you'll find structured games where the bet size doubles on the turn and again on the river. For the river bet, players have an option to either bet the size of the turn bet or to bet double that amount. Typical examples are 3/6/12 or 10/20/40. On the river, you have a choice between betting $6 or $12 in a 3/6/12 game and $20 or $40 in a 10/20/40 game.

A 10/20/40 game will have two blinds, of $5 and $10, just like a 10/20 game. The only difference is the larger bet option on the end. This difference potentially has huge implications for hand value and strategy. The large river bet primarily benefits drawing hands, even with game conditions that aren't very loose. These are implied-odds games.

There is a perception among many poker writers that the double bet on the end games favors the bad players over the good players. This isn't true if you have a reasonable definition of what it means to be a good player. My definition of a good player is one who can recognize and exploit opportunities. A double bet on the end game provides many opportunities. You just have to be good enough to adapt to and exploit them.

BEFORE THE FLOP

Power Hands

You should probably not open from an early position with the dominated power hands in this type of game structure.

Drawing Hands

With this kind of game structure, the drawing hands are generally worth playing whenever you would ordinarily play the dominating power hands. It's usually worth opening from an early position with the drawing hands (excluding dominated power hands).

Speculative and Gambling Hands

In a situation where you would normally play drawing hands, you should probably play speculative hands in this structure. Also, in those situations where you'd usually play speculative hands, you should probably play the gambling hands.

Suited Hands

With very loose table conditions and a double bet on the end, many suited cards are worth playing. In the extreme I'll sometimes play any two suited cards in a spread-limit game with a double bet on the end and very loose table conditions. The implied odds from the flush potential are huge.

AFTER THE FLOP

Because of the fast, persistent escalation of the bet size, the implied odds for drawing hands are very large. That means that medium-strength–made hands like the top pair or an overpair are at great risk on the turn and river. These hands won't usually get paid off on the later rounds by lesser hands but will often be raised by better hands. This is where it's very important to know the players in these games. The top pair should frequently just fold if raised on the turn or river. This is especially true on the river where very few players will bluff a raise. Remember, with an escalating bet size, a raise on the river costs eight times as much as a bet on the flop. This is a big difference, and it tends to hinder the already few players who are capable of a bluff raise.

ON THE RIVER

When the bet size doubles on the river, it's often good to wait until then to raise. In a game where the bet size increases on the turn and the river (like 3/6/12), a raise or check-raise on the river can be a major source of your win.

However, many players in these games will turn passive on the river bet, checking the hand down rather than betting. So, if you delay a raise to the river, you need to be sure, and you must know the players. Make certain they will actually bet.

You also need to know the players if you intend to try to set up a check-raise on the river. Many of them won't cooperate and will simply showdown anything less than the nuts if you check to them on the river.

20

Kill Games

Some rooms have games with a required kill if certain conditions are met, such as winning the last pot. These are called kill games, or winner-blind games. Depending on the cardroom, if a pot reaches a certain threshold size, or if the same player wins two pots in a row, the winner is required to straddle an amount twice the size of the big blind, and the betting limits for that hand are doubled. This can sometimes change the ratio of bet size to initial blinds enough so that significant changes in playing strategy are called for.

TRADITIONAL VIEW OF KILL GAMES

Most players tend to think of kill games as just a way to play for higher stakes and to generate action. When the conditions for a kill occur, the stakes will be raised for the next hand, hence, on average, you're really playing for higher limits then the nominal limits would suggest. Also, when the kill is on, there are usually three blinds. The more live blinds, the more money the pot starts with, and the more players who will usually compete at least as far as the flop. Hence, more action.

A STRATEGIC VIEW OF KILL GAMES

The primary change in strategy occurs at the nominal structure, without the kill. If the kill is triggered by the pot reaching a certain threshold size, then the value of draws goes down significantly. The reason for this is that draws tend to win larger pots, and the pot-size threshold is likely to be triggered by making a draw. Because some of the money won will have to be put back in the form of a kill-straddle for the next hand, the pot is never as large as it seems when you're on a draw.

In a game without the kill, an Ace-high flush draw is worth a raise on the flop so long as you're fairly sure that you'll get two callers to the raise, but with a kill, because winning a large pot means you have to put up an extra blind the next hand, you'll need to be sure that you're getting at least three callers for a raise with an Ace-high flush draw. In some situations this can significantly reduce the value of a draw.

PRE-FLOP ADJUSTMENTS

To adjust for this possibility of reducing the effective pot by having to take out money to straddle the next hand, you should play a little tighter pre-flop. Specifically, some of the weaker drawing hands should probably not be played, and you should be less willing to call a pre-flop raise with suited connectors or suited Aces with small- or medium-sized kickers. The risk of triggering the kill reduces the implied odds of these hands.

21

Short-handed Games

Short-handed games are fast-paced, aggressive games. Passive play is generally always losing play. In short-handed games, passive play is a very fast way to lose.

You won't go far wrong if you play a five-handed game as if it were a ten-handed game where the first five players have folded. You won't go far wrong if you use that approach, but you will go wrong. The distribution of hands in a short-handed game will be about the same as the distribution of hands in a full game where the first few players have folded. It's not exact, but it's close. The difference is that the blinds are moving around much faster in a short-handed game.

The initial amount of money in the pot in the form of the blinds is the same whether it's a ten-handed game or a five-handed game, but in the short-handed game, the average amount each player is contributing is twice what it is in a full game. The effect of that is to increase the importance of winning more than your share of the blinds.

The major strategy adjustment for a short-handed game is to play slightly looser and a lot more aggressively than you would in a full game with the same position. Continue this strategy after the flop. Semi-bluff draws aggressively. Play the top pair as a very strong hand, and play the second and even third pair as a strong hand. Unrelenting aggression is the key to winning at short-handed games.

PRE-FLOP IN SHORT-HANDED GAMES

I'm going to consider a short-handed game as four-handed. In a game with more players, you can usually consider it a full game, and the first few players have folded. For example, if you're in a six-handed game, you won't go far wrong by just playing as if the first four players folded.

In a game with fewer than four players, the individual playing habits of your opponents become the most important consideration. When four-handed, the first two players have blinds, the last player has the button, and the UTG player is between them. Position is important when short-handed so the UTG player will almost always want to open with a raise. If you get any callers, you don't want the button to be one of them; you want only the blinds to call so that you'll have position after the flop. Raising is the best way to accomplish this, but the button will call with a lot of hands, so you will want to be selective when UTG, even in a short-handed game.

Short-handed Hold 'Em is a high-card game. It's a struggle for the antes, a contest between a made hand and a draw, and a game of hand domination. It's a game of pairs and big cards, but it's also a game of manipulation and pressure and a game of strategy and deception. The particular perspective you should emphasize in a short-handed game depends on the other players in the game.

Against Tough Players

Most of the time you shouldn't even play a game where the other players are tough, good players, but there are times when a game gets temporarily short-handed and you will want to keep the game going even though you're only competing against tough players. Only do this if you know it's a temporary situation and that other, weak players will be showing up soon. Against tough opponents, not only will you find it difficult to win consistently, but you'll also tend to experience much wider than normal swings in your results.

Hand domination is the key when playing against tough players. You just need to have the best hand. When you're short-handed, then it sometimes doesn't take much to have the best hand. A 9 is often a big card in a short-handed game.

A hand that has two cards, 9 or larger, is worth opening with a raise. A single Ace often has enough high-card value on its own that it's worth opening with a raise with any suited Ace and unsuited Aces as long as the kicker is at least about a 7 or higher. A King doesn't quite have the high-card value of an Ace, but suited Kings with a kicker at a 6 or higher are usually worth playing. Some of the midlevel connectors are also worth playing even though they don't have much high-card value, for example, 8♠6♠.

When you're on the button or the small blind and no one else has opened yet, you can play more aggressively. Raising with any Ace is often correct.

You might want to sometimes limp in with hands a little weaker than suggested by the table. In a short-handed game, the second pair is often enough to win, and with hands like 7♠5♠, it's worth seeing the flop if you can do so cheaply. Don't overdo it if the players are really tough. If you do this, it's a good idea to also limp with your very best hands, so that your opponents won't start automatically raising whenever you limp. Hands that are worth limping and then reraising if raised include big pairs, 10♥10♦ and higher, and the big suited aces, A♠J♠ and higher. If you limp and reraise with these hands and also limp with weaker hands like 8♠5♠ or 3♥3♦, you won't have to worry about becoming too readable.

Against Tight-Passive Opponents

You should play a lot more hands against tight-passive opponents for two reasons: first, they'll often give up before the flop, allowing you to steal a lot of blinds; and second, when they do call, they'll tend to continue to call when your hand is best but won't raise when their hand is best.

Against this kind of opponent, you will probably want to play all your hands with a raise because of the good chance that they'll just fold and you'll win the blinds—but you don't want to get too carried away. You should probably still avoid the very small pairs and the unsuited Aces and Kings with very small kickers. Deuces and treys just don't have much value.

Against Loose-Passive Opponents

Against loose players you won't get many chances to steal the blinds; they'll call, but they'll continue to call far past the point where they're clearly beaten. Because of that you can play many hands against loose-passive opponents if you play just fairly well after the flop.

Any pair, any Ace, and most suited Kings are strong hands in a short-handed game against loose-passive opponents. Even pocket pairs as weak as 2♦2♥ can be played strongly after the flop with the right kind of flop and the right kind of player. For example, say you open with a raise and only the big blind calls, then he checks when the flop is Q♦9♥8♠. Against a loose-passive player, you'll often get a call from a hand like 7♦5♥ if you bet. Most players will fold on the river even if they pair one of their cards if you just keep betting. I'm not saying you should always bet in this situation, but it's always something you should give serious consideration to against loose-passive opponents. Against passive opponents you can get the maximum return when you're best, but they won't extract the maximum from you when they're best.

Loose-Aggressive Opponents

If those loose opponents also tend to get a little aggressive, the situation has changed a lot. You'll need to tighten up quite a bit. Aggressive players will be extracting as much as they can from you those times they're best so you need to avoid those situations as much as possible. You don't want to entirely avoid them, you do want to go after loose players aggressively, you just want to be more careful when they're likely to be shooting back.

Against aggressive opponents you should tighten up, particularly with unsuited cards and with very low cards. Avoid very low pairs and unsuited hands such as A♥4♦. When playing against aggressive opponents, you want to have hands that are likely to have a little something extra to fall back on. For example, a hand like A♥4♥ and a flop like K♥5♦4♠ has a little more going for it than a hand like A♥4♦ and a flop like K♥7♦4♠. When your opponents are aggressive, that little extra can mean a lot by the time the night's over.

A Maniac in the Game

Maniac players can be frustrating. The strategy adjustments you need to make when a maniac is in the game don't always follow conventional wisdom. That can be especially true in short-handed games. Conventional wisdom suggests that it's best to act after other active players, but that's not always the case with a maniac in the game.

If the other players are fairly tight, before the flop you often can do better with the maniac acting after you, but before the tight players. As an example, suppose you have a hand like 10♠8♠ UTG and there is a maniac on the button with an 8♦6♥ and a tight player on one of the blinds with Q♥10♦. If you open with a raise, and the maniac reraises, the tight player is likely to fold his hand. That leaves you with a situation where you're heads-up with the maniac with a hand that dominates his. If the positions of the maniac and the tight player were reversed, then the tight player would probably call your raise before the flop with the Q♥10♦ in late position, leaving you with a three-handed contest where your hand is the one dominated.

Opening Hands When UTG in a Four-Handed Game

Against tough opponents	4♠4♣	A♠2♠	A♥7♦	K♠6♠	K♥9♦
	Q♠9♠	Q♥9♦	J♠9♠	J♥9♦	10♠9♠
	10♥9♦	9♠7♠	9♥8♦	8♠6♠	
Against tight-passive opponents	4♠4♣	A♠2♠	A♥5♦	K♠5♠	K♥9♦
	Q♠7♠	Q♥9♦	J♠7♠	J♥9♦	10♠7♠
	10♥8♦	9♠6♠	9♥8♦	8♠5♠	7♠5♠
	6♠5♠				
Against loose-passive opponents	2♠2♣	A♠2♠	A♥2♦	K♠4♠	K♥9♦
	Q♠7♠	Q♥9♦	J♠7♠	J♥9♦	10♠6♠
	10♥8♦	9♠8♠	9♥8♦	8♠7♠	
Against loose-aggressive opponents	6♠6♣	A♠2♠	A♥5♦	K♠8♠	K♥J♦
	Q♠8♠	Q♥10♦	J♠8♠	J♥10♦	
	10♠9♠	10♥9♦	9♠8♠	8♠7♠	
Maniac on the button (others tight)	4♠4♣	A♠2♠	A♥8♦	K♠8♠	K♥J♦
	Q♠9♠	Q♥10♦	J♠8♠	J♥9♦	10♠8
	10♥9♦	9♠8♠	8♠7♠		
Maniac on the blind (others tight)	5♠5♣	A♠4♠	A♥8♦	K♠8♠	K♥10♦
	Q♠9♠	Q♥10♦	J♠9♠	J♥10♦	10♠9♠
	9♠8♠				
Maniac on the button (others loose)	4♠4♣	A♠2♠	A♥7♦	K♠5♠	K♥10♦
	Q♠8♠	Q♥10♦	J♠8♠	J♥10♦	10♠9♠
Maniac on the blind (others loose)	4♠4♣	A♠2♠	A♥8♦	K♠7♠	K♥10♦
	Q♠9♠	Q♥10♦	J♠9♠	J♥10♦	10♠9♠

Legend: A pair, such as 5♠5♣, means a pair of 5s and any larger pair.
A♠4♠ means an Ace with a card of the same suit, 4 or higher.
Q♥10♦ means a Queen with a card, of any suit, 10 or higher.
Other hands should be interpreted similarly.

Of course, this example is contrived, but it illustrates the point that having the maniac on your immediate left allows you to manipulate the betting pre-flop in way that more than compensates for the lack of position you'll have after the flop. You can do the same thing, of course, by sitting to the maniac's left and reraising whenever he opens with a raise. The key is for the other players to act after you and the maniac before you. The key is to isolate him and eliminate the tight players. If you can do that, then you can play much weaker hands than you can if you can't accomplish it.

If the rest of the field is mostly loose players, isolation of the maniac isn't as likely to work and you generally need to play fewer hands. You'll have to give up a lot of hands before the flop. By sticking to premium starting hands, you should more than make up for the loss of blinds while you're waiting for them by getting multiway action when you do play.

22

Tournaments

A tournament is a poker game where everyone starts with the same number of chips and usually plays until only one player remains with chips. Generally the blinds and limits of the game are raised at fixed times in order to force the action and ensure that the tournament ends within a reasonable time. The exact structure differs from event to event.

In some cases you can buy more chips within the first hour or some other specified period. Sometimes you have to lose all your current chips to be eligible to buy more, sometimes not. Some tournaments don't allow rebuys at all.

The payout schedule differs from event to event. Seldom does that last player get all the money, a certain percentage goes to second place, third place, and so on.

A winning strategy for tournament play is not the same as a winning strategy for a regular poker game. Tournament strategy depends on the particulars of the event: the rebuy policy, the payout schedule, and the escalation of blinds and limits. I'm not going to talk about specific tournament strategy in this book—just a little about tournaments themselves.

You can find tournaments with buy-ins as low as $10. Small buy-in tournaments can be an excellent way to learn a new game while keeping a limit on your risk. They are different from "ring games" (the term for a regular full game), but the mechanics of the play is the same in tournaments and ring games.

In a tournament you can't pick your seat, and you can't pick your table. Because these are the two most important factors in determining whether you're a winning poker player, the skills needed to win at tournaments are very different from the skills needed to win in ring games, but tournaments do provide an excellent training ground for the aspects of play that involve picking your cards.

PLAYING STRATEGIES

There are two major considerations in developing a playing strategy for a tournament: the structure and the players. By structure I mean the size of the blinds relative to the number of playing chips and the speed that the blinds escalate. When players have few chips relative to the blinds, they are often forced to play weaker hands than they might otherwise play, and the players with larger stacks will often play more aggressively than normal when they are competing for a pot with a player who has a small stack.

You won't likely be playing at any particular table for a long period of time, so you'll need to rely on stereotypes of your opponents when devising a strategy to exploit other players' mistakes. The structure and the players are what's important in any poker game and, in that respect, tournaments are no different.

STAGES OF THE EVENT

It's convenient to think of a tournament as consisting of three distinct stages. The strategic considerations differ according to the stage of the event. The beginning stages usually involve players aggressively trying to achieve an early advantage. At the middle stages, players are focusing more on a consolidation, it's much slower paced. The final stages pick up speed somewhat when the size of the blinds grows to be significant in relation to the chips.

The Early Stage—Rebuy Period

In most small tournaments, in the early stage of the event, the blinds start low and increase every twenty or thirty minutes. Even in events with large initial blinds, the small tournaments allow for rebuys in the early stages of the event, and your effective stack size is more than its actual size during this stage. It is important to be aware of the tournament stage and when the blinds will increase.

Early in the tournament, the blinds are low enough so that you can play good drawing hands, small pocket pairs, and other more speculative hands, just like in a live game. You really don't need to be making any adjustments for the tournament structure in this early stage.

The Middle Stage—Consolidation

After the rebuy period, things are different. The blinds will increase, making it sometimes as much as 25 percent of an average stack to just see the flop. Most of the players will be playing much tighter and be more cautious than they had been in the early stage. You have to wait for the big pairs or high cards of the power hands. You won't be getting enough odds to support playing drawing hands.

Your weaker opponents will not make this adjustment and will continue to play hands like Jack, 10 suited, which can be a strong hand in a limit game with many callers. You can take advantage of this selectively.

If the game becomes head-to-head and your opponent has a short stack and you are planning on calling, you should raise so your opponent has to put them all in. That way he has to make a call or fold decision. If he loses, you have knocked him out of the tournament. However, because he was short stacked, the loss should not hurt you too much if he wins.

If, however, your opponent has a much larger stack than you, you need to consider what you know about the player and play accordingly. Keep in mind, good tournament players will also be aware of your stack size, and they will play you accordingly. If possible, avoid getting into a head-to-head situation with a strong tournament player who also has a larger stack than you have.

I would not suggest trying this with some of the weaker opponents. Let's assume you have played well, luck has been with you, and you make it to the final table. As play continues, all of a sudden, it is down to the final four. This is a short-handed game, and most of your opponents are not very skilled in this area. This is the best way to eliminate an opponent.

The Late Stage—Final Table

Toward the end of the tournament, there will usually be a large mismatch among stack sizes. There will be a few players without many chips, and a few with large stacks of chips. At the late stages, most players will be picking their spots, as you should be doing. Pick your spots aggressively. Don't get involved in multiplayer situations, but play aggressive heads-up poker. This is particularly true if you have a large stack and your opponent has a small stack.

When the game gets short-handed, play it as a short-handed game. Play aggressively, but be cautious. You should be betting, not calling, unless you're trapping someone. Any two big cards are gold. Any one big card has value. The blinds are so high that on any hand you and/or your opponent are in jeopardy of being eliminated. Lots of blind stealing goes on here. You better get your share. Pick your spots where your opponents are showing weakness. But also watch out and don't get caught in a trap. With a huge hand, A,A, K,K, and so on, be the trapper. Don't be afraid to slow play here because you are not likely to get drawn out like in a low-limit game.

THE PLAYERS

Johnny Davis is a successful tournament player who's also a friend of mine. He's played in a lot of small tournaments in various locations and has developed a profile of opponent sterotypes that he's found useful. I'm presenting them here.

Live Player

This is the player who plays live games but does not have much tournament experience. This player is likely to play a tournament just like it was a live game. If they are aggressive in live games, they will be aggressive here also. If they are a rock in live games, they will be the same here. The problem for aggressive players is that if they are not hitting the flops, they will soon run out of chips. This type of player usually plans for three or more buy-ins in a live game. In a tournament, when you're out of chips, you're out of the tournament. The aggressive live player will bust out soon or build up lots of chips and could win. The problem for rocks in a tournament is they play so conservatively that they never build up enough chips to really be competitive. Against the aggressive live players, only play hands where you are the favorite. Against rock live players, you can win some pots with a semi-bluff and occasionally with an outright bluff.

Casual Player

Many players who enter small tournaments are not regular poker players. The buy-in is small enough and the payoff big enough that they are willing to take a shot. These players have almost no chance of winning. They make a lot of mistakes and you can spot them very quickly. Just play solid poker against them, and you will win.

Big-Limit Player

Many of the players who regularly play pot limit and 20/40 and above will enter tournaments just as a break. They consider the entry fee as loose change, and it is no big deal to lose it. They would like the payoff at the end, but are playing more for ego. These players like to gamble and will bluff much more than any other players. You can slow play these types and get big payoffs. There's not much in between for these players, they either get busted out early, or you will see them at the final table.

Tournament Player

Many players focus more on tournaments, and you rarely see them in a live game. They know the strategy, how to play the players, how to manage the stack, when to lay down a big hand because making it to the next level is more important than winning that particular hand. Your best bet against these players is to stay out of their way and let one of the aggressive or big-limit players bust them out.

Solid Player

This is the player who has lots of both live and tournament experience. They play a strong tight-aggressive live game and know how to alter their game for a tournament. They are the players I fear most. They will not make many mistakes, and you had better not make any against them. You just have to be careful and hope you get better cards, flops, and opportunities than they do.

Position

We know how important position is in poker. It is important in tournaments also, but being first to act, especially if you have a large stack, is sometimes better than being last to act. Middle position is the worst. If you are first, and it is late in the tournament, and you can bet enough to put your opponents all-in before the flop, you are forcing them to make a big decision. The correct decision, even if they have a good hand, is sometimes to fold because staying alive is more important than winning the pot.

23

No-Limit
and Pot-Limit Poker

In no-limit poker, the bet size is limited only by the number of chips you have on the table. You can bet all your chips at any time. So, typically, the bets on later betting rounds are much larger than the bets on the early rounds. This makes no-limit poker a game of implied odds. If you can see the flop cheaply, many hands are worth calling a small pre-flop bet because if you get lucky with the flop, you can get a very large payoff.

I'm going to point out a couple of major strategic differences. You need to think about things a little differently in no-limit.

DON'T CALL

In a limit game, whenever I'm faced with a decision about a call I always first think about raising. In a big-bet game, whenever I'm faced with a decision about a call, I always first think about folding. That's the main difference between the two structures.

Am I Beaten?

In pot-limit or no-limit, you always have to ask yourself, "Am I beaten?" Do not ask what are the odds that I'm beaten; ask, "Am

I beaten?" There is a huge difference between those questions. I started playing casino poker in no-limit games. When I later played limit games, I didn't start being a consistent winner in them until I stopped asking myself the "Am I beaten?" question. If you move from limit games to no-limit, you won't become a winner until you *do* ask that question.

POT-LIMIT

A related form of betting structure is pot-limit. In pot-limit you can bet any amount up to the size of the pot, so you can't make a really big bet in pot-limit unless you've first made the pot large. That puts slow play as a premium tactic in pot-limit. Other than the extra importance of slow play, pot-limit and no-limit are very similar.

A SAMPLE HAND

This hand was played by an acquaintance of mine in a small pot-limit game. I think it illustrates a couple of things about pot-limit and no-limit poker that are important. First, it shows the importance of implied odds, and second, it shows the importance of just folding when it looks like you're beaten.

Pre-flop

Our hero is on the blind with 7♠7♦. An early position player limped in (only called the $5 blind), and a late position player called. Our hero thought about raising, but didn't.

I think he was right not to raise. In pot-limit, it's often a good idea to put in a pre-flop raise with a pocket pair because if you do flop a set, you want the pot to be large so that you can make a large bet. In this situation, however, a raise was too dangerous. The early position player was likely to have been limping with a large pair, intending to reraise any late raise.

The Flop

The flop was J♠J♦7♥, giving our hero a full house. Pretty good flop for 7♠7♦. Our hero checked, hoping that one of the other players would bet. Checking was probably the right thing to do here. At this point the pot has only $15 in it. That's the most our hero could bet. If someone else bets first, he can then raise a larger amount. Let's see what happens.

The original opener bets $15. The late position player calls. Now the pot has $45 in it. Our hero can raise $60 now ($45 plus the $15 from the hero's call). Our hero raises.

So far, so good. Even though we've got the smallest possible full house, it appears unlikely that either of the other two players have a full house. They probably have hands like Q♠Q♥ or A♥J♥.

The original bettor folds. The late position caller raises $180. Our hero calls the raise.

Now we've screwed up. Our hero's thinking was that the guy probably had something like A♥J♥. Until that last raise, this was probably a good guess, but in pot-limit and no-limit especially, you need to constantly use new information to reevaluate the situation. Here we have a player who's been quietly calling every bet until now, when the pot has gotten very large. Only now does he take the initiative and raise. This is the behavior of a big hand. This player has a full house, and any full house will beat the full house that our pair of sevens makes. This is when you need to ask the question, "Am I beaten?" The only answer to that question is yes. It's time to fold.

In a pot-limit or no-limit game, play loose, play aggressive, don't call. If you never called a raise, you'd only be making a small mistake.

PART THREE

Special Situations

This part of the book contains some chapters that didn't seem to fit anywhere else because they don't involve strategic or tactical issues. It only has three chapters: on cheating, on playing for a living, and on self-awareness. The commonality of the chapters in this part of the book is a focus on awareness—awareness of your surroundings and of yourself.

24

Cheating

Cheating is not a big problem in poker, but it's widespread. That's not a self-contradictory statement. It means that I think a lot of cheating goes on, but most of it is so trivial or so inept that it isn't going to cost you much money. Some players are more likely to cheat than others, and some forms of cheating are more dangerous to your bankroll than other forms.

KINDS OF CHEATING

Cheating can take as many forms as your imagination can come up with, but I'll talk about three common ones: cold-decking, hold-outs, and player collusion.

Cold-decking

"Cold-decking" is when the deck is preset and introduced into the game with a false shuffle. Of course, the idea is to give you a very good, but second-best, hand. You don't see cold-decks in cardrooms much, because the players don't get a chance to get their hands on the deck when the house provides a dealer, but this form of cheating is starting to make a resurgence in jackpot games.

In a jackpot game, there is a special prize pool kept for bad beats. A bad beat is defined as getting a good hand (like Aces-full in most jackpot games) beaten. The prize is awarded to the two players involved in the bad beat. Sometimes this prize can get very large— $40,000 or more. A lot of money tends to attract a lot of thieves. There have been a few cases recently of teams of players and dealers colluding to cold-deck jackpot games.

Hold-outs

A hold-out artist holds cards out of the game. When he's dealt a card like an Ace, he'll just try to keep it, so that from that point on he's playing with an extra card. The best defense against a hold-out artist is for the dealer to frequently count down the deck and make sure he's got fifty-two cards. You'll often see dealers counting down the stub of the deck when they are finished dealing a hand. Some dealers do it habitually, other dealers only do it when they suspect a hold-out artist is in the game.

Collusion

Collusion by good players is very tough to win against. Player "collusion" is when two players use prearranged signals to trade information about their hands. They can get small edges this way by folding when their cards cancel each other in some way, for example, if they both have two Hearts. One edge that colluding players get is when one of them has a very, very good hand and they trap you in between them while they raise and reraise each other. However, such behavior will likely be noticed rather quickly. The really insidious, and difficult to detect, collusion is simple signals that allow them to fold one of the hands and play the best hand. If good players are colluding, it's very hard to defend against it. Luckily, most colluding cheats don't play well and often don't use the extra information they obtain from the signals correctly.

PROTECTION AGAINST CHEATS

Don't make the mistake of thinking that everyone who seems to get lucky is cheating. Cheating is not that prevalent. If you suspect cheating, tell the floorman your suspicions. That's about all you can do. If you're reasonably certain that someone is cheating, just don't play in that game.

Don't ever directly accuse another player of cheating. If you have strong suspicions, you should discreetly discuss your suspicisons with the floorman.

WHO IS LIKELY TO CHEAT

It's been my experience that the most likely kind of poker player to become a cheat is a mediocre poker pro who thinks that he somehow "deserves" to win because he's a better player than others.

Let's ignore the question of whether he really is a better player than others. Such a player might very well rationalize cheating with the same kind of thinking that I mentioned earlier about copyright. He'll convince himself that he's only speeding up the process, not really taking something that's not rightfully his.

That kind of rationalization is common in employee theft. Back in the 1950s, a book called *Other People's Money* was published (it's still required reading for graduate students in criminology) based on hundreds of interviews of people convicted of embezzlement. The author of that book identified three characteristics of embezzlers:

1. They have a "hidden need." They need money for some reason that would cause them embarrassment to reveal. It might be a drinking or drug problem, it might be marital problems, or maybe just personal financial problems. Whatever it is, it's of a nature that they don't feel free to share the problem with others—they don't feel like they can talk about it with others,

generally because of the potential for embarrassment. A financial planner facing bankruptcy would be an example.

2. They have opportunity. They have a job that gives them easy access to someone else's money.

3. They develop a rationalization. Generally this is either that they are only "borrowing" the money and will put it back, or it's that they are somehow "owed" the money for some imagined reason.

Subsequent research over the last forty years has found these three factors to be common across a wide range of employee theft.

I think this kind of situation also leads to cheating by poker players. Cheating at poker is more akin to employee theft than it is to burglary or robbery.

1. It's common for a mediocre poker pro to run into an extended losing streak. Often they are too embarrassed to talk about it. They are often afraid for others to find out about it for two reasons: first, they are afraid that other pros will think they are playing with scared money and will start taking shots at them, and second, they realize that there is a possibility that they are having a losing streak because they don't play as well as they think and their ego won't let them consider this possibility. That's the hidden need part of the criteria.

2. Most poker pros are well aware of many methods of cheating and are good enough to do it if they want. It's not that tough to hold out an Ace. That's the opportunity part of the criteria.

3. Many poker pros have the attitude that people who they think of as bad players don't deserve to win. They approach the game based on a idea of sharks versus minnows where the minnows have no rights that need to be respected. They basically look at weaker players with disdain.

Whenever you see a poker player who fits these three criteria, you've found a poker player with the potential of becoming a cheat. That does not mean that a player with those characteristics is likely to become a thief—it's not a predictive criminological theory; it is an explanatory theory.

This theory does help you identify poker players who are not likely to become cheats. A player who isn't shamed by losing streaks and who generally likes the people he plays with isn't likely to ever become a thief.

ETHICS AND ANGLES

More then outright cheating, you'll see a lot of angle shooting or just a general lack of ethics. By "angle shooting" I mean an attempt to gain an advantage by a ploy which is technically not cheating but is close to it. An example of angle shooting would be to make a vague wave of your hand on the river, indicating a check. Then if your opponent checks and shows down his hand, you claim you didn't check and you want to bet. This ploy often works if you're careful to wave your hand in a check when the dealer isn't looking at you.

This particular angle is fairly easy to protect yourself against. If there is any vagueness at all to a player's movements, which you think might indicate a check, just ask the dealer if the other player has checked. If you do fall victim to this angle, by the way, you should usually call. Players who pull this angle will usually only bet after they've seen your hand if they can't beat it.

Illegal Sharing of Information

One form of cheating, which is probably more of an ethical violation in the sense that it's an opportunistic form of cheating, is sharing information about others' hands with a friend. It's a form of collusion, which is cheating, but it sometimes arises at the spur of the moment, and isn't really part of a partnership play. It happens when you expose your hand to a player next to you who is not in the hand. That player may have a friend in the pot who is thinking about calling your bet. If you have a very good hand, the player you exposed it to may indicate to his friend that he shouldn't call. Maybe he'll kick his friend under that table, or catch his friend's attention and glance at you, then look back at his friend and shake his head no. Technically a player who does that is cheating.

They'll rationalize it by saying that it's your responsibility to protect your hand, and it's not their fault that you let them see your hand. Technically you shouldn't have to concern yourself with whether someone who does not have an active hand sees your hand. The reality is that you do need to be concerned about that. Protect your hand, even from players who are not active in the pot and from passersby who are not in the game.

CHEATING AND ON-LINE POKER

Playing poker on the Internet is a new venue for poker. When I began writing this book, it didn't exist. It's big now. In 1999 there was a scandal at one of the first poker sites where their random number generator sequence had been cracked, allowing players to know what cards would be dealt. This is basically on on-line version of a cold deck. A few cheats did abscond with some money. The on-line cardrooms have since improved the randomness of the deals, and it's unlikely that anyone has cracked it again. Players are also monitored in an attempt to fashion an early warning system should their system be cracked again.

Player collusion is a potentially huge problem in on-line games. The cardrooms do monitor the games, and they have access to each player's hand, so there is some protection from collusion. Unfortunately, it's an ongoing problem that will probably never be completely solved.

25

Playing for a Living

Almost every winning poker player, at some point, starts thinking something like, "Gee, wouldn't it be neat to just chuck my job and do this for a living." It seems like a glamorous, easy life. Play when you want, sleep all day, make a living by your wits, and you are able to go anywhere you want and find a game. Well, maybe the life of a poker pro is for a few people, but not very many.

For most poker pros it's just another form of the daily grind. You don't play when you want to. You play every day because you need the money. You play all night, and your personal relationships suffer because you're not on the same schedule as the rest of the world. You walk around with thousands of dollars in your pocket, but you can't spend it because you need that money to play with. For most, it's just not that glamorous. Maybe you want to do it anyway. What do you need to do for preparation?

A BANKROLL

If you're playing poker for fun, you need to have enough money to last you through the weekend. A few hundred dollars is enough, or maybe a couple of thousand if you play for higher limits. If you lose it, well, you'll get another paycheck and you can save up some more money to play with. Because no matter how good you are, there will be times when you do lose it. Of course, if you're playing for fun and win, then you have a little extra money to spend.

If you're playing poker for a living, then none of that's true. Your money is your inventory. Lose it and you're out of work. You have to keep your playing bankroll sacred—and it has to be large. Large enough to withstand weeks of losses because long streaks of losing *can* and *do* happen.

How large does your playing bankroll have to be? Let's just say pretty large. Some guidelines for minimum sizes are given in the table. Your bankroll can't be too large, and my advice is to maintain some other source of nonpoker income instead of exclusive reliance on a fixed bankroll.

These recommendations in the following table are for your playing bankroll. You'll also need a reserve for living expenses because you won't be getting a paycheck and you won't win every week, or even every month. A reserve of one year's minimum living expenses is probably about right. Also remember that the larger games often won't be available forty hours a week.

More poker pros go broke from spending their bankroll than from losses at poker. In addition to a playing bankroll, you need to have sufficient savings to allow you to pay your bills without depleting your bankroll. There will be periods when you're just not winning enough to cover your bills. Keeping at least a year's living expenses in reserve is not too much.

If you're a professional player with no other source of income, your bankroll has to be big enough to withstand a run of bad luck in which you have a very small chance of going broke. The mathematicians call this "risk of ruin." If you lose some of your bankroll due to bad luck, your risk of going broke increases. To offset that you'll often have to start playing for smaller stakes, cutting your potential income. If your bankroll gets small enough that you can't play at a limit big enough to allow you to pay your expenses, then it's probably time to give it up and get a job.

MINIMUM PLAYING BANKROLL SIZE

Game limit	Typical potential hourly earnings	Recommended minimum bankroll
1-4-8-8	$10	$3,000
10/20	$20	$7,000
20/40	$30	$15,000
60/120	$80	$45,000

Not only do you need to guard against shrinkage of your bankroll, but you also actually need to be growing your bankroll That's because without a growing bankroll you are always at risk of a short-term run of bad luck, which can greatly increase your risk of going broke. So to be a long-term winning poker player, you need not only to win enough to live on, but you also need to be winning a little extra to keep adding to your bankroll. If you don't keep adding to your bankroll and you keep playing, eventually you will run into a run of bad luck that wipes you out. It has happened to a lot of good poker players.

Playing bankroll and living expenses aren't all you need to worry about, however. Credit and insurance can be big problems for a full-time poker player. I'm a poker player, and I'm a freelance writer—self-employed. Being self-employed can make things like getting a car loan or a credit card somewhat difficult. If you're self-employed as a poker player, it can make those sorts of situations even more difficult.

The problems the self-employed can have with credit were described in an essay by Larry L. King in which he wrote about an experience he had the year he sold the movie rights to *The Best Little Whorehouse in Texas*. He decided that he needed an American Express card. So, he applied for one. They turned him down. His income that year was very large, but he was self-employed.

Larry had written a few books, so he got a letter from the publisher of most of his books that said he was employed by them as an assistant editor with a salary of $30,000 (a fraction of his actual income). He reapplied for an American Express. They gave him one.

The self-employed do really get discriminated against when it comes to credit. As for self-employed gamblers, well, what do you think?

Insurance and credit are two things that the prospective professional poker player needs to take into consideration when deciding to start playing poker full-time. The amount of money you may need to have set aside to take care of those contingencies might be even larger than the amount of money you need to have set aside as a playing bankroll. The subject of the ordinary personal finances of a gambler is seldom discussed. Be sure you don't forget to take those things into consideration. There are a couple of old jokes related to playing poker for a living. Like most jokes, they're based on an uncomfortable truth.

What do you call a professional poker player who broke up with his girlfriend? Homeless.

How do you get a professional poker player off your front porch? Pay him for the pizza.

STATE OF MIND

One of the most important characteristics a poker pro needs is a winning state of mind. You need to be mentally prepared to win. You'd be surprised how many people just aren't ready to allow themselves to win. One of the things that makes up the will to win is a willingness to lose. If you're afraid to lose, then you're putting yourself at a huge psychological disadvantage. A big part of winning is a willingness to lose.

PUTTING ON AN ACT

There is a view among many poker pros that poker is some sort of scam to run on unsuspecting dupes. Those pros look at the people they play with every day with disdain—sheep to be fleeced or fish to be hooked. The primary result of that kind of attitude is unhappiness. Most poker pros really aren't very happy people.

There seems to be a lot of different reasons for this. One of them is the cut-throat nature of the game. The profiting from the self-destructive behaviors of compulsive gamblers can sometimes harm the self-esteem of poker pros. Most poker players are not compulsive gamblers. Most recreational players lose, but they don't lose much, at least not more than they get back in the form of entertainment value—but some players are really self-destructive. When you're playing for a living, those players sometimes seem to stick in your mind. It's harmful to your self-image to realize that you're making a living by encouraging those people to just destroy themselves. Some pros are able to rationalize it, but some aren't.

I never wanted to see my opponents just lose all their money quickly. If you have a table where most of your opponents just lose money slowly, they'll keep coming forever, and eventually you'll just get it all, but when you play in cardrooms, you don't have much control over who sits down in the game. I know one pro who limits most of his play to private home games for just this reason—he would much rather make a long-term profit by winning small amounts, on a regular basis, from people who can afford it. In a private game, you can just not invite those self-destructive players, but if you play in cardrooms, you just have to get used to it.

THE ENTERTAINER

What kind of business are professional poker players in? The sentiments that a poker pro is some kind of hustler are common among pros, and suggest an attitude that playing poker professionally is akin to operating some kind of confidence game. When I was playing poker for a living, that's not the way I looked at it. I thought of myself as being in the entertainment business. It was my job to entertain folks, to give them a good time, to provide them with a reason to give me their money. I think I gave value for the money.

I think it might depend on where you play. In Las Vegas or Los Angeles, you don't have to depend on regular players to get a game up—Los Angeles has a large population and Las Vegas has lots of visitors. Out in the boondocks, however, a pro has to ensure that the supply of players doesn't dry up.

I've always tried to help any opponent who wanted help. That doesn't mean offering unsolicited comments at the table, but I don't hesitate to offer a thought if it's asked for. I'll even explain the reasons for my own play if I'm asked (I do that away from the table).

It has seldom hurt my action at all to do any of that. In fact most of the time I think it helps me, because then I know what a particular opponent thinks I have. If you're going to play poker, whether for a living or just for recreation, make sure you're having fun. There's no real point to it if you're not.

PROP PLAYERS

One way to make a living as a poker pro is to work for a cardroom. Some cardrooms use proposition players (called prop players). A "prop player" works a regular shift in the cardroom and is used to help start games and fill-in when a game gets short-handed. He's paid a wage to fill up a chair at whatever table needs a player—but he plays with his own money. A prop player differs from a shill in this respect. A shill plays with house money, not his own money. I'm not aware of any cardroom that employs full-time shills, although some do use dealers on break to shill for short periods to get a new game started.

It's certainly possible for a prop player to to lose more than his wage in the course of the shift. Of course if you do that very often, you won't be working as a prop player for long—not because the cardroom cares whether you win or lose, but because you'll just run out of money.

Prop players cannot pick their games. They have to play in whatever game is short of players. This often means games that just aren't very profitable. A game with good table conditions will usually have a long waiting list of customers wanting to play in the game.

However, if you're skilled at playing in short-handed games and can shift gears and just play tight when the situation calls for that, then you can probably do fairly well as a prop player. Working as an employee of the cardroom has some added benefits in the form of such things as health insurance and verifiable employment for creditors.

26

Know Yourself

Knowing yourself means knowing your limitations, your motivations, and your competitive advantages in the game.

KNOW YOUR LIMITATIONS

Poker is an intellectual game. Playing poker to win requires a lot of intense thought and on-the-spot analysis. You should make certain that you've done whatever you need to do in order to prepare for that. A lot of that is physical.

Get Some Rest

Thinking is tiring. It really wears you out. That means don't play when you're tired. Get some rest. Most people should limit their sessions to four to six hours. After that, take a break. Cash in your chips and leave. There will be another game when you get back. You don't have to leave for long, but leave for at least an hour. Do something refreshing: Take a walk, get something to eat, take a nap, see a movie. Relax. It's important.

Diet Does Matter

What you eat can affect your game. Foods like greasy meats will tend to tire you out more than refresh you. Avoid heavy eating before and during a session, and avoid heavy foods even in light portions. Stay away from those cardroom hot dogs. If I know a cardroom has a limited menu available, I'll often stop at the grocery store and buy some fruits and nuts to take with me to the cardroom. Having some fruit to pass out to some of the other players doesn't hurt either as making friends at the table can help in a number of ways.

I hope I don't have to tell you to stay away from alcohol while playing. You should watch your coffee intake also. If you order a cup of coffee from the waitress, ask for a glass of water to go with it. Drink at least one glass of water for every cup of coffee you drink. There are two problems caused by excess coffee. One, the nervousness that accompanies caffeine is familiar to anyone who drinks coffee, and coffee also tends to dehydrate you. So, you need to drink water with to coffee to keep yourself hydrated. Drinking lots of water is one of the best things you can do to keep your brain working at maximum effectiveness while playing poker.

Leave Your Worries at Home

If you have problems at home, don't try to use a poker game to get the problems out of your mind. Your thoughts of the problems will just distract you from the game. Take care of the problems. Then play cards.

WHY DO YOU PLAY?

In the movie *The Color of Money*, the Paul Newman character says, "Money won is twice as sweet as money earned." It's true, it is. However, money won sometimes takes more work to acquire than money earned. Poker really is a tough way to make an easy living.

If you ask poker players why they play poker they'll often respond that they play for the money. Don't believe it. First of all, few poker players are lifetime winners at the game. If 10 percent of all poker players end up winners at poker, I'd be surprised, and for those who are long-term winners, it's hard work.

Why does anybody play then? Because it's fun. Why is it fun? There are different reasons for different people. You need to ask yourself what it is that you get out of the game that makes it fun for you. The challenge? The thrill of the gamble? The social interaction? Whatever it is, make certain the game you're in is doing for you whatever it takes for you to be having fun. Winning is important, and you are much more likely to win if you're having fun.

MAINTAIN YOUR COMPETITIVE ADVANTAGE

Your advantage over the other players at the table comes from the mistakes they make—but it's not enough for them to make mistakes. You have to exploit those mistakes, you have to act on their mistakes to profit from them. That's your competitive advantage. You can sometimes do things that cause your opponents to make mistakes, but most of your winnings will come from mistakes they make all on their own. You maintain your competitive advantage by learning as much as you can about the mistakes your opponents are making and by constant vigilance for opportunities to exploit what you know.

Use Your Intuition

I'm not sure what a good way to define intuition is. It's some kind of gut feeling about a situation. I've actually had experiences at the table where images of cards flashed in my brain. An example is the time I had A♥K♥, and the flop was 2♥4♥6♥. I bet and was raised by a late-position player. When he raised, an image of the 3♥5♥ flashed in my head. I had a mental picture of those two cards. This was not a premonition or fear. When I flop the nut flush, I don't get worried about someone having a straight flush after one raise, but something about that player and the way he made that bet put the picture of those two cards in my head. I knew he had that hand. Well, I didn't really know, so I didn't fold, but I did call his raise and I checked-called the next two betting rounds.

Intuition is not premonition. If you sit down at a table and quickly find yourself winning a few hundred dollars, you might feel an impulse to get up and cash in so you don't throw the money back. That's not intuition. That's fear, dread, a premonition of disaster, but it's not intuition. Intuition is that sense of knowing what is—not knowing what will be. When I lost to that straight flush, I didn't have a feeling that he was drawing to a straight flush and was going to make it—that's premonition and it's based on superstition, not on reality. Intuition, however, is something sub-conscious, some clue that your subconscious brain has picked up and processed and told you the conclusion. All that you're con-scious of is that conclusion, you don't really understand how you arrived at it. It's no less real and it's no less logical or analytical than reading a tell. Listen to it. Just be sure it's intuition talking and not premonition.

Control Your Demons

I think that the best poker players tend to be compulsive gam-blers who don't care about money. When I played no-limit draw every day, I used to go bust almost like clockwork, but I didn't care, it didn't bother me. I didn't blow my money off in a game though, I'd spend most it, then end up sitting down with what was left of my money and going bust because I just didn't have enough money left to withstand the normal swings of the game. Back then there were afternoon, $10-buy-in, 10-cent ante, no-limit games that I could get into and start over again anytime I busted.

When I play poker every day, I just start losing perspective on life. Things like money and relationships start to lose value for me. The fact that the money doesn't have any value to me does (I think) make me a tough poker player. I think that to be a tough poker player you either have to have so much money that it doesn't matter or just not care about the money. A lot of people think that if you don't care about the money, then you don't care about winning. That's not true at all though. Winning is what matters to me. It's just that winning matters because I like to win, not because I covet the money I'll get when I do win. I liked Stu Ungar's response after his first World Series of Poker win when some idiot reporter asked him what he was going to do with money. He said something like, "I'm going to invest it for my kids' college fund," then he busted out in a fit of giggles and laughter and said, "I'm gonna piss it away gambling. What the hell did you think?" What you have to do, I think, is just get used to it.

Know the Players

Of course you want to do more that think about yourself. Most of your attention should be devoted to getting to know the other players. Try to learn how they think. Whenever you see them do something you think is unusual, ask yourself why they did it.

One important question to ask yourself about the other players is, "What do they think about me?" Knowing the answer will often help you predict how they will react to your different behaviors.

ANALYZE THE RESULTS

I used to play no-limit draw every day. It was a long time ago, but one of the characteristics of no-limit games is that the results for a particular session almost always hinge on the outcome of one or two key hands. You don't know ahead of time what hands they're going to be, but you almost always end up with at least one major situation where you end up with all the money in the pot and you win or lose it. One mistake, or the failure to exploit an advantage just one time, can make all the difference.

In limit games you don't get punished that much for a single mistake, but even in a limit game you can often look back at the session and pick out a few key hands that made a difference. I've gotten into the habit of picking out one or two hands and spending an hour or two after a session going over those hands. I'll sit down by myself with a pencil and paper and analyze everything I can remember. I'll figure out the actual odds, try to identify what I did wrong and what I did right.

PART FOUR

Playing Some Hands

This part of the book contains two short chapters that illustrate thinking about poker from an *odds perspective*. I didn't play either of the hands discussed; they were both played by others and discussed on the Internet. One of them is about playing a draw and thinking in terms of betting odds; the other is about playing a small pocket pair and thinking in terms of pot odds. Both hands illustrate errors that are often caused by a persistence in thinking about the game in terms of *best hand versus a draw*.

27

Playing a Draw

In this chapter I'm going to analyze a hand that was played in a 15/30 game at the Bellagio in Las Vegas. This hand was posted on the Internet by the pro player who played it, and was discussed extensively. I think it's a hand that illustrates why loose-aggressive games are so profitable; it also illustrates why many otherwise good players don't seem to do well under those kinds of game conditions.

Many poker pros who play in Las Vegas argue that the best games are loose-passive games and that loose-aggressive games are not profitable games. The way the pro played this hand illustrates why many would think that. The reason is that he doesn't properly adjust his play to exploit the mistakes that players in a loose-aggressive game are making.

Of course in Las Vegas there is a reason for this. There are more poker pros per capita in Las Vegas than anywhere else, and an aggressive game is usually a sign that the table has a larger than normal contingent of pros. Passive games usually indicate a lot of tourists at the table so Las Vegas pros do tend to find passive games more profitable than aggressive games. They just wrongly conclude that the game conditions themselves are the cause of that.

The reason we're looking at this hand is to illustrate the importance of modifying your play to exploit the table conditions.

THE SITUATION

It's an unusually loose-aggressive game—at least unusual by Las Vegas standards. The table had several very aggressive players and several very loose players. No one other than our hero was a top local pro. Our hero in this hand is on the button and is dealt 9♠7♠.

PRE-FLOP BETTING

Five players had called the blind by the time the action got to our hero with the 9♠7♠. Should he call, fold, or raise? If you're taking an *odds* perspective to the game, then you need to think about a raise in this situation. There is a popular misconception, repeated in many poker books, that you should only raise if your hand figures to be the best hand. That's not how to get the money in Hold 'Em. You should raise whenever your chances of winning are greater than the odds you're getting on the raise.

Based on Turbo Texas Hold 'Em simulations, 9♠7♠, from late position against a field of from five to seven loose players, will win over 20 percent of the time. That makes the hand about a 4-1 underdog. With five players already having called, and the two blinds left to act, you'll get between 5-1 and 7-1 on a raise. If you know that the blinds will call a raise, then there is profit in a raise, and you should take that profit. However, with only five sure callers, a raise with 9♠7♠ would be marginal. If the players in the hand play very badly after the flop, you might want to raise. In general though, five players are not quite enough to raise with this hand.

There are arguments for not raising, based on different theoretical perspectives. I won't go into those arguments here because when you're in a hand with four or more active players the dominant perspective to take is an *odds* perspective. Our hero called. That's probably the best play in this situation. It's a close decision.

The small blind folded and the big blind raised. Everyone called, including our hero, but our hero made a mistake by not reraising. Now there are six active players, and getting 6-1 odds when you're only a 4-1 underdog is a pretty good proposition. That's the case even though you can usually expect a player who raised from one of the blinds to have a much better than average hand. That's because even weak players tend not to raise with many hands from the blinds because they will be in poor position in all future betting rounds.

THE FLOP

Seven players are in for a flop of 8♠7♥4♠. This is a very good flop for our hero. The main feature is a flush draw against a large field. Played properly, flush draws against large fields are very big money winners, but this flop is even better. Second pair might actually be the best hand. Additionally the 9♠ kicker is an overcard, and there is a three-card straight. Counting the three-card straight as one out, and counting the 9♠ overcard as three outs, this hand might already be the best hand and has as many as thirteen outs if it's not best. That's enough to make this hand only a small underdog against one player. Against two or more players, this hand is probably worth a raise. Against three players this hand is certainly worth a raise if you're certain that three of them will call. Of course it would be nice to have everyone fold and win the pot right now, but as that isn't likely to happen, you'd like to have as many callers as you can get so that you get maximum odds on your draw.

The first three players checked. There was a bet. The next player raised. The sixth player called, and our hero called. Then the pre-flop raiser, who had initially checked, reraised; the other two players who had checked folded; and everyone else called.

Let's look at this in two stages. First the initial call on the flop by our hero. An argument can be made for not raising initially on the

flop because there were still three players who hadn't had a chance
to call, and he didn't want to discourage them from calling. With
three players who will almost certainly call a reraise, a raise would
not be wrong, but it's a situation calling for table judgment. If you
have reason to think that a couple of the the players who had initially checked will call for two bets when they wouldn't call for three
bets, then just calling and going for the overcalls is the right thing
to do. If, however, you think that an extra bet won't affect whether
any of those three players will call, you should go ahead and raise.
You should also check, intending to back-raise, if you think that one
of the early position players was planning a check-raise.

In any event, our hero called the first round, and the situation
was such that it's not really possible to be sure that calling isn't
better than raising here. After the big blind check-raised, however,
our hero should put in the last raise when the betting gets back
around to him. He's last, and there is no one else behind him who
might raise; everyone has already called a bet and two raises, so
they'll call another raise. With a flush draw and many callers, you
want as many players calling as many bets as possible. With the
extra features of this flush draw, that becomes even more important.

In the Internet discussion, our hero explained why he didn't
raise. It was because he was concerned that someone might be
drawing to a bigger flush than his 9-high. That's a common concern among players who habitiually take a made-hand-versus-a-
draw perspective to Hold 'Em. It's also a common concern among
Hold 'Em players who play a lot of seven-card stud.

In seven-card stud, if you have a flush draw then the chances
that someone else also has a flush draw are higher than they would
be if you didn't have a flush draw. Their draws are likely to be in
a different suit than yours. The reason is that if you have four
Spades, then the remainder of the deck has a higher proportion of
Hearts, Diamonds, and Clubs than it normally would. If you have
four Spades, then the chance of someone else having four Hearts
is larger than it would be if you had one card of each suit. So, in
games such as seven-card stud that don't have shared cards, you

should be very careful in drawing to flushes that aren't headed by an Ace. A 9-high flush can often be beaten by a larger flush.

Hold 'Em is very different. Because of the nature of the shared cards, you cannot have flush draws in two different suits on the flop. If anyone else has a flush draw, it must be in your suit. Between the two in your hand and the two on the board, there are only nine cards of your suit left. There are thirteen unseen cards of two of the other suits and twelve unseen cards of the fourth suit. If another player has suited cards, the odds are very high that the suit is not the same suit as your flush draw. It's very unlikely that two players both flop a flush draw in Hold 'Em. One player with a draw is what makes it unlikely that another player also has a draw.

The other thing which works in your favor is that if you have a flush draw in those situations (where someone else actually does have a bigger flush draw) the chances that you will make your flush are very slim. That means it's unlikely that you'll make your hand, and you'll be beaten by another flush, which can be expensive those few times it does happen.

The 2-1 odds of making a flush takes into account those times that someone else has a draw and your chances of making it are worse than that. If no one else has a flush draw, then your odds are actually better than 2-1, and having the extra edge of three or four callers is more than enough to compensate for those few tragic situations where you do get beaten by a bigger flush. The risk of putting in the last raise here is more than compensated for by the profit you will get from that raise. Failure to raise before the flop was a small mistake. Failure to raise on this flop was a huge mistake.

THE TURN

The turn card made the flush with the K♠8♠7♥4♠K♠. The first player checked, the next player bet, everyone called.

Why didn't our hero raise now that he's made the best hand he had a draw to? Again, he was concerned that someone else might have a better flush. That's way too timid. It's the kind of timid play in a multiway pot that players who take a fixed perspective on the game tend to make. If you have a flush, then the chances of someone else having a flush are fairly small. Here the K♠ is one of the cards on the board, making it even less likely that, even if someone else has a flush, it's larger than our 9-high flush. Failure to raise in this situation is just way too timid; it's an example of weak-tight play. Three players have already called a bet. At least two of them would call a raise. That means that in the worst case you get 2-1 on a raise. You might even have everyone call, giving you 4-1 on the raise. The chances that your hand is best are probably better than 10-1. Even if you estimate that it's even money that someone else has a higher flush, the odds you will get on the raise from the number of callers you will get compensates for that risk.

It's common for players to be hesitant to raise when they make a flush that's not the best possible flush. That's a mistake. Hands such as 9♠7♠ are profitable in multiway pots. The reason they are profitable is that they sometimes make flushes with the potential for a big pot. You aren't going to realize that profit if you don't raise with these hands when you make them.

THE RIVER

The river card made a straight possible: 8♠7♥4♠K♠9♦. The first three players checked, and one of the players who had just been calling bet. Our hero called.

It's even more important to raise now. Because no one raised when the flush card hit, the bettor is very likely to have made a straight and be convinced it's the best hand. Raising here might very well get a reraise from a player with a straight. Sometimes it is better to just call a bet on the river in a multiway pot in the hope that players who haven't called yet will call but they won't call a raise. That's called "going for the overcall." When the pot gets large, and in this case the pot is large, the kind of players who tend to populate loose tables will often call a raise with fairly weak holdings. The pot is just too large for them to just give up. Because the board looks as if it's possible someone has a straight and they probably think a straight is the best hand, a raise may very well entice them to reraise.

But, our hero called. Then the player who had originally raised on the flop raised. A check-raise on the river with a board that shows a possible flush and a possible straight is a show of great strength, but this player didn't check-raise when the K♠ fell on the turn, and he could have. So it's unlikely that the check-raiser has a flush. A straight is the most likely hand that the check-raiser has, although it would be surprising if he'd raised before the flop and continued to call to the river with a hand that would make a straight.

In any event, our hero called the raise. I think a reraise was called for. The trade-off between overcalls and a raise is now gone. Although the check-raise by the pre-flop raiser does show strength, I think the pattern of the play of the hand suggests that it's very unlikely that anyone else has a flush. Our hero's judgment at the table was that there was a great risk of another player having a higher flush, and he just called. His judgment may well have been right. He was there, I wasn't.

THE SHOWDOWN

The pre-flop raiser had made two pair on the river. He had K♣9♣. The other player in the showdown had a straight. Our hero won the pot with his flush.

SUMMARY

I think this hand serves as a classic example of the kinds of mistakes that players make when they tend to always think of Hold 'Em as *a confrontation between the best hand and a draw*. They believe that adding more callers increases the chances that the best hand is a very high hand. The reality is that adding more callers just serves to increase the odds you're getting; enough so that it's often good enough just to have the best hand, particularly when your hand has many outs.

In a loose game, particularly a game that's very loose and very aggressive, players tend to have some weak hands, and they often tend to overplay those weak hands. That's where the profit comes from in these games. Having a lot of callers who tend to play weak hands does not increase the likelihood that the best hand is a very good hand. Just the opposite: it increases the odds that a better-than-average, not top, hand will get action from weak hands. To get that action, you have to be prepared to take some risk. It is a risk to reraise on the river with a flush that might not be the best flush. It is a risk to raise on a draw to a hand that might not be the best hand, but there is a very high payoff available to those willing to take those risks in the right kind of game conditions.

In a loose or very loose game that's also aggressive or very aggressive, it's important to take control, play your hands aggressively. That means raising and reraising when you think you probably have the best draw. That also means raising when you make a flush. If you aren't willing to take the risk associated with taking control in these kinds of games, then it might just be that these kinds of games aren't for you.

28

Playing a Pocket Pair

Long discussions about the play of a hand often crop up on Internet discussion groups. Players extensively debate the pros and cons of particular actions of some real-life hand that someone has played. This chapter examines another hand played by by a Las Vegas pro in a 15/30 game at the Bellagio. I think this hand was played pretty well.

I picked this particular hand because I think that the options at each betting round were close, there was no clear-cut best thing to do, and an analysis of the possibilities of playing this hand illustrates the kinds of thinking, and shifts in thinking that you need to do at the table.

THE BEGINNING

Our hero is in late position, one seat to the left of the button, and is dealt 4♠4♥. It's a fairly loose game, not very aggressive. I'd probably categorize the game as loose-typical. An early position player opens by calling the blind and three more players call. It's now up to our hero.

A PRE-FLOP CALL

Should our hero call? It's actually close. A pocket pair of fours isn't much of a hand; it's a speculative hand that needs four to five callers to get a good enough combination of pot odds and implied odds. If we know that we won't be raised by the button or one of the blinds, then this is a pretty clear call. If we estimate that the chances are that one of the players still behind us will raise, then a call becomes a little marginal. All in all the table is fairly passive, we're in late position, four players have already called, and the blinds will probably play. This is a good call, but folding wouldn't be a big mistake. What did our hero do? He called, of course. If he hadn't, then we wouldn't have a story.

I would have thought about raising in this situation—but only thought about it. You need a little larger pair to raise in this situation with only four sure callers. In a loose game, you need to look at the game in terms of the kind of odds you're getting. A pocket pair of fours before the flop needs very high odds, probably about 8-1, to justify a raise.

With a pocket pair, the odds of flopping a set are a little more than 7-1. That's the primary way that a small- or medium-sized pair will win. Of course you can win with these hands in other ways. Sometimes they make a straight. Sometimes they end up winning unimproved. You can even flop a set and still lose also. The smaller your set, the greater the chance that someone will make a higher set. The larger the pair, the more ways they have to win and the fewer callers you need to justify a raise. With a pair of Aces, you only need one caller to justify a raise. With a pair of 4s, you need about eight callers to justify a raise. With only four or five callers, you probably shouldn't raise with less than about a pair of 8s, but I do try to always think about raising, even if it is just to keep reminding myself that a lot of good things can happen when you raise. However, our hero correctly only called.

The Rest of the Pre-flop Action

As soon as our hero calls, the button raises. Oops! We hadn't counted on that, but both blinds call, all the other callers just call, and no one reraises. It's our hero's turn to act again. Time to think about a raise again. Now there are seven other players in the pot, each has already called two bets. We have that pocket pair of 4s and are a little worse than a 7-1 underdog to flop a set. Should we raise? It's a close call. At our first action in the betting, there were not enough active players for a raise, but three more players have shown action. Whether you should raise now depends somewhat on how badly the players in the pot tend to play in later betting rounds. With eight callers a raise is almost automatic with a pair of 4s. With a pair of 6s, a raise would be automatic with six callers. I might have raised. I'm not sure. If raising is a mistake, then it's not a huge mistake, but just calling isn't a huge mistake either. Our hero just called. That was probably the right thing to do, but it's important to at least think about raising.

THE FLOP

The flop was 9♦8♠3♦. The first player bet and two players called. What should our hero do now?

The conventional wisdom says to fold. The argument for a fold is simply that we only called based on the chances of flopping a set. We missed the flop, so give it up and wait for the next hand. On the other hand, we have a pretty good-sized pot here.

Let's look at what kind of odds we're getting for a call. Eight people called two bets each before the flop. That's sixteen bets that went into the pot before the flop. Now we have one bet and two callers, adding three bets to the pot. We're getting at least 19-1 to call if no one raises.

What are the chances that the next card will be a 4? We've seen five of the fifty-two cards. That leaves forty-seven cards in the deck. Two of them are 4s. Two out of forty-seven cards will make our set, and forty-five out of the forty-seven will not help us. The odds are 22.5-1. The pot odds aren't quite that large, but if we do make the set of 4s on the next card, we'll probably win a few extra bets on the last two betting rounds. Usually I look for odds of about 20-1 to call a bet on the flop with a small pair in the hopes of spiking the set. We don't quite have that, but with at least three other players active, we can be fairly certain that we'll gain more than just one or two extra bets on the last two betting rounds, and they are double-sized bets. So, based purely on current pot odds, our hero should probably call. The combination of the large pot and our implied odds from future bets is big enough.

When thinking about calling on the flop to draw to a small pocket pair, we not only need to think about the pot odds we're getting on the call, but we also need to be certain that we really will get those pot odds, that no one is going to raise. In addition we need to consider the likelihood that our three of a kind will be the best hand should we get lucky and spike the third of our rank on the turn card. In this situation we have one player left to act, and that player had raised before the flop. The risk of him raising now might be large. This is a situation where tells come into play. Most players will frequently telegraph what they intend to do by putting on a false act. The important thing to do is to distinguish between when they are acting and when they are behaving naturally. A player who is not paying attention to the action and is behaving naturally probably really doesn't care what's happening and is going to fold, but a player who is acting in such a way that he clearly wants you to think that he's not paying attention is probably very interested in what's happening and is very likely to raise.

What about the likelihood that a 4 on the flop will make someone else a better hand at the same time it makes your hand? With a flop of 9♦8♠3♦, a 4 won't make anyone a straight, and one of our 4s is a Diamond, matching the suit of the potential flush draw. That means that a 4 can't make anyone a flush. This second consideration is very important. No matter how large your pot odds, if there is a potential flush draw on the flop, it's almost never right to take one more card off in the hopes of turning your pocket pair into a set unless you have a card in the flush suit. That's because making three of a kind with the same card that makes someone else a flush can be a disaster. It's a disaster that's best avoided.

There are some other arguments against calling. It is possible that someone else has a pocket pair of 8s or a pocket pair of 9s, meaning that you would essentially be drawing dead, but that's very unlikely. In general it's not worth worrying about someone having a larger set unless there is some specific reason to think they do, and there's no reason here to think that. Our hero called the bet. The button called but didn't raise.

THE TURN

The turn card was another 3, giving a board of 9♦8♠3♦3♥. Now we get a surprise. The first three players checked.

Until now it was pretty safe to assume that someone had an 8 or a 9, and that our pocket 4s were not the best hand, but with everyone checking it starts to look as if everyone has some kind of a draw. Maybe flush draws, straight draws, or overcards. With the 9 and 8 on the board, a lot of players would call a bet on the flop with a hand like K♠J♠ and then check on the turn. If that's the case, it's important to bet.

Betting requires a major shift in thinking at this point. Until now we were playing passively, assuming we didn't have the best hand and would have to passively play catch-up in order to end up with the best hand. Now it looks like we might actually have the best hand. It even looks as if no one else has much of a draw, but a lot of cards can still beat us. The other players just don't realize it. A bet may very likely cause players who have nothing except cards larger than a 4 to fold; they won't realize that they are getting the right pot odds to beat our measly pair of 4s.

Our hero bet. This bet was probably a key play in this hand. A couple of the players folded, a couple of them called.

THE RIVER

The last card was a Queen, and it didn't make the flush. The final board was 9♦8♠3♦3♥Q♠. Everyone checked. Our hero showed his pocket 4s; everyone folded. The 4s were enough to win it.

Without knowing more about the players, checking was really the only reasonable option our hero had. If we knew more about the other players though, there are times when it would be right to bet in this situation. There are players who don't call often enough on the river and would fold an 8. There are also players who call way too much and might call with an Ace for high. If two remaining players have those kind of habits, a bet might be considered. Under normal circumstances though, checking is pretty automatic.

CONCLUSION

This was an unusual hand, with an unusual outcome. Our hero got very lucky, but it wasn't all luck. His quick-wittedness on the turn by taking advantage of an unexpected turn of events probably saved the day for him. One of the players who had folded on the turn gave a noticeable wince when the Queen fell on the river. It is very likely that player had folded a hand with a Queen in it.

The point of this hand is both that you need to consider pot odds when calling, as our hero did before and on the flop, and you need to be alert to changes in the situation, taking advantage of information as the hand unfolds.

PART FIVE

Continuing Education

This final part of the book contains chapters on tools and resources for self-study. Some mathematical tools useful in the analysis of some poker situations and tactics are explained. Reviews of other Hold 'Em books are provided; the reviews focus on the kinds of theoretical perspectives that various books tend to take. Also, computer tools and Internet resources are described. This collection of tools and resources should prove helpful to most poker players in continuing to improve both their understanding of the game and their playing performance.

29

Mathematics of Poker

INTRODUCTION TO PROBABILITY AND STATISTICS

Most mathematical analyses of Hold 'Em are based on theories of probability and statistical computation. Probability and statistics are not the same topics, although they are closely related. Probability is devoted to the description of the theoretical outcomes from random events. Statistics is devoted to the description of actual, observed outcomes from random events.

There are other ways to distinguish between probability and statistics, and the one I've chosen may seem somewhat subtle, but it works well enough for our purposes. Probability is about *theoretical* outcomes whereas statistics is about *observed* outcomes.

PROBABILITY

A "probability" is a number, between zero and one, which represents the relative frequency of a particular outcome occurring as a result of a random event. A probability of zero means the outcome cannot occur. A probability of one means the outcome will occur with certainty. A probability of 0.5 means the event will occur one-half of the time.

For example, shuffle a deck of cards and turn over the top card. That's a random event. One of the possible outcomes is that the card is black, either a Spade or a Club. The probability of this particular outcome is 0.5. This means that one half of the time the card you draw will be one of the black suits.

A "probability distribution" is a list of all possible, mutually exclusive outcomes and their associated probabilities. By "mutually exclusive" I mean that the outcomes don't overlap in some way. Each outcome is defined in such a manner as to be unique from other outcomes. For example, still considering our event of shuffling the deck and turning over the top card, one probability distribution we could define would be:

OUTCOME	PROBABILITY
Black card	0.5
Red card	0.5

Law of Averages

The "law of averages" is a limit theorem that says the sample mean gets arbitrarily close to the actual mean as the sample gets larger. "Mean" is a technical term for average. "Actual mean" for our purposes is the theoretical average that's implied by a probability distribution; "sample mean" is about actual observed results. A sample mean is the mathematical average of some actual result.

For example, in our black-card red-card probability distribution, think about a black card as representing the value 1 (you win a dollar if the card turned up is black) and a red card is the value 0 (zero). The mean of this distribution is 0.5. On the average you win $.50 for every turn of the card. Half the time the card is black and you get $1, and half the time the card is red and you get nothing.

If we shuffled the deck and turned over a card ten times, *on the average* we'd get a black card five times, but we might get six black cards, or four black cards, and in some unusual results, we might even get a black card all ten times. Let's suppose that happens, we shuffle and turn a card ten times, turning over a black card every time. What does the law of averages tell us about the results from the next ten times we turn a card? The next 100 times? The next 1,000 times?

It actually doesn't tell us anything about the individual results from future events. It tells us something about the overall average for a large number of replications. All the law of averages really tells us is that the sample average won't be affected by any short-run results if we make our sample size large enough.

The law of averages tells us our results should look like this if we start off with ten black cards:

Sample Size	Black Cards	Sample Mean
10	10	1
100	55	0.55
1,000	505	0.505

Our sample mean gets closer and closer to the actual average of 0.5 because of the increased sample size. The more cards we turn, the less effect on the total those first ten cards have. Luck does not even out. The first ten black cards don't get offset by a run of ten red cards. Luck averages out because in the long run short-term results don't have a big effect. This difference between luck averaging out and good luck being offset by bad luck is important. If you get lucky, then you just got lucky. The gods of chance aren't going to take it away from you.

The law of averages is often misinterpreted to mean such things as "red is due" at roulette because it hasn't hit in a while. That's because people tend to think that the process that causes the sample mean to get close to the true mean is that sequences on one side of the mean get offset by sequences on the other side, that is, that a run of ten blacks will, at some time, be offset by a run of ten reds. However, that's not what makes the sample mean converge to the actual mean. It's just a large sample size that does that.

Remember this the next time you miss twenty flush draws in a row. That is not going to mean that you are due to make the next draw. *The cards don't have a memory.*

Counting Methods of Calculating Probabilities

We can calculate the probabilities of various outcomes in card games by using mathematical counting methods. We've already done some of that at various places in this book. The probability of an event can be calculated as a relative frequency. You count the total number of possible outcomes and the number of outcomes that correspond to the event. For example, in the shuffle-the-deck-and-turn-a-card trials, the total number of possible outcomes is fifty-two. There are fifty-two cards in the deck, and any one of them could be the one turned over. If the event that we are interested in is that the card turned over is a black card, then we have twenty-six possible outcomes that correspond to the event. The probability of the event is then twenty-six divided by fifty-two. That's 0.5.

In Hold 'Em we're often interested in calculating the probabilities of hitting our outs on the next card. For example, in a gutshot straight draw on the flop, say the flop is 9♠5♥2♦ and we have 7♣8♣.

We have four outs, any 6 makes a straight for us. What's the probability of this happening? We need to count two things: the total number of possible outcomes and the number of those outcomes that makes our straight. We've already counted the second of these, four cards will make your hand. The total number of possible cards that can be turned up on the next card is forty-seven. That's just the fifty-two cards in the deck minus the five cards that we know can't be turned up (the three on the flop and the two in our hand). Because we don't know anyone else's hand, we just consider all the other cards to still be in the deck. We only subtract out those cards that we specifically know can't be turned up next. Therefore, the probability of making our inside straight draw on the turn card is 4 ÷ 47 or about 0.085. Expressed another way, it's about a one in twelve chance, or 8.5 percent.

How about the probability of making an inside straight in the next two cards? The probability that either the turn or the river card is a 6?

Before we look at that, we need to consider two rules of calculating probabilities of joint events. By joint events I mean a trail that consists of two distinguishable events, in this case the turn card or the river card.

The first of these rules is called the addition rule. Whenever we want to know the probability of something occurring one way or another way, we can calculate the two probabilities separately and add them together if the two ways of occurring are mutually exclusive. The addition rule is applicable whenever our statement of our two events uses the word "or"—the turn *or* the river. The events need to be mutually exclusive. We can't add probabilities for two things that overlap. In the case of a 6 falling on the turn or the river, we have to be concerned with double counting those times that a 6 comes on both the turn and the river. If we counted the number of ways a 6 could fall on the turn, then counted the ways a 6 could fall on the river and added them together, we would be counting some sequences of cards twice. (I'll give you a way to avoid this in a minute.)

The second rule is a multiplication rule. This rule is for two independent events when we are interested in the probability of them both occurring. This rule says that to get the probability of two things both happening, we can calculate the probabilities of each of them and then multiply. This rule applies whenever we have a joint statement that uses the word "and." A card comes on the turn, *and* one comes on the river.

We can sometimes convert a complicated statement that uses the addition rule to a simple statement that uses the multiplication rule by using the rule of complements. The probability of something not happening is just one minus the probability of it happening.

In the case of our inside straight draw, we can simplify the computations by looking at the probability of not making the draw rather than directly calculating the probability of making it. We will not make the straight in the next two cards if the turn card is not a 6 and the river card is not a 6. We can compute the probability of this by invoking the multiplication rule.

On the turn, we have forty-seven unseen cards and forty-three of them are not a 6. On the river we will have forty-six unseen cards and, if the turn card was not a 6, forty-two of them will not be a 6. We can therefore compute the probability as $(43/47) \times (42/46) = 0.835$. That's the probability of not making the straight. To get the probability of making the straight, we just subtract that from one, giving us a probability of making an inside straight draw in two cards as 0.165. That's 16.5 percent, or about a one-in-six chance.

Counting methods can get more complex than this, using the mathematical concepts of combinations and permutations, but most situations of interest in Hold 'Em can be calculated using these simple rules.

Converting Probabilities to Odds

There is a direct relationship between probabilities and odds. You convert odds to probabilities as follows: If the odds against something happening are 2-1, that means that it will happen one time and fail to happen two times of every three times, making the probability 1/3 or 0.33. If the odds are a to b of it happening, then the probability of it happening are $a \div (a + b)$. That's the number of ways it can happen divided by the total of ways it can and can't happen. Odds of 9-1 are a probability of 1/10 (10 percent or a one-in-ten chance).

To convert probabilities to odds, you just reverse the procedure. If the probability is p then the odds to 1 would be $p \div (1 - p)$. For p = 0.33, the odds are 0.33 ÷ 0.67 or 0.5-1 in favor. That is the same as odds of 2-1 against.

Probabilities of Flush Draws

On a few occasions in the book, I've said that you should count a backdoor flush draw as the equivalent of about two outs. We can use these simple counting methods of computing probabilities to demonstrate why I suggest this.

First, let's compute the probability of making a two-out draw in the next card. A draw with two outs would be something like having a 4♠4♥ when the flop is 9♥8♦3♥. There are forty-seven unseen cards, two of them are 4s, the probability of making three 4s on the turn is $2 \div 0.47 = 0.04$ (4 percent or a one-in-twenty-four chance; note that one-in-twenty would be 0.05, so this is a little more than one-in-twenty).

To make a backdoor flush draw, you need two running cards of your suit. For example, if you hold K♥Q♥ and the flop is A♥7♠6♠, then you need the turn card and the river card both to be a Heart. There are forty-seven unseen cards, and ten of them are Hearts. If the turn card is a Heart, then there will be forty-six unseen cards, and nine of them will be Hearts. Using the multiplication rule, we can calculate this probability as $(10/47) \times (9/46) = 0.04$.

The probability of making two running cards to complete a three-flush is the same as the probability of the turn card making you three of a kind when you have a small pocket pair. In a probabilistic sense, a backdoor flush draw is equivalent to two outs.

Variance

"Variance" is a measure of the dispersion of a probability distribution. The larger the variance, the more likely that a calculation of a mean from a sample result will differ meaningfully from the true mean. Variance is sometimes thought of as a measure of risk, although, as we'll see in a moment, it's not always a good measure of risk in gambling situations.

The computational definition of variance is the mean of the squared deviations from the average. Before we give a formula for it, we need a definition of expected value.

The expected value of X is written E(X) and is equal to

$$\text{sum}\{p(X) \times X\}$$

where the summation is over all values of X and p(X) is the probability of a particular value of X occurring.

Now we can define the variance of X as

$$V(X) = E(X^2) - E(X)^2$$

Let's look at an example. We can analyze the play of a small pocket pair using mean and variance. Generally a small pocket pair will only win if it flops a set. There are other ways to win, but we'll ignore them in this model. The probability of flopping a set can be calculated by looking at the probability of not having a matching card on the board.

$$(48/50) \times (47/49) \times (46/48) = 0.88$$

so the probability of flopping a set (or better) is 0.12 (12 percent, or about a one-in-eight chance).

Generally if you flop a set, you'll win about 88 percent of the time. That's based on empirical results from the Turbo Texas Hold 'Em simulations.

Now the question becomes how large the pots are. We'll analyze the question of whether you should call a raise pre-flop with a small- or midsized pocket pair when there are four other active players. We'll assume that the game is a 10/20 limit and that the pot gets to $300 by the river.

The process we want to model then is that we call $20 before the flop: 88 percent of the time we miss the flop and fold, 10 percent of the time we go to the river and win, 2 percent of the time we go to the river and lose. If we go to the river, we will put an extra $90 in the pot. That assumes that there is a raise and reraise on the flop, one raise on the turn, and one bet on the river. To see how implied odds affect the outcome, you can modify the assumptions I'm making about pot size and analyze this with different assumptions about the action that will occur after the flop.

With these assumptions the range of outcomes is that we can lose $20 (88 percent of the time), lose $110 (2 percent of the time), or win $190 (10 percent of the time). The expected value is then

$$0.88 \times (-20) + 0.02 \times (-110) + 0.10 \times 190 = -0.6$$

This means that calling a raise with only four other callers will lose about $.60 on the average. This result is sensitive to assumptions about how these players play after the flop and how large the pots will get after the flop. We can calculate the variance of this situation as

$$(0.6)^2 - 0.88 \times (-20)(-0.20) + 0.02 \times (-110)(-110) +$$
$$0.10 \times (190)(190)$$

or

$$(352 + 242 + 3610) - 0.36 = 4203.64$$

Notice that the variance is a very large value. We often use the square root of the variance, which gives us a value in scale with the expected value. The square root of the variance is called the "standard deviation." In this example the standard deviation is 64.9.

A large variance is common in poker situations. In this case it's interesting to note that most of the variance comes from our 10 percent of large wins. This demonstrates that having a large variance is not always a bad thing. To use variance to reflect risk, we can use what's called a semivariance. That's computed by adding up only the terms in the variance that result from negative outcomes. In this example the semivariance is 352 + 242 = 594, with a semistandard deviation of 24.

Risk is a fundamental element of gambling. Without risk, there is no gamble. Whenever you have uncertain outcomes, you have risk. The usual view of risk is that the more uncertainty about the outcome, the more risk. Sometimes you'll see a perspective that the more likely the outcome is to result in a loss, the higher the risk. This view of risk would suggest that buying a lottery ticket is high risk because the probability that your ticket will lose is very high. This is the kind of result that you get if you use variance as a proxy for risk, but as we've just seen, it's usually a better idea to use semivariance as a measure of risk.

STATISTICS

Statistics is about the analysis of actual results—data analysis. It's kind of science of information reduction. Statistical analysis involves estimating a small group of parameters that somehow gives a description of the distributional properties of a large set of data. The usual parameters of interest are the mean and variance. You can compute these from actual data rather than from the probability distributions. This book is not intended as a primer on data analysis, and you should refer to any standard text on statistical methods for the formulas to use in analyzing actual data.

30

Other Books on Hold 'Em

INTRODUCTORY HOLD 'EM BOOKS

The last twenty years have seen a lot of poker books on the market, and many of them have been on Hold 'Em. Some are pretty good books, and some are not so good, but I think even the bad books have something to offer. Hold 'Em is a complex game, and every author has added a little bit of unique insight into its various aspects.

In most cases each book looks at the game from a slightly different perspective. This book is no exception. Although I've tried to look at the game from a variety of perspectives, most of this book has focused on an *odds* perspective. I believe this is a neglected perspective among the Hold 'Em books. To get a broader view of some of the perspectives I haven't covered quite as fully, there are a number of other books on the market. You should plan on reading them all eventually. In this chapter I give a short summary of the perspectives taken by the major books on Hold 'Em.

292

David Sklansky, *Hold 'Em Poker*,
Two Plus Two Publishing, 1997

This book was originally published by Gambler's Book Club, a Las Vegas bookstore, in 1978. It was the first major book written on Hold 'Em. It's a classic, and every Hold 'Em player should read it, if only for its historical value. When the book was first written, the usual blind structure was different than it is today. Games typically had only one blind, the amount of the blind was half of the small bet size. That's not much money in the pot to start with. As a consequence structured betting games of the time didn't play that much differently from the spread-limit games of today. The book was updated in 1997 to reflect the change in blind structure that had occurred. However, the update was generally superficial, in many places consisting of just footnotes that say that some of the advice is really no longer true—still it's a good book. Many of the general principles discussed apply to any structured-limit game. For example, Sklansky has a good discussion of semi-bluffing.

Sklansky primarily takes a *hand-domination* and a *made-hand-versus-a-draw* perspective on the game in this book. He was heavily influenced by the games in Las Vegas at the time, and those games tended to be fairly tight by today's standards and compared with typical games outside of Las Vegas. If you find yourself in a tight-passive or loose-passive game, then much of what Sklansky has to say in this book will be useful to you.

Ken Warren, *Winner's Guide to Texas Hold 'Em Poker*,
Cardoza Publishing, 1996

This book focuses on 1-4-8-8 spread-limit games. It's the only book on the market that I'm aware of that has a focus on spread-limit games, where the initial blind money is very small compared with the size of future bets. Warren does take somewhat of a multiperspective view of the game, but his primary perspective is that of *money flowing from bad players to good players*. That's a natural way to look at the game when you're talking about relatively low-limit games. Such games are often populated by many bad players, and a common strategy for those games is to just sit and wait for the money to flow to you.

Lou Kreiger, *Hold 'Em Excellence: From Beginner to Winner*, Conjelco, 1999; and Lou Krieger, *More Hold 'Em Excellence: A Winner for Life*, Conjelco, 1999

Both these books were originally published by B&F Enterprises, *Hold 'Em Excellence* in 1995 and *More Hold 'Em Excellence* in 1997. A major plus for both these books is that Kreiger is both a writer and a poker player; as a consequence these books are well written. That's not the normal situation in most poker books.

Although the two books don't really overlap much, they are very similar. In both books, Kreiger takes an approach based on patience and discipline. His primary perspective seems to be *hand domination*, which is very dominant in the first book. *Hold 'Em Excellence* is aimed more directly at the beginning player, and most of the advice is aimed at keeping the reader out of situations that cause trouble. It's a good approach for beginners and a valuable book to read.

To Lou, poker is a *game of discipline*, and in *More Hold 'Em Excellence*, he has more of a focus on a *money-flows-from-bad-players-to-good-players* perspective than he did in *Hold 'Em Excellence*. This book is aimed at the more experienced player and has more discussion on how to exploit the mistakes of others rather than how to avoid mistakes yourself.

Lee Jones, *Winning Low Limit Hold 'Em*, 2nd edition, Conjelco, 2000

Like the Warren book, this book is aimed at playing in low-limit games in public cardrooms, but it is about low-limit with structured betting, rather than spread limits. The difference is that the structured games have more blind money in the pot to start, and it's important to play more aggressively from the beginning. Jones takes a combination of an *odds* perspective and a *domination* perspective in this book. That's the best approach to take in structured games of mostly loose-passive players, and those are the kinds of games at which he aims the book.

Even if you don't play in the low-limit games Jones addresses, this is a good book to read if you often find yourself in loose-passive games.

D. R. Sherer, *No Fold 'Em Hold 'Em*, Poker Plus Publications, 1997

This is something of a unique poker book. It's not a book for beginners. Its perspective is that money flows from bad players to good players, and its focus is on how to exploit the errors of the typical weak-tight player. The main problem with the book is that Sherer doesn't explicitly tell you his focus. If you take the book at face value, it might seem like a book that suggests that hands such as 7♠5♥ are strong hands that should be played aggressively. The book is about how to play hands like that aggressively, but the context of the play is when you are able to get heads-up against a tight player who at times tends to give up too easily and at other times falls in love with his hand.

The book also has some discussion on hand value in very loose and very passive games that's valuable, but the real benefit is learning when you don't need to have the best hand in a confrontation between a *made hand* and a *draw* if the other player has exploitable weaknesses. However, the book is written by a poker player, not a writer, and it isn't written well enough for someone without a lot of table experience to profit from it.

David Sklansky and Mason Malmuth, *Hold 'Em for Advanced Players*, Two Plus Two Publishing, 1999

This book was originally published in 1988. A more recent edition, with some new material, has recently been published. The book has a strong orientation toward perspectives of *domination* and *deception*. It's geared mostly toward attacking loose-passive players with a strong focus on plays like semi-bluffs. It provides good coverage of many profitable deceptive plays that work well against small fields of weak players and covers a lot of material that gives you strong clues in reading tougher players that you're likely to find at tight or typical tables. If for no other reason than it's a widely read book, this book is a must read for any serious Hold 'Em player. Your tougher opponents have read this book. You need to read it, too.

The new material that's been added in the second edition is mostly on short-handed play and playing in loose, wild games. The heads-up material in the short-handed play section is good and well worth reading. The material for play in loose, wild games suffers from the author's tendency to stress perspectives of domination and deception, two perspectives that don't really add much value to play in very loose and very aggressive games.

T. J. Cloutier and Tom McEvoy, *Championship Hold 'Em*, Poker Plus, 2000

Championship Hold 'Em tries to be a lot. It presents itself as a book aimed at all Hold 'Em players: novices and professionals alike. That's a pretty big target. When writing a book, the big targets are much harder to hit than the small ones. It has a strong focus on *domination* and *made-hand-versus-a-draw*. A wide range of players will find the book interesting, but it's not a book for a rank beginner.

The structure is unusual. In some ways it's an editor's book. It has some chapters written by T. J. Cloutier and written by Tom McEvoy, though most of the book consists of transcripts of conversations between Cloutier and McEvoy. That's not a typical book format, but it works well here.

The first chapter, by Cloutier, sets the tone with a list of eighteen "Key Concepts for Winning at Limit Hold 'Em." The traditional list of this sort might contain items such as Hand Selection or Check Raising. Not T.J.'s list. He has items in his list like Watch Your Opponents and Remember That Kickers Are Important. He doesn't give you a set of rigid rules, but gives you guidelines for thinking. Although the book does go into technical details about hand selection, when to raise, and other topics, this first chapter sets the tone of the general approach—this book is about thinking during the game.

If I have any criticism of the book, it's probably that I think the idea of avoiding trouble is overemphasized. If you're going to make mistakes, that's a mistake that is often not a mistake.

The book has coverage of a lot of topics often avoided in poker books. Kill-pot games, jackpot games, and the difference between raked and time-collection games are discussed. As you might expect from these writers, they have an extensive chapter on limit Hold 'Em tournaments.

GENERAL POKER BOOKS

There are also a few more general poker books that should be read by any serious poker player.

Mike Caro, *Caro's Fundamental Secrets of Winning Poker*, Cardoza Publishing, 1991

This book is a collection of short guidelines on a variety of poker topics, from picking a game to playing straight draws in Hold 'Em. Caro is a top-notch poker theorist and analyst, and anything he writes is well worth reading. It's a short book with a wealth of things to think about.

David Sklansky, *The Theory of Poker*, Two Plus Two Publishing, 1987

The *Theory of Poker* is actually the third version of this book. The initial edition was published by Gambler's Book Club, which was followed by an expanded edition by Prentice-Hall. The current edition is based primarily on the first edition. If you can find a copy of the Prentice-Hall version in a secondhand bookstore, you should snap it up. It was coauthored with a professional writer and is much better written than the current version.

This book is a must read. It's probably the most important book ever written about poker. It's not really about theory as much as it is about tactics and strategic considerations; it covers most of the major strategic considerations of the game and has influenced every poker writer and every serious poker player.

Topics such as semi-bluffing, free cards, inducing mistakes, slow playing, and playing draws are all covered in this book. Sklansky uses clear examples from various forms of poker, including Hold 'Em, but also seven-card stud, Razz, and other forms of poker. *Read this book*.

Mike Caro, *The Body Language of Poker*, Lyle Stuart, 1982

This book is also a must read for every serious poker player. Unfortunately it's currently out of print. The good news is that it should have been republished by the time the book you're reading goes to press. Caro intends to update the book and republish it under his own publishing imprint of Mike Caro University. Because Caro's reputation as a top poker theorist is only surpassed by his reputation as a procrastinator, I can't give you a publication date, but watch for it. Buy it when it comes out.

The book discusses tells—player behaviors that give you clues to the strength and weaknesses of their hands. It's complete with photographs illustrating the behaviors. If any book can directly and immediately translate into money won at the table, it's this book.

Mason Malmouth, *Gambling Theory and Other Topics*, Two Plus Two Publishing, 1987

Most reviews of this book have been favorable, although I don't like it. I include it here because Malmuth has a nice introduction to statistical analysis of poker results in the book. His coverage of the topic is not complete but does provide a good introduction to the interpretation of sample variance.

OTHER REVIEWS

A good source of short reviews of gambling books of all types can be found at my Internet Web site: www.garycarson.com.

31

Poker and the Internet

The resources available on the Internet to learn poker and to improve your game are just awesome. Discussion groups, games you can play for fun, games you can play for money, books, and discussion archives are all over the Internet. No serious poker player should be without access to these resources.

POKER DISCUSSION

There are a number of poker discussion forums on the Internet. They differ somewhat in terms of activity and topic.

rec.gambling.poker

The oldest and most popular discussion group is the poker newsgroup rec.gambling.poker. The discussion threads cover a wide range of poker topics, and it has a large, diverse group of contributors, from novice poker players wanting to know whether a straight beats a flush to well-known poker writer and personality Mike Caro. Even poker legend Doyle Brunson is heard from now and then on rgp.

Your first stop on the Internet should be rec.gambling.poker. It's accessible from most mail and newsgroup readers. The Web site maintains large, searchable archives. It's free although it does require that you set up an account.

The newsgroup is very active and somewhat anarchistic. Some of the threads have only a nebulous relationship to poker, but the poker discussions can often be deep and enlightening. If I were to suggest only one thing to read about poker, it wouldn't be a book, it would be the archives of this newsgroup. If you're serious about poker, get yourself Internet access and start reading this newsgroup.

www.twoplustwo.com

Another threaded discussion group is a Web-based forum hosted by Two Plus Two Publishing Company. Known as the *twoplustwo forum*, it's devoted to the theory and strategy of poker. Sometimes other gambling topics pop up, but if you post a question like What's the best hotel to stay at during the World Series of Poker? you'll be quickly corrected by one of the site hosts, poker writers David Sklansky and Ray Zee or poker book publisher Mason Malmuth. Stick to strategic playing issues on this forum.

The twoplustwo forum has many rich threads on topics of poker tactics and strategy. It is, however, censored. You won't find much discussion about the drawbacks of the perspectives suggested in books published by Two Plus Two. You also won't find much discussion of the benefits of perspectives suggested in books that are published by mainstream publishers. Even though the perspectives that dominate the discussion threads on this forum are limited, some of the regular posters to the forum have some very useful insight into the game. I don't post to this forum; when I do get involved in discussions on the Internet, it's usually on rgp, but I do read the forum regularly. It can be a rich source of ideas.

www.pokerpages.com

PokerPages.com hosts two discussion forums: one on poker and one devoted to poker for women. Extensive coverage of tournament news and feature articles from many different poker writers are also provided. I write for them.

E-mail Discussion Lists

Les Smith hosts an E-mail discussion group, called TexasHoldem. It's pretty much open to any poker or poker-related topic, but most of the threads are on subjects that are of particular interest to newer poker players. To subscribe, send a blank E-mail to TexasHoldem-subscribe@egroups.com.

I host an E-mail list of my own. It's a small list, used mostly by me to get early feedback on whatever my current writing project might be. You're certainly welcome to join the list if you're interested. There's a button to sign up on my Web site, www.gary carson.com.

Although it's not a discussion list, Mike Caro also has an E-mail list. It's a one-way list; Mike sends out announcements of seminars and other events. Just send a blank message to caro-on@mail-list.com.

There are also a number of poker newsletters offered by various Web sites.

Poker Chat Rooms

Pokerpages.com maintains a Web-based poker chatroom. It's not very active, although they do sometimes use it for scheduled chats with some of their columnists or other poker writers.

The best place for poker chat is at the Internet Relay Chat (IRC) poker games. These are fun games only, played for funny money, no cash involved. A free graphical client for IRC poker and chat can be downloaded from a site maintained by Greg Reynolds (webusers.anet-stl.com/~gregr/). Many of the frequent posters to rgp hang out at this IRC site.

PLAYING POKER

Playing without Money

There are a few Internet sites that offer fun-only poker games. Some provide a limited range of games that are very unrealistic, and some provide a wide range of realistic games.

IRC Poker

The best of the on-line poker games played without money are on an IRC channel, irc.poker.net. A graphical client can be downloaded free from Greg Reynold's Web site. Players from Europe and Japan can often be found on this site, so there is always a game, no matter what time it might by in your time zone. Hold 'Em is the most popular game, but you can select from channels that provide seven-card stud, Omaha hi/lo, seven-card stud hi/lo, Omaha/8, pot-limit Hold 'Em, and pot-limit Omaha.

There are other Internet locations that provide games which can be played with no money. Yahoo has one, for example, but the games on the IRC channels are the closest to real games in terms of the play of the other players that I've seen. They do tend to be very loose and very aggressive, but the players who frequent the IRC channels include some very good poker players and the games can be a rewarding challenge. I recommend it highly.

World Rec.Gambling.Poker Tournament

The World Rec.Gambling.Poker Tournament (WRGPT) is an annual poker tournament played by E-mail. The tournament begins in the fall, and usually lasts many months, to the complete aggravation of some of the players. The game played is no-limit Hold 'Em.

The most recent event attracted about a thousand players from all over the world. Starting with almost one hundred tables, the game began in September, and by July there was only one player left. The prize is bragging rights until the next game. To find out about the game, ask on rgp. Most of the WRGPT players are readers of rgp.

Playing for Money on the Internet

There are new Internet sites hosting on-line poker every day. The sites are hosted in locations that regulate Internet gambling, and they are legal operations. Depending on the state you're located in, it may not be legal for you to play on them, however. This area of law is still somewhat in flux.

I've played on some of these sites, and the games are good games; the site operators go to great pains to keep the games good. However, player collusion is a serious potential problem that cannot be eliminated in Internet poker games. The sites do attempt to monitor the games and investigate any activity that suggests that two players might be sharing information about their hands. The sites themselves are legitimate.

Play on these sites at your own risk, however. As legitimate as the sites themselves are, you cannot eliminate player collusion. Most cheats don't really play very well and don't get that much of an edge by collusion, but if two good players are colluding and sharing information about their hands, it would give those players a tremendous advantage. Just be wary.

COMPUTER GAMES

Many casino game software packages contain a poker game. Most are weak games. They don't offer many realistic options, and their computer opponents play weak-predictable strategies.

An exception is Turbo Texas–Hold 'Em. Wilson Software distributes games for Hold 'Em, seven-card stud, Omaha-8, and

Omaha High. There are both ring-game and tournament versions, and they run on Windows systems.

I'm mostly familiar with the Hold 'Em version, which is much more than a game. It's a very flexible poker simulator. Computer players are driven by large tables describing each decision point. The tables can be modified to create player profiles to match the playing habits of the players you most frequently play against in your live games. Developing profiles on your regular opponents can be invaluable for use in testing various strategic questions. You can simulate alternatives against the exact game conditions you face.

Glossary

All-in   The table stakes rule says that you can only bet up to the amount of money you had in front of you at the start of a hand. When you've bet (or called) up to that amount, you're said to be all-in. You've put all the money into the pot that you can for that hand. Other active players can continue to bet among themselves, but they'll compete for a side pot. Your hand will compete for the pot at the point where you were able to match all bets.

Angle   An action that's not explicitly against the rules, but is considered a serious ethical violation and unfair act.

Angle-shooting   Angle-shooting is the use of angles to gain an unfair advantage.

Backdoor   A draw where you have three of the five cards you need on the flop. To make your hand, you need the right cards on both the turn and the river. Three cards to a flush on the flop is a backdoor flush draw.

Back-raise   Calling a bet, then reraising when someone raises. Sometimes called sandbagging, it's a form of slow play.

Bad beat   When a very good hand is beaten by a hand that had to make a long-shot draw, such as a backdoor draw, then it's called a bad beat.

Bet odds   The odds you get from the number of callers on a betting round. If you bet and four players call, then your bet odds are 5-1.

Blind An initial forced bet that is put out before the cards are even dealt is called a blind bet. It's used in Hold 'Em to replace the ante to get some initial money into the pot.

Blind, big The larger of two blinds. Usually this blind is the same size as the bet size on the first betting round.

Blind, small The smaller of two blinds. Usually this blind is half the size of the bet size on the first betting round.

Bluff A bet that can't win if you're called. There are generally two ways for a bet to win. One is for the opponent to fold, conceding the pot, the other is for the opponent to call and your hand prevail in a showdown. A bluff has only one way to win.

Board The community cards in the middle of the table are called the board. It consists of either three, four, or five cards, depending on the betting round.

Book player A player who plays in a rigid style. Book players tend to overvalue the concept of patience and tend to think that hand value is determined by the cards themselves. Waiting for an obviously superior hand is their primary approach to the game.

Burn card A burn card is the card on the top of the stub of the deck that's discarded by the dealer before dealing cards for the next betting round. This is done to minimize the advantage a player would get if he caught a glimpse of the top card, knowing that card would be dealt to the board for the next betting round.

Button The last player to act, before the blinds, is called the button. The button player is designated by a plastic disk, which rotates among the players. It is used to designate the player who holds the dealer's position in the betting order.

Call When another player bets, you must either call by putting an amount equal to the bet into the pot (sometimes called equalizing the pot) or fold. If you don't have enough chips to completely equalize the pot, you can go all-in and call for only the chips you have.

Calling station   A loose-passive player who will seldom bet or raise but will call bets with very weak hands.

Capping   *See* four-bet.

Check-raise   A form of slow play. Checking with the intent of raising if another player bets.

Cold-call   Calling a bet and a raise all at one time. If a player in front of you bets, a second player raises, and you call, then you've cold-called the raise. If a player in front of you bets and you call, then someone else raises and you call the raise, you've then called the raise, not cold-called it.

Cold-decking   A form of cheating where a prearranged deck is put into the game and given a false shuffle.

Dog   *See* underdog.

Dominated power hands   These are hands that are strong enough to be worth raising with from early position, but are probably not strong enough to call a raise from an early position raiser unless two or three other players have already called.

Dominating power hands   These are hands that are very strong and should almost always be played, even in situations that mean calling a raise from an early position raiser.

Drawing dead   When your hand can't win even if it makes the improvement you're hoping for. An example is when the flop is all of one suit and someone has a flush and you've got a straight draw.

Drawing hand   In general use, a drawing hand on the flop is one that probably has to improve to win. Before the flop, drawing hands are those two-card combinations that hope to flop a drawing hand. A hand like 7♦6♦ is a drawing hand. You're hoping to flop either a flush draw or a straight draw. In this book I used the term *drawing hand* to categorize a group of hands that have sufficient chances of winning to be worth calling a raise if two or three other players are active, even though the hand is probably not the best starting out.

Fancy Play Syndrome (FPS)   A tendency to try to be tricky when it's unwarranted. A player with FPS bluffs too much, semi-bluffs too much, and generally plays too aggressively.

Fish   A bad player who can be counted on to lose his money.

Flop   The first three of the five community cards that make up the board.

Fold   To concede any claim on the pot by discarding your hand rather than calling a bet.

Four-bet   To four-bet is to make the last raise. Most cardrooms have a limit of one bet and three raises per round, so the fourth bet is the third, and last, raise. Sometimes it's called capping it. To cap the betting is to four-bet it.

FPS   *See* Fancy Play Syndrome.

Gambling hand   A hand that isn't immediately the best hand but has long-shot chances of developing into the best hand. These hands are usually playable pre-flop when six or more other players are active. Usually you should not call with these hands if the hand is going to be heads-up, but if seven or more players will call a raise, these hands are often worth a raise pre-flop when you're in a late position.

Gutshot   An inside straight draw. An outside straight draw has eight outs. That's a hand like 6,7,8,9. An inside straight draw is a hand like 5,6,8,9 and has only four outs.

Heads-up   Heads-up is a two player contest. Whenever there are exactly two active hands, the hand is said to be played heads-up.

Implied odds   The odds you are getting from an expectation of calls on future betting rounds.

Kicker   The highest odd card when you have a pair. If you have a pair of Aces with a King, a 10, and a 7 then you have a pair of Aces with a King kicker. It's often used to denote the lower of the two cards in your private hand. For example, if you have an Ace and a 10, you have an Ace with a 10 kicker. If your 10 pairs a 10 on the board, then you have a pair of 10s with an Ace kicker.

Kill   A kill is an extra blind that doubles the limit. If the game is a 10/20 limit game with 5/10 blinds and a player puts out a $20 kill, the game becomes a 20/40 game with three blinds for that hand.

Kill blind   *See* kill.

Limp   Calling the blind bet in the pre-flop round of betting without raising. Also called limping into a pot. If this is done as a sandbag, it's sometimes called a limp-reraise.

Live   Used in the context of either live hand or live one.

Live hand   A live hand is a hand that has not been folded when all bets have been equalized.

Live one   A live one is a player who can be expected to lose chips quickly.

Main pot   If a player goes all-in, the amount of the pot that's been equalized is set aside as the main pot. Any further action by other active hands goes into a side pot that the all-in player does not compete for.

Maniac   A wild, very loose, and very aggressive player. He plays a lot of hands and almost always raises when he plays. He will frequently raise on a bluff or with a very weak hand.

Morton's Theorem   A technical result that shows there are certain combinations of pot odds and outs that your opponents can have which create a situation where you don't profit from a bet if they all call. They all profit from the call, and the largest portion of the profit goes to the best draw.

No-limit   A betting structure where the only limit on bet size is the amount of chips on the table.

Nuts (also nut hand)   The best possible hand. For example, if the board does not contain a pair, and no player has a pair, then an Ace-high hand is the nuts.

Odds   *See* bet odds, implied odds, and pot odds.

Open-raise   On the first betting round, the first player to voluntarily put money into the pot can do so by either calling the blind or by raising. A raise by the first player to voluntarily put money in the pot on the first betting round is called an open-raise.

Outs The number of cards that can be turned up on the next round that will improve your hand to a probable best hand.

Overcall Usually refers to bets and calls as the last action on the river. If there is a bet and a call, the second caller is called an overcall. It generally takes a stronger hand to overcall than to call.

Overpair A pocket pair higher in rank than the highest card on the board.

Pocket Your private two-card hand.

Pocket pair A pair of cards of the same rank as your private two-card hand.

Position Your order in the betting sequence. If you are one of the first players to bet, then you're in an early position. If you're one of the last players to act, then you're in a late position. If there are one or more players who act before you and there are one or more players who will act after you, then you are in a middle position.

Pot odds The odds the current pot size is giving you to make a call. It is based on the number of bets in the pot, and is the ratio of the number of bets you have to call to equalize the pot and the number of bets in the pot.

Pre-flop The first betting round. It's the betting round after you've been dealt your two-card hand, but before the flop is dealt.

Prop player A proposition player is employed by a cardroom to play. He's used to start new games or to sit in on short-handed games to keep them going for a while. A prop player plays with his own money and plays in the games he's assigned, but makes his own choices about how he plays. (*See also* shill and stake-player.)

Raise You raise by putting an extra bet in the pot, requiring other active hands to either equalize the pot by calling your raise or fold.

Rake   Money taken out of the pot by the house dealer. How much is taken is a small fixed percentage of the pot and varies according to the bet limits. Also called the cut. This is the fee the house extracts for covering the overhead associated with the game.

Reraise   A reraise is a raise after a previous raise by someone else.

Reverse tell   Faking a tell.

Ring game   A regular game, as opposed to a tournament.

River   The last card is called the river card. In Hold 'Em this is the fifth community card put on the board. The river betting round is the last betting round of the hand.

Rock   A usually passive, very tight player.

Sandbagging   A form of slow play. Usually means calling a bet when players are left to act behind you, intending to reraise if someone in a later position raises. Sandbagging on the pre-flop round of betting is often called a limp-reraise.

Semi-bluff   A bet made with more cards to come when you probably don't have the best hand, but have outs if you're called.

Set   A form of three of a kind where you have two of the rank in your hand and one on the board. Because of the community card nature of Hold 'Em, this is a much stronger hand than three of a kind made with one card from your hand matching a pair on the board. That's because with a pair on the board any player who has the fourth card of that rank also has three of a kind. If you have, for example, three Kings made as a set, then no other player can hold three Kings.

Shill   A shill is a cardroom employee who helps start new games by sitting in with house money. He doesn't get any portion of his winnings and is not responsible for his losses. Often he's given a set of rules to play by; generally he'll play tight and passive. (*See also* prop-player and stake-player.)

Showdown   When all the cards are out and all the bets have been equalized, the active hands show themselves to determine what the winning hand is.

Side pot   Bets made after one player is all-in are put in a side pot.

Slow play   Playing a strong hand in a way that suggests you have a weak hand. Sandbagging and check-raising are forms of slow play. The term slow play often refers to checking and calling on the flop, intending to bet and raise on the turn, when the bet size increases.

Slowroll   On the river, waiting until everyone else involved in the showdown has turned over their cards before showing yours, even when you think you have the best hand. This is considered bad etiquette by some.

Speculative hand   Speculative hands are a group of hands that aren't immediately the best hand but are getting sufficient odds for a pre-flop call if four to five other players are active in the pot.

Spread-limit   A betting structure that allows any bet size within a specified range.

Stake-player   A stake-player is a player who has a financial backer. This is very common in tournaments, where one backer will stake more than one player in return for a percentage of their winnings. (*See also* prop-player and shill.)

Steal-raise   On the pre-flop round of betting, when everyone has checked, an open raise from late position that hopes to make everyone fold and win the blinds.

Stone killer   An extremely tight-aggressive player.

Straddle   A straddle is a voluntary extra blind. Unlike a kill, it does not raise the limits. It's just a blind raise within the nominal limits.

Structured limits   A betting structure that specifies a bet size at each betting round.

Tell   An involuntary action that gives observers a clue as to the cards you are holding.

Tight-aggressive player   A player who plays few hands, but when he does play he plays very aggressively, betting and raising often.

Tilt (going on tilt)   A psychological state where you're playing very badly. The term is borrowed from pinball.

Turn The fourth card placed on the board as a community card. The betting round after the turn is usually at a bet size double the size of the bets on the previous round. The previous round is the flop round.

Under the Gun The first player to act.

Underdog An underdog has the odds against him.

Underpair A pocket pair smaller in rank than the highest card on the flop.

UTG *See* under the gun.

Value bet On the river, a bet that should win if called.